Austria Supreme (if it so wishes) (1684)
A Strategy for European Economic Supremacy

ECONOMIC IDEAS THAT BUILT EUROPE

Economic Ideas That Built Europe reconstructs the development of European political economy as seen through the eyes of its principal architects and interpreters, working to overcome the ideological nature of recent historiography. The volumes in the series – contextualized through analytical introductions and enriched with explanatory footnotes, bibliographies and indices – offer a wide selection of texts inspired by very different economic visions and stress their complex consequences and interactions in the rich but often simplified history of European economic thought.

SERIES EDITOR
Sophus A. Reinert – Harvard Business School, USA

EDITORIAL BOARD
David Armitage – Harvard University, USA
Steven L. Kaplan – Cornell University, USA
Emma Rothschild – Harvard University, USA
Jacob Soll – University of Southern California, USA
Bertram Schefold – Goethe University Frankfurt, Germany

Oesterreich
Uber alles
wann es nur will.
Das ist:
wohlmeinender
Fürschlag
Wie mittelst einer wol-
bestellten Lands = Oeconomie, die Kayserl. Erbland in kurzem über alle andere Staat von Europa zu erheben / und mehr als einiger
derselben/ von denen andern Independent zu ma-
chen.

Durch einen Liebhaber
der Kayserl. Erbland
Wolfahrt.

Gedruckt im Jahr Christi
1 6 8 4.

Austria Supreme (if it so wishes) (1684) A Strategy for European Economic Supremacy

Philipp Wilhelm von Hörnigk

Edited with an introduction by Philipp Robinson Rössner
Translated by Keith Tribe

ANTHEM PRESS

Anthem Press
An imprint of Wimbledon Publishing Company
www.anthempress.com

This edition first published in UK and USA 2018
by ANTHEM PRESS
75–76 Blackfriars Road, London SE1 8HA, UK
or PO Box 9779, London SW19 7ZG, UK
and
244 Madison Ave #116, New York, NY 10016, USA

Part of The Anthem Other Canon Series
Series Editor Erik S. Reinert

British Library Cataloguing-in-Publication Data
A catalogue record for this book is available from the British Library.

ISBN-13: 978-1-78308-820-1 (Hbk)
ISBN-10: 1-78308-820-6 (Hbk)

This title is also available as an e-book.

Wir sind doch nunmehr gantz, ja mehr denn gantz verheeret!
Der frechen Völcker Schar, die rasende Posaun
Das vom Blutt fette Schwerdt, die donnernde Carthaun
Hat aller Schweiß und Fleiß und Vorrath auffgezehret.
Die Türme stehn in Glutt, die Kirch ist umgekehret.
Das Rathhauß ligt im Grauß, die Starcken sind zerhaun,
Die Jungfern sind geschänd't, und wo wir hin nur schaun,
Ist Feuer, Pest, und Tod, der Hertz und Geist durchfähret.
Hir durch die Schantz und Stadt rinnt allzeit frisches Blutt.
Dreymal sind schon sechs Jahr, als unser Ströme Flutt,
Von Leichen fast verstopfft, sich langsam fort gedrungen,
Doch schweig ich noch von dem, was ärger als der Tod,
Was grimmer denn die Pest und Glutt und Hungersnoth,
Dass auch der Seelen Schatz so vielen abgezwungen.

– Andreas Gryphius, *Tränen des Vaterlandes* (1636)

Be't Kinder, bet't
Morgen kommt der Schwed'
Morgen kommt der Oxenstern
Wird die Kinder beten lern'n
Bet't Kinder, bet't
Die Schweden sind gekommen,
Haben alles mitgenommen,
Haben's Fenster eingeschlagen,
Haben's Blei davon getragen,
Haben Kugeln daraus gegossen
Und die Bauern erschossen.

– *German lullaby, Thirty Years War*

CONTENTS

ACKNOWLEDGEMENTS

The translation of Hörnigk's 1684 volume was financed by the the Institute of New Economic Thinking (INET) as part of their grant to Sophus A. Reinert and Francesca Viano. The editor wishes to thank Erik S. Reinert and The Other Canon Foundation for assistance throughout the project, and Fernanda and Erik S. Reinert for assistance in a crucial point of the translation.

Chapter One

PHILIPP WILHELM VON HÖRNIGK – HIS LIFE, TIMES AND PLACE IN HISTORY

A Long-Forgotten Algorithm for Europe's Rise to Greatness: The Hörnigk Strategy

How does a country grow rich? Why do some countries grow rich much faster than others? Why do some nations experience growth and prosperity, while others don't? Why did Europe eventually overtake the rest of the world, becoming the first region to industrialize and experience a progressive economic advantage over the rest of the world? These are the big questions asked in the modern social sciences, not only in more recent times (as witnessed by the post-2000 Great Divergence debate fuelled by two books by scholars working at the University of California),[1] but also since the days of Karl Marx or Max Weber.[2] Philipp Wilhelm von Hörnigk's[3] 'Austria Supreme' provides a concise and powerful answer to them.[4] People had even raised them way before. In

---

1 E.g. Roy Bin Wong, *China Transformed: Historical Change and the Limits of European Experience* (Ithaca, NY: Cornell University Press, 1997); Kenneth Pomeranz, *The Great Divergence: China, Europe, and the Making of the Modern World Economy* (Princeton, NJ: Princeton University Press, 2000). See also Andre Gunder Frank, *ReOrient: Global Economy in the Asian Age* (Berkeley: University of California Press, 1998); more recently Prasannan Parthasarathi, *Why Europe Grew Rich and Asia Did Not. Global Economic Divergence, 1600–1850* (Cambridge: Cambridge University Press, 2011). A slightly different viewpoint (sometimes labelled 'Eurocentric') was taken in David S. Landes, *The Wealth and Poverty of Nations. Why Some Are So Rich and Others So Poor* (New York: W.W. Norton, 1998), or Eric L. Jones, *The European Miracle: Environments, Economies and Geopolitics in the History of Europe and Asia*, 3rd ed. (Cambridge: Cambridge University Press, 2003).
2 See the account in Parthasarathi, *Why Europe Grew Rich*, introduction, especially 3–4.
3 More than 34 different spellings of this name are known. This is not at all unusual, given that in early modern Germany, neither family names nor general orthography were in any way standardized. 'Hörnigk' was the spelling given by his father Ludwig, when he obtained his Imperial Nobilitation privilege in 1629.
4 Karl Theodor von Inama-Sternegg, 'Hörnigk, Philipp Wilhelm von', in *Allgemeine Deutsche Biographie (ADB)*, vol. 3 (Leipzig: Duncker & Humblot, 1881), 157–58, gives 12 editions, see ibid. For more reliable accounts on Hörnigk's life and times, see Gustav Otruba, 'Hörnigk, Philipp Wilhelm von', in *Neue Deutsche Biographie (NDB)*, vol. 9, (Berlin: Duncker & Humblot, 1972), 359–61; the introduction by Horst Knapp to '*Österreich über alles, wann es nur will*' / *Philipp Wilhelm von Hörnigk*, ed. Hannes Androsch et al. (Vienna: Edition Brandstätter, 1983), 11–24; Roman Sandgruber, '*Österreich über alles*'. *Programmatik und Realität der Wirtschaft zur Zeit Prinz Eugens*, in Erich Zöllner and Karl Gutkas, eds, *Österreich und die Osmanen – Prinz Eugen und seine Zeit* (Vienna: Österreichischer Bundesverlag, 1988), 153–71; as well as the introduction to Gustav Otruba, ed.,'*Österreich über alles*', *wenn es nur will* / *Philipp Wilhelm von Hörnigk, Nach d. Erstausg. von*

the eighteenth-century Enlightenment discourses, these questions were at the core of the 'rich' country versus 'poor' country debates. All major epigones of the Scottish Enlightenment, including David Hume and Adam Smith, would comment on this problem.[5] But this discourse was even older than that. It had been raised in early modern European political economy discourse at least since the sixteenth century and the days of Giovanni Botero, the Italian author who wrote a major treatise on cities and economic development.[6] It is not usually acknowledged that the big rift that developed in economic fortune between Asia and the West around AD 1800 had a prehistory that predates the industrial revolution – one major element and cause of the Great Divergence – by centuries. Nor is it well understood what role ideas played in this process – that is, the intellectual history of industrialization and Europe's eventual economic supremacy. With the present text, written by a seventeenth-century diplomat living in Habsburg, Austria, who no schoolchild and social science student of today would be expected to have heard of, we have an answer at last, however partial or incomplete. It was the 'Hörnigk Strategy' that made European nations rich. Perhaps, there is something to be learned from this. At least, this man should receive the fame he deserves.

During his own lifetime, Philipp Wilhelm von Hörnigk, as he is usually known, must have been formidably famous. At least his work was, as people maintained, even long after his death in 1714. The preface of the 1723 edition of '*Oesterreich über alles*' was the first to disclose the author's true identity, years after his death. The original 1684 issue, as well as all other editions up to 1723, had been published anonymously.[7] When Austrian political economy professor Joseph von Sonnenfels (1732/33–1817) was appointed to the

---

1684 in Normalorthographie übertr. u. mit d. Aufl. von 1753 kollationiert sowie mit e. Lebensbild d. Autors versehen (Vienna: Bergland, 1964), 11–43. The most reliable and detailed surveys can be found in Heinz-Joachim Brauleke, *Leben und Werk des Kameralisten Philipp Wilhelm von Hörnigk: Versuch einer wissenschaftlichen Biographie* (Frankfurt etc.: Peter Lang, 1978), esp. 4–43; Herbert Matis, 'Philipp Wilhelm von Hörnigk: Leben, Werk und ökonomisches Umfeld', In ibid. et al., eds *Vademecum zu einem Klassiker absolutistischer Wirtschaftspolitik: Philipp Wilhelm von Hörnigks "Oesterreich über alles"* (Düsseldorf: Verlag Wirtschaft und Finanzen, 1997), 67–136; Heinz-Joachim Brauleke, 'Vom Frankfurter Gelehrtenspross bis zum Passauer Mandatsträger in Regensburg. Imposante Stationen auf dem Lebensweg des Kameralisten Philip(p) Wilhelm von Hörnigk', *Ostbairische Grenzmarken. Passauer Jahrbuch für Geschichte, Kunst und Volkskunde* (1991), 76–88. Walter Braeuer, *Handbuch zur Geschichte der Volkswirtschaftslehre. Ein bibliographisches Nachschlagewerk* (Frankfurt am Main: Klostermann, 1952), 41ff.

5   Istvàn Hont, 'The "Rich Country – Poor Country" Debate in Scottish Classical Political Economy,' in ibid. and Michael Ignatieff, eds, *Wealth and Virtue. The Shaping of Political Economy in the Scottish Enlightenment* (Cambridge and New York: Cambridge University Press, 1983), reprinted in Istvàn Hont, *Jealousy of Trade: International Competition and the Nation State in Historical Perspective* (Cambridge, MA: Belknap Press of Harvard University Press, 2005).

6   Giovanni Botero, *Delle cause della grandezza delle città* (On the Causes of the Greatness of Cities, 1589). See *The Reason of State and the Greatness of Cities. By Giovanni Botero*, Translated From the Italian by P. J. Waley, with an Introduction by D. P. Waley (London: Routledge & Kegan Paul, 1956)

7   1723 and 1727 ed. (Regensburg/Ratisbon: Johann Conrad Peetz). See Table 1 in the text for a history of editions.

chair in Cameralist economics at the University of Vienna in 1763, he was required to draw up a list of textbooks on which his lectures were to be based, as well as indicate the textbook he would actually use in class. While academic bookshops still haunt university lecturers in a similar way by asking them to submit reading lists at the start of every academic year, ironically, the main reason this was required from Sonnenfels by his superiors in the university was that he was a self-confessed ignorant in political economy. He had prepared to lecture on Hebrew and translation. But it was not at all unusual to appoint people who were ignorant in the subject they were supposed to be lecturing on (again, this is not necessarily different today!). But what counts here is that, among a longer list of more modern authors he had (or was going to) read, Sonnenfels included Hörnigk's *Österreich über alles* (as well as Schröder's *Fürstliche Rentkammer* and Becher's *Politische Discurs*) on his reading list as a natural starting point (Seckendorff's *Teutscher Fürsten Stat* from 1655 seems to be missing from the list).[8] On the one hand, this story seems to testify to the rather dubious qualities and obscure qualifications of some eighteenth-century university professors. On the other hand, it marks and underscores Hörnigk's position and rank as a towering figure in the long and venerable genealogy of modern economics and political economy.

As mentioned above, the initial editions were published anonymously. Well into the 1750s (e.g. 1750) the book's cover page only featured the initials *Ph. W. v. H.* This was with good reason, as Hörnigk was in the services of high-ranking diplomats on the Imperial level, whose business was often top-secret. But Hörnigk published, in 1684, a bestseller; a book that would become the most widely read economics book on the continent, at least in the German-speaking lands, before Adam Smith wrote his 1776 *Inquiry into the Causes and Nature on the Wealth of Nations*. We may not call Hörnigk's opus a textbook in the modern sense; this literary genre evolved later on, in the eighteenth-century German lands under the auspices of Cameralism and Cameral Science as taught at universities. But the work was much more than a mere pamphlet, the most common literary genre in early modern European economic thought, especially when it came to framing economic questions and questions of economics scientifically. '*Oesterreich über alles' wann es nur will* went through at least eighteen editions between 1684 and 1784. The fact that it was still famous and available in print a hundred years after its first issue (1784) set it apart from most contemporary textbooks in the economic sciences. There were three editions of the work already in 1685, that is, one year after its initial publication.[9] In fact, Hörnigk's treatise went through more editions than his brother-in-law Johann Joachim Becher's (*Politischer Discurs*, 1673)[10] or Wilhelm von Schröder's *Fürstliche Schatz- und Rentkammer* (1686), works that represented, alongside Veit Ludwig von Seckendorff's

---

8 Herman Freudenberger, *Lost Momentum. Austrian Economic Development 1750s–1830s* (Cologne/Weimar/Vienna: Böhlau, 2003), 88.
9 See Brauleke, *Leben und Werk*, 91, for the most reliable (ac)count (as in n. 4).
10 On Becher, see Herbert Hassinger, *Johann Joachim Becher 1635–1682. Ein Beitrag zur Geschichte des Merkantilismus* (Vienna: Verlag Adolf Holzhausens NFG., 1951).

Teutscher Fürsten Stat (1655), 'early' Cameralism and German economics in its prime.[11] The author of the preface to the 1750 edition (Frankfurt and Leipzig) remarked that most of the previous editions had gone out-of-stock rapidly, and that it would be time for a new one, especially as the Cameral sciences had advanced so considerably now. In fact, as the editor of the 1750 edition pointed out, many an active cameralist author or project-maker would have to fear a new edition of Hörnigk's *Oesterreich über alles*, as such an edition would give away the true origin and basic foundations of Cameralist economic theory, thus, relieving many of the contemporary economics professors of their claim to originality, turning their works into plagiarism.[12] While this assessment is certainly too harsh, especially given the theoretical height and analytical depth found in the works of Johann Gottlob Heinrich Justi (1717–71, the man who developed Cameralist economics into a full-blown and unified economic theory – as far as one could possibly get with then-contemporary economics), it does contain an element of truth. Hörnigk's ideas may not have been so profoundly original as many of his contemporaries and later eighteenth century economists often suggested (there were important precursors, such as Antonio Serra or Giovanni Botero), but they were usually admired for their radicalism and purity of expression (while Hörnigk's language and discursive style were quite complicated, ponderous and laborious in places). The work must have been so prominent that contemporaries in the 1750s were not only ready to admit that Austria had made good economic progress because of the Hörnigk principles, but that the book could also be seen as the scientific foundation of Cameralism as a university discipline. Both assumptions may be doubted on many counts, as will be shown later in this book, but there remained a grain of truth in them. Surely the conditions would have changed between the first appearance of the book and the later eighteenth century, when contemporaries still sung Hörnigk's praises in the highest tunes. But the principles remained in place over time, so that Benedict Franz Hermann, the editor of the much-altered 1784 version, was able to state with pride that over the past century or so, Austrian industry and commerce had flourished, rising to unequalled prominence, and that Hörnigk's book was responsible for this. Hermann acknowledged the rather archaic nature of some of Hörnigk's core principles, including the uncompromising protectionist stance; the condemnation of fashion as a driver of economic change (which was a late seventeenth-century *topos*), and the rather negative stance on merchants and traders, which comes across clearly from the Hörnigk text. Most importantly, Hermann conceded, on page 15 of the 1784 commented edition of Hörnigk's *Austria Supreme*, that Austria's backwardness

---

11 Ibid., 91. If we include mid-sixteenth century writers such as Melchior von Osse (1506–1557), Georg Obrecht (1547–1612), or Kaspar Klock (1583–1655), then there would have been even 'earlier' Cameralists; the issue is, of course, to an extent a question of nuance. See Erhard Dittrich, *Die deutschen und österreichischen Kameralisten* (Darmstadt: Wissenschaftliche Buchgesellschaft, 1974), 40–49, and on Klock, as well as 'early' Cameralism in a wider sense, the excellent introduction by Bertram Schefold in ibid., ed., *(Kaspar Klock) Tractatus juridico-politico-polemico-historicus de aerario, sive censu per honesta media absque divexatione populi licite conficiendo, libri duo* (Hildesheim and New York: Olms-Weidmann, 2009).

12 1750/1753/1764 ed. (Frankfurt and Leipzig), preface.

compared to France, England and Holland in terms of manufacturing, which Hörnigk had complained about a hundred years earlier, was still true. The only real change that had occurred in between was that England had now surpassed all the other nations in terms of economic wealth and stealth. With the benefit of hindsight, we know that this was to a significant extent due to England's trajectory as the 'first industrial nation' – which rested on a state economic policy that was formidably close to what Hörnigk laid out in his *Austria Supreme*.[13] Literally all nations of contemporary Europe adopted Hörnigkian measures to some extent; some with more, others with less success. It was long after the mid-nineteenth century that modern social sciences came to condemn, as something 'unnatural' and contrary to the cosmic order and the natural market optimum effected by the virtuous forces of the 'invisible hand', the very strategies that had made the north-western European nations rich since the Middle Ages (Table 1).

Until the 1930s, some doubts remained about Hörnigk's authorship;[14] including the hypothesis that *Oesterreich über alles* may have been written by his brother-in-law, eminent German early 'Mercantilist' (or Cameralist) Johann Joachim Becher. Since then however, Hörnigk's authorship has been asserted without doubt.[15] As far as is known, this work was never translated into English and, as yet, we have no secure knowledge of possible contemporary translations into other languages. Parts of the work were translated into English by Arthur E. Monroe in the 1920s.[16] The next edition was the one (in German) in 1948 by August Skalweit;[17] in 1949 there was a New York edition, with part translation into English, by K. W. and L. L. Knapp.[18] After that, all scholarly efforts directed at Hörnigk took place in the German tongue. We have the 1964 commented edition by Otruba.[19] In 1978, there appeared a facsimile reprint of the 1753 edition.[20] This was before google.books. In 1983, a facsimile appeared in the Austrian 'Klassiker der Österreichischen Nationalökonomie' series, again with a brief introduction.[21] In 1997, a similar launch was made in its German equivalent, the Düsseldorf project, accompanied

---

13 *Herrn Johann von Horneks Bemerkungen ueber die oesterreichische Staatsoekonomie*, ed. Benedikt Franz Hermann (1784; no place of publication given), preface, 15, 20, notes.

14 Otruba, '*Österreich über alles*', 9.

15 Ibid., 28.

16 Arthur Eli Monroe, *Early Economic Thought: Selected Writings from Aristotle to Hume*, 8th ed. (Cambridge: Harvard University Press, 1965).

17 Hörnigk, Philipp Wilhelm von, '*Österreich über alles', wann es nur will*, ed. August Skalweit (Frankfurt: Klostermann, 1948).

18 Karl William Kapp and Lore L. Kapp, *History of Economic Thought: A Book of Readings* (New York: Barnes & Noble, 1949).

19 Gustav Otruba (ed.), '*Österreich über alles', wenn es nur will*. Nach der Erstausg. von 1684 in Normalorthogr. übertr. und mit der Aufl. von 1753 kollationiert sowie mit einem Lebensbild des Autors versehen (Vienna: Bergland, 1964) (as in n. 4,14,15).

20 '*Österreich über alles', wann es nur will / Philipp Wilhelm von Hörnigk, Unveränd. Neudr. d. Ausg. Frankfurt u. Leipzig 1753* (Vaduz/Liechtenstein: Topos-Verlag, 1978).

21 *Philipp Wilhelm von Hörnigk, 'Österreich über alles', wann es nur will*, ed. Horst Knapp, Hannes Androsch, Helmut Haschek and Franz Vranitzky (Vienna: Edition Wirtschaft / C. Brandstätter, 1983).

Table 1 Publication history of Hörnigk, *Oesterreich über alles*

---

1. German edition, [Nuremberg?], *Gedruckt im Jahr Christi, 1684.*
2. German edition, [n.d., 1684?], not located.
3. German edition, [n.p.], 1685. * Published in Passau according to Otruba.
4. German edition, [n.p.], 1705.
5. German edition, Leipzig/bey Thomas Fritschen, 1707.
6. German edition, Regensburg (Ratisbon)/Verlegts Joh. Zacharias Seidel, 1708.
7. German edition, Regensburg/Verlegts Joh. Zacharias Seidel, 1712.
8. German edition, Regensburg/ Verlegts Joh. Zacharias Seidel, 1717.
9. German edition, [n.p.], 1719.
10. German edition, Regensburg/Verlegts Johann Conrad Peetz, 1723.
11. German edition, Regensburg/Verlegts Johann Conrad Peetz, 1727.
12. German edition, Franckfurt, 1729.
13. German edition, Franckfurt u. Leipzig/Franckfurt und Leipzig, 1750.
14. German edition, Frankfurt u. Leipzig/Franckfurt und Leipig, 1753.
15. German edition, Franckfurt und Leipzig, 1764.
16. German edition, Berlin und Stettin, Bey Friedrich Nikolai, 1784.
17. German-language pirated edition, [n.p.], but Vienna, [Vienna: Georg Philipp Wucherer], 1784.
18. German-language pirated edition, n.p., probably Vienna, 1784.

Source: Ken Carpenter, formerly librarian at Kress Library, Harvard University. Communicated via email. Further sources: Otruba (See full citation in n. 19); Brauleke, Otruba (ed.), *Österreich über alles*, editor's introduction (in German), 93–97 and the chapter by Reinert and Carpenter in Philipp Robinson Rössner, ed., *Economic Growth and the Origins of Modern Political Economy: Economic Reasons of State, 1500–2000* (Milton Park and New York: Routledge, 2016). From 1707 on, the additional *Anhang oder unvorgreiffliches Projekt zu Stellung einer Armee von hundert tausend Mann aus den Kayserl. Erbländern* was added, for which Hörnigk's authorship is in much doubt.
Note that Leipzig was among the most favoured places for publication as the censorship laws were comparatively mild there compared to Austrian lands.

by a *Vademecum* or companion volume series.[22] The present volume, therefore, presents the first fully annotated and commented translation of this important text into the English language.

Hörnigk's text is odd in more than one way. Contemporaries such as Johann Joachim Becher and his *Politische Discurs*, or Veit Ludwig von Seckendorff with his *Teutscher Fürsten Stat* (1656) wrote treatises that often numbered more than a thousand pages. They could easily have condensed them down to the size of Hörnigk's work without losing substance (and Hörnigk may have done the same: a thirty-page volume would have done the trick in terms of bringing home his main points). But only today's epistemology, manifested in the modern paradigm in economics and general calls for parsimony in saving resources

---

22 *Philipp Wilhelm von Hörnigk, 'Österreich über alles', wann es nur will, das ist … Faksimile Ausgabe* (Düsseldorf: Verlag Wirtschaft und Finanzen, 1997) and the commentary Monika Streissler, Herbert Matis and Erich W Streissler, eds, *Vademecum zu einem Klassiker absolutistischer Wirtschaftspolitik* (Düsseldorf: Verlag Wirtschaft und Finanzen, 1997), with an excellent introduction by Bertram Schefold and a very informative paper by Keith Tribe on the semantics of Cameralism.

for printing would suggest such a strategy. Three hundred years ago, in the age of Baroque, things were much different. People had time to read longer texts. The language and discursive strategy of baroque economics were different. Moreover, *Oesterreich über alles* was not a 'textbook' in the same way, for instance, as Seckendorff's *Fürsten Stat* or the Cameralist literature of the eighteenth century à la Johann Heinrich Gottlob Justi's *Staatswirthschaft* (Principles of Economics, 1755) would have been. It was much more akin to a pamphlet, written in an opaque language, cliché ridden and full of exaggerations, hyperboles, digressions and excursions. Style and syntax were not nearly as economical as students would now expect from an economics textbook. Rather than coming straight to the point, Hörnigk, very much like his brother-in-law J. J. Becher, loved huge sentences that meandered all over the place, often without finding a real ending or coming to the point. They contained a sometimes exhausting level of detail, some of it perhaps obsolete to the modern reader. But the core of his economic programme was very similar to what another 'German' economist would, about 150 years later, formulate as the core strategy of catch-up economic development and a blueprint for many a modern development economic textbook. In his works, Friedrich List (1789–1846) argued, inter alia, that it was vital for an economy to build up a manufacturing sector that was competitive in international markets; that it would be imperative to nourish domestic industry so long as it remained uncompetitive, by protective tariff walls and government intervention so as to raise overall productivity, and that it was good to have free trade – but only when the nation was considered to be fit for it. List was, as were Hörnigk, von Seckendorff and Becher, reiterating a stance other theorists had formulated previously, most prominently Giovanni Botero, in his *Della Ragion di Stato* (1589) and Antonio Serra, *Breve trattato delle cause che possono far abbondare li regni d'oro e argento dove non sono miniere* (1613). The Serra text was one of the earliest texts containing a systematic analysis of manufacturing and its role in economic growth and development.[23] In fact it seems as though Botero's *Ragion di Stato* – a treatise explaining why wages were higher in cities and why manufacturing as an economic activity generated positive scale economies, thus adding value to the economy where agrarian activities wouldn't – would have been the intellectual inspiration of many an economic treatise of the time, including Hörnigk's *Austria Supreme*. From Veit Ludwig von Seckendorff – the 'Adam Smith of Cameralism' (Albion Small) – it is known that he had read and greatly admired Botero's work. He recommended it as compulsory reading to the Duke Ernest of Saxony-Gotha, and the princely library at *Schloss Friedenstein* in Gotha contained numerous editions of Botero's *Ragion di Stato*. Seven translations into German and twelve translations into Latin were published in Germany between 1596 and 1670, which explains not only the huge number of volumes found in the library at *Friedenstein* Castle but also allows us to draw a direct line between Giovanni Botero and German Cameralism via Veit Ludwig von Seckendorff's *Additiones* (1665) to his *Teutscher Fürsten Stat* and his spells as a princely librarian in the service of the Saxon Dukes.[24] It was

---

23 See *Antonio Serra, A Short Treatise on the Wealth and Poverty of Nations (1613)*, ed. Sophus Reinert (London and New York: Anthem, 2011), with an excellent introduction by the editor.
24 And more than 84 editions of Botero's *Relazioni Universali* (1591–98) were printed between 1591 and 1796, making it arguably one of Europe's best-selling economic treatises. See

not unusual in those days to not fully disclose one's sources, and footnotes or annotations were, for the time being, rather rare in scientific treatises. Hörnigk would have known Botero's works as intimately as Seckendorff's and the other cameralists.

Hörnigk got forgotten over time, as did, in a way – looking at the modern economics curriculum taught at university level – Botero, Serra and many Germanic economists yet to come, up to Friedrich List and the earlier and later so-called 'German Historical School'.[25] Their ideas continued to live on into modern economic thought and practice, but sometimes without explicit acknowledgement. Europe grew rich on these ideas. Only specialists are nowadays aware of these economists' contribution to the ideas that built (and in many ways continue to build) Europe, as well as the non-European world.[26]

Who Was Hörnigk?

Who was Philipp Wilhelm von Hörnigk, then? We even lack a portrait of Hörnigk, so conspirative were his political activities as a diplomat in the service of high-ranking imperial politicians and officials. But we do have an engraving showing the portrait of his father Ludwig (von) Hörnigk, a polymath and native of the Imperial City of Frankfurt who had obtained, during his academic career, three doctorates (an LLD, a PhD in philosophy as well as an MD) and may, in fact, according to obscure sources, have been an illegitimate son of Louis V, Landgrave of Hesse-Darmstadt (1577–1626).[27] Most of his time as an active administrator and secretary during the 1660s to 1690s, Hörnigk worked undercover, in the services of great Catholic politicians such as

Giovanni Botero, *Le relazioni universali*, 2 vols., ed. B. A. Raviola (Turin: Nino Aragno, 2015). Sophus A. Reinert, 'Cameralism and Commercial Rivalry: Nationbuilding through Economic Autarky in Seckendorff's 1665 *Additiones*', *European Journal of Law and Economics*, 19 (2005), 271–86, at 277f., as well as personal communication with Erik, Fernanda and Sophus Reinert.

25 Good overviews can be found in Johannes Burkhardt and Birger P. Priddat, eds, *Geschichte der Ökonomie* (Frankfurt: Deutscher Klassiker Verlag, 2009), Bertram Schefold, 'Der Nachklang der historischen Schule in Deutschland zwischen dem Ende des zweiten Weltkriegs und dem Anfang der sechziger Jahre', in Karl Acham, Knut Wolfgang Nörr and Bertram Schefold, eds, *Erkenntnisgewinne, Erkenntnisverluste. Kontinuitäten und Diskontinuitäten in den Wirtschafts-, Rechts- und Sozialwissenschaften zwischen den 20er und 50er Jahren* (Stuttgart: Franz Steiner, 1998), 31–70, and Peter Koslowski, ed., *The Theory of Ethical Economy in the Historical School: Wilhelm Roscher, Lorenz von Stein, Gustav Schmoller, Wilhelm Dilthey and Contemporary Theory* (Berlin: Springer, 1995).

26 The role of old German economists in the story of how Europe developed a successful industry and economy since the Middle Ages has most recently been stressed in Erik S. Reinert, *How Rich Countries Got Rich…And Why Poor Countries Stay Poor* (New York: Carroll & Graf, 2007); there is a host of recent specialist literature, referenced at the appropriate sections below, which has dealt with this heterodox or 'Other Canon' in close detail. Scholars that have made notable advances in the field include, apart from Reinert, Bertram Schefold, Birger Priddat, Jürgen Backhaus, as well as Andre Wakefield and Keith Tribe. Sophus Reinert, *Translating Empire: Emulation and the Origins of Political Economy* (Cambridge, MA: Harvard University Press, 2011) has opened up a new agenda for treating pre-Smithian (pre-classical) economics, but without a Germanic focus.

27 Barbara Dölemeyer, *Frankfurter Juristen im 17. und 18. Jahrhundert* (Frankfurt: Klostermann, 1993), 81.

Cardinal Lamberg or Bishop Cristobal de la Rojas/Royas, a man who toured the Empire during the 1670s and 1680s on a mission to reunify the Christian Faith amongst the German nations and territories. In effect, this project would have amounted to a full re-Catholization of the Empire if it had been successful. Hörnigk is alleged to have adopted the title of his magnum opus, which he wrote within a few months during his intermittent spell at Dresden in Saxony (1683–84), from a pamphlet of similar character, content and argumentation, dating from the same year, entitled *Teutschland über Franckreich / wenn es klug seyn will.*[28] The phrase made it into the infamous nineteenth-century *Deutschlandlied* by August Heinrich Hoffmann von Fallersleben, which was sung to the tune of the current national anthem of the Federal Republic, but whose first verse was banned (in 1952) due to its nationalist undertone and racist abuse after 1933.[29]

Philipp Wilhelm von Hörnigk can be found in the written record as *Horneck, Hornigk, Hörnigk, Hornek, Hornog* and many more; in total 34 alternatives of the name and spelling have been found so far.[30] But this was usual for those times. 'Hörnigk' would perhaps be the most appropriate version; at least that was the name by which his father went when he obtained his imperial nobilitation privilege issued at Prague in 1629. According to economic historian Inama-Sternegg, our protagonist referred to himself as *Hornick* during later years of his life and in his testament of the 1690s.[31] The literal meaning of this name is either 'horny' or 'horned'. Whatever may be true with regard to the original prominence of the name, the imperial coat-of-arms received in 1629 features a white unicorn as a pictorial translation.

Philipp Wilhelm von Hörnigk wrote a series of pamphlets either anonymous or under pseudonym such as the Francopolita; therefore more texts written by the man may exist than we know for certain.[32] What we know about his life in terms of direct biographical dates is much less than could be expected from the prominence of his work. His life is not easy to reconstruct, as he left no coherent or complete set of personal records. Most of what we know about him comes from 'mirror' sources: documents produced by people Hörnigk met with, or the praise and acclaim his work received posthumously. It was only during the eighteenth century that *Oesterreich über alles* was formally acknowledged to be Hörnigk's work (and controversy as to the authorship would remain into the twentieth century, see earlier in the chapter). Like Becher and Schröder, the other two of the tripartite gang of the older Austrian Cameralists, Hörnigk was a convert to the Catholic faith (a re-convert from the point of view of the Old Faith). This influenced (or was influenced

---

28 Brauleke, 'Vom Frankfurter Gelehrtenspross', 84; Walter Dührkoop, *Einzelwirtschaftliche Erörterungen in den Hauptwerken der alten österreichischen Kameralisten: Becher, Hörnigk, Schröder* (Bottrop i. W.: Postberg, 1935), 67.

29 Under the Hitler regime the first verse of the *Deutschlandlied* was sung as the national anthem, followed by the Horst-Wessel-Lied.

30 Brauleke, *Leben und Werk*, chapter IX.

31 Karl Theodor Inama-Sternegg, 'Über Philipp Wilhelm von Hörnigk', *Jahrbücher für Nationalökonomie und Statistik* 36 (NF 2) (1881), 194–200, at 194.

32 Heinrich Gerstenberg, 'Philipp Wilhelm von Hörnigk', *Jahrbücher für Nationalökonomie und Statistik*, III. Folge (1930), 813–71, at 816–17.

by) his later professional career as a man of the Church and simultaneously the Emperor and the Imperial Cause. Theirs was the Catholic cause.[33] If one thing is for certain it is that Hörnigk travelled a lot; not so much outside Austria and the Holy Roman Empire, which contained, at that time, several hundreds of different states and other formally independent territories. Quite unlike his brother-in-law Becher (1635–82), who made it to England and Scotland, or Wilhelm von Schröder (1640–88) who even became a member of the Royal Society in London, Hörnigk seems to have remained tied to the German-speaking lands. But nevertheless he spent most of his professional career on the road before he retired to his post of secretary and archivist of the Prince Bishop of Passau in the 1690s. For a man of his age and profession this was anything but unusual. When he compiled the Austrian industrial census or statistics in 1673, he travelled between August and December through wide stretches of Bohemia, Silesia, Moravia and Lower Austria. By then he had visited and compiled a detailed set of economic statistics for about 110 cities and market towns in total, when he returned to Vienna three months later, on 30 December, 1673 (he was suspected to be a spy). In the late 1670s, when his magnum opus would have germinated in his head, he accompanied bishop Christopher de la Royas on his political mission (reunifying the church), visiting, among many other cities, Salzburg, Augsburg, Nuremberg, Frankfur, Munich, Ulm, Regensburg, Mannheim, Mainz, Fulda, Kassel, Cologne, Paderborn, Osnabrück, Hanover, Celle, Lübeck and Mecklenburg. He was at the Saxon Court in Dresden as early as 1679, and of course, in 1682–84, where he finished *Oesterreich über alles*. Subsequently, we find traces of his time in Hamburg, as well as Berlin and many other princely residences, accompanying imperial legate Cardinal Lamberg.[34] So he would have had a profound knowledge of German political and economic geography; but his knowledge about the Netherlands and England was clearly second-hand.

He was born presumably in Frankfurt, but older sources also have Mainz, the capital and residential place of the Archbishop of Mainz. His most likely date of birth is 23 January 1640; his accepted death date is 23 October 1714.[35] His family may, according to a side remark by his biographer, Hans Joachim Breuleke, have been of Swedish origin. But we do not know how far back a Swedish lineage would have reached. Other sources have suggested, with similar lack of firm evidence, that – based on the etymology of the name Hörnigk – the family may have come originally from somewhere east of the Oder-Neisse line.[36] Both stories are equally plausible but impossible to corroborate (and not ultimately important). As mentioned earlier in the chapter, another legend has him as an

---

33 Konrad Amann, 'Ein Kameralist in Passauer Diensten. Philipp Wilhelm (von) Hörnigk', *Ostbairische Grenzmarken* 42 (2000), 59–74.

34 Otruba, *Österreich über alles*, 21–27.

35 Inama-Sternegg, 'Über Philipp Wilhelm von Hörnigk', 196 has 1638 as his birth year, as does Kurt Zielenziger, *Die alten deutschen Kameralisten. Ein Beitrag zur Geschichte der Nationalökonomie und zum Problem des Merkantilismus* (Jena: G. Fischer, 1914), 278. Various similar as well as other suggestions (e.g. 1636) may be found in the older literature. The current state of the art has 1640 as Hörnigk's birth year.

36 Breuleke, *Leben und Werk*, 8.

offspring of the illegitimate son of a Hessian Landgrave. His father Ludwig had made it into Imperial Nobility in 1629 with a privilege and certificate allowing him to carry the title 'von' as well as have a custom-made coat-of-arms.[37] His grandfather was, according to the other legend, said to have been a piper of Darmstadt in Hesse about twenty kilometres south of the Free Imperial City of Frankfurt. He may have come from a place called Borna, although it cannot be ascertained with ultimate certainty if this was the Borna near Leipzig in Saxony.[38] Ludwig von Hörnigk had been in the service of Count of Solms-Rödelheim, but when at Frankfurt, he entered the service of Johann Philipp von Schönborn, Archbishop of Mainz, and converted to Catholicism in 1647. Hörnigk was, in a sense, born into a family of servicemen to prominent Catholic Princes during a *Sturm-und-Drang* period; a time of bitter struggle for imperial unification, political as well as religious (the Thirty Years War raged on still), and a time that saw the Ottoman army stand at the doors of the Empire. Perhaps the change in confession was simply a matter of convenience: it got the Hörnigks the jobs they obviously wanted.

Philip von Hörnigk matriculated 1654 at the University of Mainz at the tender age of 14 and became friends with his later brother-in-law Johann J. Becher who would subsequently marry Hörnigk's sister, Maria Veronika von Hörnigk. As the father Ludwig von Hörnigk was at the time Dean of the Medical Faculty it was him who conferred the doctorate to Becher, his son-in-law, at Mainz in 1660–61. Hörnigk moved to Ingolstadt to study Law, graduating in 1661. There has been a long controversy whether or not Hörnigk ever earned a doctorate (LLD);[39] the current state of the art has it that he didn't. His father had collected three of them (as listed earlier in this chapter); four degrees in the family may have been enough for the Hörnigk clan. But he wrote a dissertation in Church Law, somewhat paving the way for an administrative career in the services of the church, the Empire and the Catholic Cause, very much as his father did. We find Hörnigk, over the next twenty years, in the service of Bishop Christoph de Roya (also written as Rojas, Roxas, Rochas, or Cristóbal de Royas y Spínola, circa 1626–1695, the occasional titular Bishop of Tinia in Croatia, a Franciscan born in Flanders (the Habsburg or Spanish Netherlands) and an Imperial Legate. Hörnigk was also with Cardinal Johann Philipp von Lamberg or Lambert, sometime Prince-Bishop of Passau. Lamberg was, as was Royas, an ardent advocate of confessional and economic (re-)unification of the Empire, bringing

---

37 The original document can be consulted at the Sächsische Staats- und Universitätsbibliothek Dresden online: http://digital.slub-dresden.de/fileadmin/data/327505214/327505214_tif/jpegs/327505214.pdf (last accessed 20 January 2015).

38 This could be possible inasmuch as some sources suggest that the father, Ludwig von Hörnigk, may have been born at Leipzig. The problem is, of course, 'which father?', as other sources have claimed that Ludwig von Hörnigk was an illegitimate son of Landgrave Ludwig V of Hesse-Darmstadt (1596–1626). See Wilhelm Stricker, 'Ludwig von Hörnigk. Ein Charakterbild aus der Geschichte der Medizin', *Archiv für Frankfurts Geschichte und Kunst*, 4–5 (Frankfurt: Heinrich Keller, 1869), 237–47, at 237.

39 See a chapter especially devoted to this problem in Brauleke, *Leben und Werk*, ch. VI. Zielenziger maintains that Hörnigk obtained a doctorate (*Die Alten Kameralisten*, 278) but there is no written evidence for this.

the confessional landscape back to the pre-1517 status quo changed by the Monk from Wittenberg. 'Imperial Mercantilism' was the chosen political economic programme of the day as a way to achieve political and religious-confessional unity by using economic means for wealth creation and economic development of the German territories (which is an interesting aspect in itself and resonates with late twentieth-century attempts at creating political unification in Europe by using the tools of economic and monetary integration).[40]

Hörnigk repeatedly travelled, in company with his brother-in-law Johann Joachim Becher, who was said to be the intellectual father of the German 'imperial Mercantilism'. They visited German courts to enforce the imperial edict prohibiting the import of French goods (7 May 1676), one of the prime expressions of Germano-Austrian 'imperial Mercantilism'. In effect this edict – as most of the subsequent imperial economic legislation – more or less came to nought. The Holy Roman Empire lacked many of the key executive functions characteristic of a 'state' and 'empire'. The political interests of the territorial states that made up Germany more often than not proved irreconcilable. Nevertheless, 'Imperial Mercantilism' unfolded an enormous discursive power and created a lot of work and travel expenses for skilled negotiators, journalists and schemy administrators in those times. From 1663 onwards we find the 'permanent' imperial diet (*Immerwährender Reichstag*) in place, based at Regensburg (Ratisbon). One crucial aim was to achieve an increase in political integration through increased economic cooperation, such as customs unions and a common tariff against countries outside of the imperial umbrella.[41] These aspects set the context within which Hörnigk's *Oesterreich über alles* ought to be placed. The main impetus, alongside the political danger posed by the Ottoman Empire, was directed at France, the emerging political and economic power and Europe's biggest and most powerful economy of the day, if measured in terms of absolute population size times their purchasing power or 'per capita gross domestic product'. (We may identify this accounting concept, or 'GDP', as *economic potential* denoting the potential market size of a country as opposed to relative productivity and wealth which is captured most usually under the term *per capita gross domestic product/per capita GDP*.)[42] While in terms of per capita GDP France ranged alongside the continental average, its total GDP or 'market size' placed her at the top. France was, if we disregard Russia and composite monarchies (such as Poland-Lithuania-Saxony and Habsburg, comprising the Austrian, Hungarian and Bohemian lands as well as other smaller territories) the biggest country in Europe. It was, accordingly, Europe's biggest market economy, far ahead (but only in terms of market size) of the Holy Roman Empire, the Netherlands, Italy and England.[43] France

40 The basic and only fundamental study still remains Ingomar Bog, *Der Reichsmerkantilismus. Studien zur Wirtschaftspolitik des Heiligen Römischen Reiches im 17. und 18. Jahrhundert* (Stuttgart: Gustav Fischer, 1959), 14.

41 Joachim Whaley, *Germany and the Holy Roman Empire* (Oxford: Oxford University Press, 2012), vol. II, 58–9.

42 For an interesting approach, see Paul M. Kennedy, *The Rise and Fall of the Great Powers: Economic Change and Military Conflict From 1500 to 2000* (New York: Random House, 1987).

43 According to the Maddison database (see below): http://www.ggdc.net/maddison/oriindex.htm (last accessed: 23 January 2015).

was for German manufacturers what modern sports language has as the *Angstgegner*, the antagonist to be feared, the arch-enemy. French imports into the Empire would have numbered, according to Becher's more or less fantastic estimates (but whose estimates weren't fantastic those days?), around 4 million Thalers every year. Gottfried Wilhelm Leibniz, the prominent philosopher, reckoned them to be ten per cent of the German national product, an estimate that was, of course, as fictitious as Becher's, especially in terms of comparability with modern accounting concepts, but also on account of the somewhat limited reliability of contemporary statistical coverage. Nevertheless such estimates did the trick, inasmuch as they served to drive home a fundamental point. The French were the most important suppliers of manufactured imports into the German lands. France was the biggest danger to German economic health, if health was defined as the potential to build up a competitive export industry, with a focus on manufacturing (a prime point on the agenda of Mercantilist and Cameralist economics). The Imperial Edict from 1673 was directed at French luxury imports and manufactures with a high value added: gadgets, such as clocks and watches, high value garments, fabrics, hats, buttons, brocade and so forth.[44] Similar import lists exist for seventeenth- and eighteenth-century Scotland, another of the poorer economies of the day, suggesting a similar commercial dominance of the French in the high-value-added manufacturing sector.[45] Late seventeenth-century discourses, especially at Europe's periphery, were full of fears relating to the 'French danger'.

The text of the 1673 Imperial edict directed at prohibiting French manufacturing imports specifically referred to the high outflow of money and the underemployment of domestic productive resources as a consequence of a monetary outflow to a nation that also classified – for many, but by no means all German states – as a political enemy. At that time, people made much less fuss about 'political' enemies; many German princes entered into alliance with the French Sun King to protect their interests. But the discourses were sharp and charged with undertones that often came close to hate propaganda.[46] The preceding decade had seen attempts at political and economic integration between the Austrian lands and Bavaria, coupled with plans to develop seaports for international trade, projects that usually met with mixed success due to the Empire's rugged physical, political and economic geography.[47] German philosopher Leibniz and Samuel von Pufendorf stressed the principal possibility of achieving economic autarky for the German lands; a dubious proposition if seen from a modern vantage point. Autarky is often seen, in the modern discourse, as the opposite of 'good economics'; both unrealistic and economically unfeasible or 'stupid', as nations striving for autarky basically forfeit

---

44 Bog, *Reichsmerkantilismus*, 76ff. Konrad Amann, 'Ein Kameralist in Passauer Diensten. Philipp Wilhelm (von) Hörnigk', *Ostbairische Grenzmarken* 42 (2000), 59–74, a not so original paper as it draws heavily on Brauleke (as in n. 33).

45 Philipp R. Rössner, *Scottish Trade in the Wake of Union (1700–1760). The Rise of a Warehouse Economy* (Stuttgart: Franz Steiner, 2008), 139–40.

46 Bog, *Reichsmerkantilismus*, 78.

47 See, e.g. Florian Schui, 'Prussia's "Trans-oceanic Moment". The Creation of the Prussian Asiatic Trade Company in 1750', *The Historical Journal* 49, no. 1 (2006), 143–60.

the imputed benefits from foreign trade and specialization, to Ricardian comparative advantage. But the proposition needs to be understood in the political context of the 1650s and 1660s. The edict was also specifically directed at certain commodity flows but not, as in a general situation of warfare, against French subjects and individuals generally; exports to France should remain intact. The document carried a sort of Listian undertone inasmuch as it favoured the education of an underdeveloped economy whose industrial spirit should be raised in order to participate more equally in international trade and manufacturing exports. These issues would become cornerstones of eighteenth-century political and economic discourses on 'civilized' economies and 'polite' societies in the models proposed by Scottish philosophers and theorists, from David Hume and Adam Smith to Sir James Steuart in the second half of the eighteenth century.[48] As early as 1679, we find an expert reference, written by Augsburg merchants who doubted very much that German producers would be able to craft high-value woollen and silk fabrics such as Serge des Nîmes, de Châlons, de Reims etc. Outright prohibition of French imports would pose the risk of these goods being imported into Germany via the Netherlands; this would only increase their costs and thus the German import bill.[49] When the Free Imperial City of Hamburg counteracted a second imperial edict in 1689 – as Germany's biggest and most competitive sea port, the Imperial edict of 1676 was diametrically opposed to Hamburg's commercial interest (free trade with everyone) – , the Emperor levied a hefty fine of 100,000 Rix dollars in retaliation.[50] Of course, the imperial Mercantilism edict would have been impossible to enforce effectively. It collided with too many vested interests, especially those of the individual states and territories that made up the empire. Hamburg alone developed, during the eighteenth century, an increasingly powerful oceanic trade in colonial goods, for which France, the Netherlands and England turned out to be the chief suppliers.[51] Strictly speaking, Germany was not the place where a programme of 'imperial' Mercantilism could ever be imposed as a 'national' strategy of development. It could, and would, be implemented successfully only on the individual state level. But still the hopelessly utopian illusion of 'Imperial Mercantilism' was important for the political and economic landscape of central Europe towards the later seventeenth and well into the eighteenth century. Ideas matter, after all – in the same way as practices do.

Thus, many battles of the economic wars fought in the period were fought out on paper. But this does by no means belittle or berate their historical significance. The English Navigation Acts (1651 under Cromwell; 1660 under Charles II) are proverbial; less famous but similar in tone and approach is the Scottish Navigation Act of 1661. An

---

48 Hont, *Jealousy of Trade*. (as in n. 5).

49 Bog, *Reichsmerkantilismus*, 90.

50 Friedrich Lütge, 'Außenwirtschaftspolitische Maßnahmen des Deutschen Reiches im Zeitalter des Merkantilismus', in Otto Stammer and Karl C. Stammheim, eds, *Festgabe für Friedrich Bülow zum 70. Geburtstag* (Berlin: Duncker & Humblot, 1960), 257–70, at 265–67.

51 Klaus Weber, *Deutsche Kaufleute im Atlantikhandel, 1680–1830: Unternehmen und Familien in Hamburg, Cádiz und Bordeaux* (Munich: C. H. Beck, 2004). Statistical figures for Hamburg's import trades from 1733 onwards have been tabulated in Jürgen Schneider, Otto-Ernst Krawehl and

edict with a similar consequence would be issued in Sweden in 1664, as contemporary German documents relating to the formulation and preparation of the imperial prohibition of 1676 suggest. The imperial edict of 1676 was based on an Austrian Mercantilist model tested and applied under Emperor Leopold in 1674. Accompanied by Hörnigk in 1678–79, Bishop Royas (Spinola) went on an imperial mission through several territories of the empire. His programme of political unification using economic integration in many ways prefigured, as far as we can determine from the written record of this period, what Hörnigk would write later in his 1684 main work. The programme covered cornerstones of 'Mercantilist' reasoning, including the prohibition of exporting valuable raw materials such as hides, wool and flax; and the call for high-value manufactures such as fabrics using the French pattern, but manufactured domestically. French imports should be generally prohibited. Workhouses were to be erected for fast-track education of expert spinsters and weavers (and vagabonds were to be put into the workhouses: the Dark Side of Mercantilism). Domestic merchants should be reimbursed for foregone profits on imports that were now banned. Manufactured imports were to be prohibited as long as domestic production was not completely sold on the domestic market or elsewhere. Sliding import tariffs were then to be applied following the English example.[52] This programme is again very 'Listian' in approach and nature, as Hörnigk's pamphlet is in many places. We may call this approach the 'Hörnigk Strategy' or alternatively, 'Enlightenment economics', to give credit to modern developments in the intellectual history of political economy. But this enlightenment economics was different from what later mainstream research has, in a shorthand way, identified as 'enlightened' (which we prefer to call free market economics, in the wake of Scottish philosophers such as David Hume or Adam Smith).[53]

Whether or not the Mercantilist discourse and measures of the 1670s, in which Hörnigk took on an increasingly active function, were ever turned into practice or were 'effective' is a moot point. Any definition of 'effectiveness' or 'efficiency' (of a peculiar policy or strategy) is controversial in this context.[54] Moreover, we lack the quantitative evidence that would be necessary for testing such hypotheses. It has been said sometimes, in a similar vain, that Germany's trade balance with France would have turned from passive in 1648 to positive around 1705.[55] Again

Markus A. Denzel, eds *Statistik des Hamburger seewärtigen Einfuhrhandels im 18. Jahrhundert. Nach den Admiralitätszoll- und Convoygeld-Einnahmebüchern* (St Katharinen: Scripta Mercaturae Verlag, 2001). See also discussion in Philipp Robinson Rössner, 'Structural Change in European Economy and Commerce, 1660–1800. Lessons from Scotland's and Hamburg's Overseas Trades', *The Bulletin of the Institute for World Affairs, Kyoto Sangyo University*, XXVII (2011), 25–62.

52 Bog, *Reichsmerkantilismus*, 102–3.

53 Masterfully analysed in the first chapter in Reinert, *Translating Empire*, with a useful précis and update in ibid., 'Rivalry: Greatness in Early Modern Political Economy', in: Philip J. Stern and Carl Wennerlind, eds, *Mercantilism Reimagined: Political Economy in Early Modern Britain and Its Empire* (Oxford: Oxford University Press, 2013), 348–70.

54 See the good discussion in Regina Grafe, 'Mercantilism and Representation in a Polycentric State: Early Modern Spain', in Stern and Wennerlind, eds *Mercantilism Reimagined*, 241–62.

55 Whaley, *Germany and the Holy Roman Empire*, II, 59.

this is impossible to either falsify or confirm. What matters is the discourse programme of development, the mind map that was in place, and that the scientific discourse in economics was increasingly based upon quantitative evidence that would later become known as economic statistics, however fictitious or unreliable from a modern vantage point.

Hörnigk spoke Spanish and some French and did in fact accompany Royas on a voyage to Spain; both returned in 1665 to the Imperial Court at Vienna. We have seen him already compiling, in 1673, a *Gewerbestatistik* (industrial census) for the Austrian lands (see earlier in the chapter).[56] Hörnigk moved to Vienna in 1665–68 and returned in 1673. Baroque Vienna had emerged as an important intellectual centre; with the Catholic Enlightenment, however intolerant of protestant sentiments, which laid the foundation for later Josephinian Reform. Austria became a leader in terms of elementary and industrial schools, generating cultural techniques able to generate and improve 'useful knowledge', but still lagging behind protestant countries in terms of university training.[57]

Hörnigk became administrator of the *Pfarre Hartberg* in East Styria and secretary to Bishop Royas; he thus gained the practical experience necessary for managing a Mercantilist micro-territory for nine years.[58] During 1676, he toured through Germany, inter alia Augsburg, Nuremberg, Ulm, Frankfurt, then Mainz and Cologne. In the Upper German merchant and trading metropolis of Augsburg he learned the techniques of the cashless payments mechanism (especially the Augsburg-Lyons bill of exchange business) and about the practice of how outstanding debts for imports from France were settled with native merchants. In 1676, he commenced his intellectual exchange with Gottfried Wilhelm Leibniz (1646–1716), the German philosopher king, mainly through written correspondence that can be traced from the Leibniz letters. This exchange lasted until 1709.[59] In 1680–82 Hörnigk can be found in the service of the imperial ambassador Count Johann Philipp von Lamberg to the court of the Margrave of Brandenburg. *Oesterreich über alles* is likely to have originated at Dresden, while in Lamberg's service, where Hörnigk would have stayed most of the time between summer 1682 and 1684.[60] While in Saxony, he read the anonymous pamphlet *Bedencken von Manufacturen* ('On Manufacturing', Jena 1683) attributed to Mercantilist author Johann Daniel

56 Otruba, ed., '*Österreich über alles*', 17–20.

57 Anton Schindling, *Bildung und Wissenschaft in der frühen Neuzeit, 1650–1800* (Munich: R. Oldenbourg, 1999), 6–8.

58 Otruba, 'Hörnigk, *Philipp Wilhelm* von' (NDB), 360; Ingomar Bog, 'Christoph de Royas y Spinola und die deutschen Reichsstände. Forschungen zu den Reichseinigungsplänen Kaiser Leopolds I', *Jahrbuch für Fränkische Landesgeschichte* 14 (1954), 191–234.

59 *Gottfried Wilhelm Leibniz: Sämtliche Schriften und Briefe, Reihe 1: Allgemeiner politischer und historischer Briefwechsel* eds Leibniz-Archiv der Gottfried-Wilhelm-Bibliothek, Niedersächsische Landesbibliothek Hannover, vol. 3. 1680–83, 2nd reprint of the original, Leipzig, Koehler, 1938 (Berlin: Akademie-Verlag, 1990).

60 Dührkoop, *Einzelwirtschaftliche Erörterungen*, 65; Heinrich Gerstenberg, 'Philipp Wilhelm v. Hörnigk', *Jahrbücher für Nationalökonomie und Statistik*, 78 (3) / 133 (1930), 813–71, at 834–35, 847–48.

Krafft/Crafft.[61] According to his own testimony, Hörnigk drew much inspiration from this work for his magnum opus.[62]

Crafft had been born in Miltenberg on the Main; after travelling in the Netherlands, France and North America and studying medicine, botany and chemistry – a typical university training for economists in those days – he entered the service of Johann Philipp von Schönborn, Archbishop of Mainz (who had also employed Hörnigk's father) in 1670, where he was responsible inter alia for running several industries, including iron and glass works. Upon the archbishop's death in 1673, Crafft entered the service of the Saxon Duke Johann Georg, establishing a series of bigger manufacturing enterprises (with mixed success) in Leipzig and Dresden, including a large silk manufactory. In the 1680s and 1690s, he was in Bohemia, among other places, still establishing new industrial ventures, as this was his main occupation as a true Cameralist 'project maker' (around 1689, he put forth proposals advocating the introduction of gas lighting in Vienna). Crafft died comparatively poor in Amsterdam in 1697.[63]

From the Leibniz letters, it seems as though Crafft, Hörnigk and Leibniz had been debating the manufacturing and import substitution issue for years (since about 1680), as a means to raise the Austrian and German economies' powers vis-à-vis France. Similar economic ideas had been voiced by Royas / Spinola in the later 1670s.[64] Their ideas were to be communicated widely amongst the rulers of the several territories of the Empire (*das ganze teutsche Manufactur und commercien Wesen und deßen Balance mit den Auslaendern und sonderlich mit … gruendtlich zu untersuchen; und underdeßen in den Erblanden zu wuercklicher Execution anstalt machen zu helffen, auch denen gemaeß die Propositionen bey den vornehmsten teutschen Hoefen einzurichten*).[65] Leibniz also speculated about the viability of revitalizing the Bohemian and Hungarian silver mines, as well as promoting manufactures, in a memorandum addressed to the Emperor in July 1680.[66] Hörnigk's '*Oesterreich über alles*' thus picked up some ideas put forth by Crafft, in his 1683 pamphlet, relating to population and immigration as a source of cultural transfer and useful knowledge. Perhaps his remarks on mining and the finance of unprofitable mining ventures were formulated against the background of Saxon mining. Many of the Saxon mines and pits yielded negative profits and had to be constantly supported by *Zubusse*, something which seems to have been a sort of quasi-patriotic exercise especially in the eighteenth century. Leipzig composer Johann Sebastian Bach possessed several *Kuxen* which do not seem to have yielded impressive proceeds, but the Saxon lands were geared towards and built upon silver rocks. Mining was the

---

61 Justus Nipperdey, *Die Erfindung der Bevölkerungspolitik: Staat, politische Theorie und Population in der Frühen Neuzeit* (Göttingen: Vandenhoeck & Ruprecht, 2012), 323–24.

62 Gerstenberg, 'Philipp Wilhelm v. Hörnigk', 829.

63 Ursula Forberger, 'Crafft (Kraft), Johann Daniel', in *Sächsische Biografie*, ed. Institut für Sächsische Geschichte und Volkskunde e. V. / Martina Schattkowsky, Online issue: http://www.isgv.de/saebi/ (last accessed 20 January 2015).

64 Bog, 'Christoph de Royas y Spinola', 216.

65 E.g. the letter and memorial from Leibniz for Daniel Crafft, circa early July 1680, in: *Leibniz: Sämtliche Schriften und Briefe*, Reihe 1, Vol. 3 (1680–83), 400–3, 408.

66 Ibid., 403–6.

pre-eminent pre-industrial industry. Multiplier effects would double or triple the initial investment in mining – at least that was expected. Above all, supporting the silver rock would have been seen as a patriotic duty.

In 1684, Hörnigk was appointed Imperial Secretary ('Titul dero Kais(erlichen) Secretarii') with a yearly pension of 300 Rhenish florins, which was not a gigantic sum of money, but certainly something on which he would have been able to live well.[67] From 1690, he was in the services of Cardinal Lamberg as Prince-Bishop of Passau (located in today's Bavaria, on the Danube), to which Lamberg had been elected in 1689. The Passau period was the longest time spent at one place; it was at Passau Hörnigk would eventually meet his maker. He remained involved in matters of high politics, with Lamberg being Principal Imperial Commissionary (*kaiserlicher Stellvertreter*) at Regensburg 1699 (*Gesandtenkonferenz der drei Stände*); possibly he became emissary to the Imperial Diet in 1702. Hörnigk died from a stroke during the night of 23–24 October 1714, almost certainly before midnight (various death dates therefore). He left no wife or children behind.

---

67 Brauleke, *Leben und Werk*, 25.

Chapter Two

AN AGE OF REASON? ENLIGHTENMENT AND ECONOMICS

Economics Enlightened

The concept of 'Enlightenment' is, of course, a treacherous one. Adorno and Habermas were neither the first nor the last to discover this. Ratio and rationality were gradually inscribed into Europe's scientific and philosophical mind map since the mid-seventeenth century, including the field of economics and political economy (which have been given far less attention by intellectual historians than other fields, such as the natural sciences). Contrary to a widely-cherished textbook notion, the eighteenth-century Physiocrats weren't the first to entertain the notion that economics should be interpreted as a science in itself, with the subject of study – the economy – being understood as a separate realm of analysis that followed its own mechanisms and 'laws' of motion. The Cameralists were here long before the Physiocrats, but it was the latter who drove the notion to its extreme, describing the realm of economy using the morphology of *physics* (which during the later nineteenth century became an even more popular analogy in the modern economic sciences). The Cameralists on the other hand (and many Mercantilists) understood the economy to be an 'organism', a living being (which it was and is and always has been: economics is about interaction between humans) – something for which biological analogies may be invoked, but certainly not abstract physical laws or working mechanisms. In the modern economic sciences post-1880, when the 'Marginalist' or Walrasian Revolution had finally taken hold, this interpretation of the economy as a *physical* mechanism or system (rather than a *biological* organism) finally teamed up with a quasi-ethical standpoint of 'valueless-ness' (*objectivity*) coupled with what would become known and cherished as the *homo oeconomicus* principle (rational individual with perfect overview on chances, available menu of options and ability to precisely calculate/quantify opportunity costs, maximizing benefits at a given cost structure or, alternatively, minimizing costs in a given framework of desires).[1] In the days of Hörnigk, most of these ideas would have sounded alien; there were large overlapping areas between chemistry

---

1   The literature on this is considerable. An excellent survey may be found in Bruno Ingrao, 'Free Market', in Richard Arena and Christian Longhi, eds *Markets and Organization* (Berlin etc.: Springer, 1998), 61–94, as well as Lisa Herzog and Axel Honneth, eds *Der Wert des Marktes: Ein ökonomisch-philosophischer Diskurs vom 18. Jahrhundert bis zur Gegenwart* (Berlin: Suhrkamp, 2013). A provocative recent account of the evolution of a 'free market' discourse can be found in Bernard Harcourt, *The Illusion of Free Markets: Punishment and the Myth of Natural Order* (Cambridge, MA: Harvard University Press, 2011). See also Peter D. Groenewegen, *Eighteenth Century*

and economics, as many of the 'economists' of the day had studied medicine, botany and chemistry (and many of them engaged in *alchemy*). In late seventeenth-century Sweden, for instance, there was a sizeable economic-improvement discussion based on advancing the production frontier by using the physical and biological remedy which Mother Nature had provided.[2] Right about the same time, Swedish iron exports began to take off, from an average of about 12,000 tons per year around 1640 to about 33,000 tons by the 1710s (peak values of 51,000 or 52,000 tons were reached by the 1790s). Swedish wrought iron was thought to be surpassed by no other, leading to a quasi-monopoly on European markets, including copper exports. This domination would only change with England's industrialization and the industrial production of iron that matched Swedish (and Russian) qualities by the early nineteenth century. By the later seventeenth century, Sweden's import statistics also began to feature significant imports of grain, indicating a growing integration into the international processes of specialization and division of labour, marking Sweden as one of the slightly 'more developed' economies of the pre-industrial age. With its relatively weak nobility and native peasantry enjoying an unusual degree of economic and political freedom and with its cultural homogeneity, coupled with a relatively strong state, Sweden, although an 'agrarian' economy well into the nineteenth century, still enjoyed some key preconditions for successful subsequent industrialization that were laid in earlier centuries.[3] So we find mutual feedback processes between economic improvement discourses and improvements in the real economy. Earlier, in the days of Martin Luther and the later medieval scholastic authors, economics had been embedded within academic theology, that is, religiously-framed. To view economics as an independent and quasi-technical science rather than a panoptic-holistic and ultimately cultural discipline is a rather modern, and in many ways peculiar, development.[4]

A major achievement of the Enlightenment and enlightenment economics was, of course, the discovery of the human being as a subject and protagonist in God's chosen world order. Scholastic and Neo-Aristotelian economics had been different in terms of their anthropology. The new discovery meant that this order could be *modified* to the benefit of mankind and modelled, that is understood by scientific analysis, using the technique of scientific observation and reasoning. This represented an important, if gradual, departure and emancipation from an earlier theological determinism that had

Economics: Turgot, Beccaria and Smith and their Contemporaries (London and New York: Routledge, 2002), 3–99.

2   See the ongoing research by Carl Wennerlind, 'Hartlibian Political Economy in Sweden – Johan Classon Risingh's Improvement Discourse', in Philipp Robinson Rössner, ed. *Economic Reason of State. Reconfiguring the Origins of Modern Political Economy, 1500–2000 A.D.* (Milton Park and New York: Routledge, 2016).

3   Bertil Boethius and Eli F. Heckscher, eds *Svensk handelsstatistik, 1637–1737* (Stockholm: Bokförlags Aktiebolaget Thule, 1938), xlv–lviii; Lars Magnusson, *An Economic History of Sweden* (London and New York: Routledge, 2000); Chris Evans and Göran Rydén, *Baltic Iron in the Atlantic World in the Eighteenth Century* (Leiden and Boston: Brill, 2007).

4   I have discussed this in regard to Martin Luther extensively in Philipp Robinson Rössner, *Martin Luther on Commerce and Usury* (London and New York: Anthem, 2015), especially ch. 1.

dominated European philosophy and economics since the Middle Ages.[5] The goal now was not to prove the immovable nature of a pre-ordained creation, but rather to obtain proof of God and the beauty of God's chosen order through reason and empiricism – by discovering natural laws and working mechanisms of the world through scholarly observation. This included, at the turn of the eighteenth century, quite obscure practices still, such as alchemy and the burning of child witches.[6] Nevertheless, the epistemological paradigm that developed over the course of the seventeenth and eighteenth century was formidably new and quite different from medieval neo-Aristotelian social ethics and economic equilibrium theory.[7] It included aspects seen as critical nowadays, especially by post-modernist and post-structuralist social theory, such as the discovery of 'European Civilization', strange discourses about orientalism and wild natives, as well as the belief that improvement and infinite growth – or enlargement of the menu of choices relating to decisions and consumption – were principally possible. 'Improvement' became a key-word in many a social, technical and political conversation.

The enlightenment consisted of networks of scientists and philosophers, learned societies directed at scientific observation and agrarian development. The cornerstone was the Royal Society founded in 1660 – eminent 'early' (*älterer*) Cameralist Wilhelm von Schröder even became a member. Johann Joachim Becher, another one of the late seventeenth-century Austrian or 'old' Cameralists (Hörnigk was, as we have seen, the third) had associates in the English learned world. Samuel Hartlib, Prussian émigré since 1612, even founded a learned circle in England, to which he gave his name.[8] Philipp Wilhelm von Hörnigk was part of this intellectual tradition and network, albeit he certainly didn't travel as far as many of his contemporary German and Austrian polymath-economists, and – out of the trio of Austrian Cameralists – he may have represented the most parochial one. Contrary to a widely-cherished notion, Mercantilist and

---

5   On medieval economic theory, see in particular, Odd Inge Langholm, *Economics in the Medieval Schools: Wealth, Exchange, Value, Money and Usury According to the Paris Theological Tradition 1200–1350* (Leiden: Brill, 1992); id., *The Legacy of Scholasticism in Economic Thought. Antecedents of Choice and Power* (Cambridge: Cambridge University Press, 1998); id., 'Monopoly and Market Irregularities in Medieval Thought', *Journal of the History of Economic Thought* 28 (2006), 395–411, and id., 'Martin Luther's Doctrine on Trade and Price in Its Literary Context', *History of Political Economy* 41, no. 1 (2009), 89–107, as well as Raymond de Roover, 'Scholastic Economics: Survival and Lasting Influence from the Sixteenth Century to Adam Smith', *The Quarterly Journal of Economics*, LXIX (1955), 161–90. Other good recent studies include Diana Wood, *Medieval Economic Thought* (Cambridge: Cambridge University Press, 2002), and Germano Maifreda, *From Oikonomia to Political Economy: Constructing Economic Knowledge from the Renaissance to the Scientific Revolution* (Farnham; Burlington, VT: Ashgate, 2012).

6   Rainer Beck, *Mäuselmacher oder die Imagination des Bösen. Ein Hexenprozess 1715–1723* (Munich: C. H. Beck, 2011) tells a gripping story of how child witches were burned in eighteenth-century enlightened Germany.

7   Karl Pribram, *Geschichte des ökonomischen Denkens*, vol. I (Frankfurt: Suhrkamp, 1994), is very informative on the evolution of early modern economic thought.

8   A fascinating panorama of Hartlibian economics can be found in Carl Wennerlind, 'Money: Hartlibian Political Economy and the New Culture of Credit', in Stern and Wennerlind, eds *Reimagining Mercantilism*, 74–96.

Cameralist economists were part of this 'Enlightenment' economic culture – the foundation of modern economics, even though many historians and economists still reserve the term 'enlightenment economics' to David Hume, Adam Smith (or liberal theory) and Physiocracy.[9] These scholars neglect the fact that the Scottish enlightenment was quite peculiar and that not only were there many rival 'enlightenments' in early modern Europe, but also competing epistemologies in economics and, accordingly, economic theories – until today.[10]

Manufacturing Matters, Useful Knowledge and the Deception of Free Markets

Two basic ideas that once held importance in European economic discourse were forgotten over time as economic discourse and economic theory evolved and attained their characteristically 'modern' shape. These ancient insights were that (a) manufacturing mattered, and (b) that a strong and pro-active state was important to safeguard and nurture the precarious plant, which became known later as *economic growth and development*. Names have been given to these ideas, as well as the theories embodying them, such as 'Mercantilism', 'Colbertism' (in France) or 'Cameralism', denoting differences more in terms of nuance and context-specific economic practice rather than theoretical content. For reasons of convenience, and due to the fact that such labels have frequently become emotionally charged, we may, perhaps, subsume them under the more neutral term 'Economic Reason of State' (a term borrowed from Hartman/Weststeijn), reflecting the mutual interest and feedback processes between state, finance and economy that influenced the writing of these theories. These ideas were widely shared across Europe. It is known, for instance, that around 1589, Bavarian Duke Maximilian read (and tried to implement in his Bavarian possession) Botero's *Della ragione di Stato libri dieci* upon recommendation of his Italian secretary and emissary to the Papal Court, Minuccio Minucci.[11]

The pedigree of these ideas is ancient. They even continue to matter today, particularly in the light of the current crises in the world economy. If we look at pre-industrial Europe, we find that many of the key ingredients and ideas usually identified as crucial to 'modern' economic growth were already in it – for a long time. A strong manufacturing base? Known to sixteenth-century Italian economic writers. The role of knowledge management, technology and science? Known to early seventeenth-century Swedish thinkers. The notion that infinite growth is principally possible? Again, Sweden, around 1600. A strong state that safeguards its subjects' economic interests and property rights,

9 Sophus A. Reinert, 'The Empire of Emulation: A Quantitative Analysis of Economic Translations in the European World, 1500–1849', in id. and Pernille Røge, eds *The Political Economy of Empire in the Early Modern World* (Houndmills, Basingstoke: Palgrave Macmillan, 2013), 105–28.

10 Reinert, *Translating Empire* (as in ch. 1).

11 Heinz Dollinger, 'Staatsräson und Staatsfinanzen in Bayern im 16. und frühen 17. Jahrhundert', in Aldo De Maddalena and Hermann Kellenbenz, eds *Finanzen und Staatsräson in Italien und Deutschland in der frühen Neuzeit* (Berlin: Duncker & Humblot, 1992), 249–68, at 265–6.

up to the point of actively promoting growth and development? We find this idea in seventeenth- and eighteenth-century German economic discourse, but, of course, much earlier in the texts produced in Renaissance Italy. We also find states that repeatedly tried to apply these ideas in practice. The best example perhaps is post-1688 England. Here we find, as new research has pointed out, an increasingly developmental-protectionist state that laid the foundations for the subsequent transition into the 'first industrial nation'. Less-well understood, however, is how deeply influenced continental Europe's intellectual landscape was by these ideas. We also lack a deeper understanding of the interaction between these ideas and economic practice and policy. But very early on, the idea existed of a state that *actively promoted* development with a focus on *manufacturing* – around 1500 AD at the latest (the idea is certainly much older). We find the concept, both in economic discourse and applied in practice, in sixteenth-century Italy, or seventeenth-century Germany and Sweden, or in the nineteenth-century continental economic theory called *Nationalökonomie* (e.g. the German Historical School of Economics). But we also see, in pre-industrial European economic discourse, ideas that are fairly different from what would subsequently, that is, after 1800, be portrayed as 'mainstream'; especially the free-trade ideology. If we adopt a comparative European focus, we observe that free trade ideas never represented the mainstream outside the Anglo-British context. And, contrary to much previous belief, a lot of the more protectionist political economy ideas inherited from the pre-classical 'Economic Reason of State' theory survived unscathed into modern political economy discourse.

That ideas and theories varied over time, attaining different configurations over different spaces seems only natural; but just how they unfolded differently in different contexts (*idiosyncrasy*) has seldom been studied. However, recent works have begun to cast more light on this.[12] That ideas may also change according to political climate and social context – that is, may represent vested interests of the actors formulating the 'theories' as can be shown by a study on France under Colbert and Britain towards the end of the American War.[13] Good examples are the free trade and comparative advantage ideologies, two of the most prominent discursive figures and concepts in modern economic theory. Useful knowledge, that is, science and knowledge management were as important in pre-Enlightenment economic thought as they were later in the 'classical' context – contrary to a widely-held notion.[14] Finally, the idea that the state should interfere with the economy is not only ancient, but also one that is to be found in many other places outside

---

12 See, e.g. Moritz Isenmann, 'From Privilege to Economic Law. French Origins of Comparative Cost Theory', in Rössner, ed. *Economic Reason of State* (See n. 2) which studies the evolution of the comparative advantage argument in early eighteenth-century French production (wine exporting provinces vs. manufacturing and export oriented French provinces) as well as, within the same volume, the paper by William Ashworth, 'Industry, Fiscal Pressure and the Collapse of Mercantilism in Britain 1763–1842', on the adoption of more liberal ideas governing trade and production in Britain towards the end of the American War of Independence.

13 See previous note.

14 Explicated as late as 2009 in Joel Mokyr, *The Enlightened Economy: An Economic History of Britain, 1700–1850* (New Haven: Yale University Press, 2009).

Europe. The idea seems to have worked exceptionally well in Europe since the Middle Ages. Neither modern historians nor economists have paid much heed to the concept in recent times. Hörnigk's text (1684) wrapped up these ideas quite nicely.

The Origin of Modern Economics

Thus, rather than focusing on somewhat misgiven ideas of *breaks* in tradition, or radical *differences* in paradigm (before, say pre-classical and classical economics), or a clearly misplaced assumption of a *discontinuous evolution of modern economic knowledge*, new research has emphasized the long-term *continuities* and shared traits in modern economic thought.[15] Even Heckscher, in his magnum opus on Mercantilism, had been doing something similar but came (not surprisingly, given the task he had set himself) to the conclusion that neither Cameralism nor Mercantilism mattered for the evolution of modern economic knowledge, or for liberal economic thinking. Modern research has disagreed.[16]

To a large extent, the problem hinges, of course, upon what is defined as 'modern' economic reasoning. Competing notions and definitions certainly exist, which cannot be pursued further here, as many apt and scholarly contributions have shed light on this ornate and winding path. By the seventeenth century, economic theory had advanced far beyond the conservative-static scholastic or Neo-Aristotelian view of the economy as a big household or *oikos* – as it has often been portrayed in the more traditional accounts on the history of economics – in which a just *distribution* of resources was cherished as a prime goal, but not so much the idea of *extension* of the physically available ('economic growth'). As seen earlier in the chapter, seventeenth-century Swedish improvement discourse already entertained the notion of infinite growth as a principal possibility, effected through scholarly observation of nature and the subsequent taming and domestication of nature's forces for the services of mankind. While esoterically-framed from a modern vantage point (but inherently logical from a seventeenth-century perspective), alchemy remained a firm part of this theory. But there were many aspects in it which are as crucial for modern economic theory and development, such as the generation and systematic application of cultural techniques, scholarly education and useful knowledge, as they were back then. Such ideas would have floated hither and thither across Europe. It would be reasonable to assume sufficiently strong connections, for instance, between Sweden, from which the Hörnigk family may have initially come, and Germany. Sweden produced a rich agrarian household economics literature during the sixteenth and seventeenth centuries, a prime example of which may represent Per Brahe's (1520–90) *Oeconomia*, typical of which was a household calendar (depicting the activities required during the agrarian cycle – something we find in similar if not identical shape in the later German

---

15 See William D. Grampp, 'An Appreciation of Mercantilism', in Lars Magnusson, ed. *Mercantilist Economics* (Boston: Kluwer, 1993), 59–85.

16 Eli F. Heckscher, *Der Merkantilismus*, trans. G. Mackenroth, 2 vols. (Jena: Gustav Fischer, 1932), II, 240. On the Mercantilist heritage in modern liberal and neoclassical thought, see Grampp, 'An Appreciation of Mercantilism' (at n. 15).

Hausväterliteratur, for example, Caspar Jugel's *Oeconomia*, Johannes Coler's *Oeconomia* (1591)[17] or Wolf Helmhard Hohberg's *Georgica Curiosa*, a treatise on agrarian household economics which went through at least six editions between 1682 and 1749.[18] Thereafter, in the words of Morell, 'While the older type of texts (in a German "Hausvater" tradition) had focused on the running of individual elite farm households, the farming literature published after about 1740 commonly concerned implications on a national level of agricultural innovations.'[19] Many of the late seventeenth- and eighteenth-century Swedish 'Mercantilists', from Oxenstierna (who was more of a politician) to Anders Berch (1711–1744), the first holder of the newly-established chair in economics at Uppsala University, had, in Lönnroth's words, 'been astute enough to defend a dissertation on the need for this kind of professorship in 1731.' This makes them somewhat akin to the German Cameralists of the eighteenth century who have been described as habitual vagabonds, always on the lookout for a job at a princely court, using their writings as 'job market papers' and evidence that they were fit to hold the post as professors (until the 1720s, mostly in law, as the first university chairs in Cameralist economics were not created until 1727) or administrators in the German mini fiscal-military states of the age.[20] Berch also advocated the idea that a country should be thoroughly surveyed so as to know which economic activity would be best placed where. This idea of *spatiality* – that space matters and codetermines the profitability and efficiency of any economic activity – and the element of regional industrial development and resource management is mostly absent from modern mainstream economics.

Surely the Thirty Years War acted as an important cultural transmitter between Swedish and German economic discourse, although we lack studies on the economic aspect of Germano-Swedish cultural exchange in the early modern period.[21] During the sixteenth century, the trend in Swedish students visiting German universities had

---

17 See the new study Philip Hahn, *Das Haus im Buch. Konzeption, Publikationsgeschichte und Leserschaft der "Oeconomia" Johann Colers* (Epfendorf: bibliotheca academica, 2013).

18 *Georgica curiosa, das ist umständl. Ber. u. klarer Unterricht v. d. adelichen Land- u. Feldleben auf alle in Teutschland übliche Land- u. Forstwirtschaften gerichtet* (1682). See Otto Brunner, 'Hohberg, Wolf Helmhard Freiherr von', in *Neue Deutsche Biographie* 9 (1972), 476–77; URL: http://www. deutsche-biographie.de/ppn118774735.html (last accessed 24 January 2015), and the relevant sections in Burkhardt and Priddat, eds *Geschichte der Ökonomie*. On the Swedish side of the discourse, see the interesting yet short account by Johann Lönnroth, 'Before Economics', in Bo Sandelin, ed. *The History of Swedish Economic Thought* (London and New York: Routledge, 1991), 11–43, especially 13–17.

19 Mats Morell, 'Swedish Agriculture in the Cosmopolitan Eighteenth-Century', in Göran Rydén, ed. *Sweden in the Eighteenth-Century World. Provincial Cosmopolitans* (Farnham and Burlington, VT: Ashgate), 69–94, at 74.

20 On Swedish economics, see Lönnroth, 'Before Economics', 19. See also Karl Willgren, 'Die Anfänge der finanzwissenschaftlichen Forschung in Schweden und Finnland', *FinanzArchiv/ Public Finance Analysis*, 28, no. 1 (1911), 141–66. Andre Wakefield, *The Disordered Police State: German Cameralism as Science and Practice* (Chicago: University of Chicago Press, 2009).

21 See, e.g. Nils Runeby, '"Der große Fleiß und Ruhm der Deutschen". Geistiger und wissenschaftlicher Austausch', in Martin Grass et al., *Schweden und Deutschland: Begegnungen und Impulse = Tyskland och Sverige: möten och impulser* (Stockholm: Svenska Institutet, 1999), 62–79.

been upward (190 registered at the Reformed Saxon University of Wittenberg, Martin Luther's former 'work place' and residence, during the sixteenth century alone). The number of Swedish students at German universities peaked towards the 1650s and 1670s. Most of them were drawn from the native nobility and clergy, with the purpose of acquiring skills that would prepare them for a later career in the Swedish administration. The three most-favoured places were Leiden in the Netherlands, Greifswald and Rostock in Swedish Pomerania, located within the Holy Roman Empire, and, of course, Wittenberg. Law and Jurisprudence were obvious candidates for chosen subjects of study; German professors of law were also appointed at Swedish universities such as Uppsala or Lund.[22] During the Great War, the Swedes were known for taking entire libraries from the German lands back into their mother country (sometimes they used them for ransom). 'Useful knowledge' was also an important item of booty, and books represented an important asset, perhaps even more so then than later on. Concerning Würzburg castle, the rich library amassed by Prince-bishop Julius Echter von Mespelbrunn between 1573 and 1617 was captured by a 'donation' from Gustavus Adolphus on 6 November 1631 (*vnserer Academien Ubsalen die allhie auffm Schloss vorhandene Bibliothek mit aller zubehör wie dass namen haben mach gnädigt geschenket*), inventoried and then prepared for dispatch to Uppsala University Library. Würzburg's university library also suffered. Prints and manuscripts dating as far back as the fifteenth century, taken from the libraries of the Jesuit colleges at Erfurt and Heiligenstadt im Eichsfeld after 1631, ended up as far as Copenhagen University Library, but mostly in Uppsala, as well as the ecclesiastical library in Linköping or at the formidable castle library at Skokloster. They were sometimes shipped via Bremen and Hamburg.[23]

If it was true that the Hörnigk family had come from Sweden (which we do not know for certain), the Swedish connection therefore may have been important in the emergence and evolution of 'Germanic' economic discourse around the early 1600s, which oscillated between a more traditional Neo-Aristotelian agrarian household economics called *Hausväterliteratur* or *oiko*-nomics in the literal sense on the one hand,[24] and the emergent 'modern' or Baconian economic sciences on the other hand,[25] of which German Cameralism represented a foundation stone. Certainly the Big War, apart from

22 Lars Niléhn, 'Swedish Society and Swedish Students Abroad in the 17th Century', in Göran Rystad, ed. *Europe and Scandinavia: Aspects of the Process of Integration in the 17th Century* (Lund: Wallin & Dalholm, 1983), 101–22, diagram on 102; see also, within the same volume, the contribution by Kjell Å. Modéer, 'Die Rolle der Juristen in Schweden im 17. Jahrhundert. Eine rechtshistorische Skizze', ibid., 123–38.

23 Otto Walde, *Storhetstidens litterära krigsbyten. En kulturhistorisk bibliografisk studie*, 2 vols. (Uppsala: Almqvist och Wiksell 1916, 1920), vol. I, 108–11; 178; quote from the original *donationsbref* (certificate or letter of donation) from 1631, ibid. appendix, 2 (p. 338), for Prussia, Erfurt, Heiligenstadt, Würzburg and Mainz. I am indebted to Erik Reinert for bringing this to my attention.

24 Keith Tribe, *Land, Labour, and Economic Discourse* (London and Boston: Routledge & K. Paul, 1978), as well as the relevant sections with commented extracts from original *Hausväterliteratur* texts in Burkhardt and Priddat, eds *Geschichte der Ökonomie*.

25 Pribram, *Geschichte des ökonomischen Denkens*. (See n. 7).

all its gruesome aspects (which will be given more detailed consideration later) also acted as a cultural transmitter, a big melting pot for culture, including economic ideas, with soldiers, generals, provisioning merchants, travelling salesmen and financiers, who would have played an important role in transmitting ideas across the German and north-central plains, transforming, adapting, modifying and reconfiguring them constantly. The seventeenth-century Swedish improvement discourse may have borrowed something from the German *Hausväterliteratur* (as well as the other way round). We find Cameralist elements in the Swedish discourse early on, and a lot of Swedish ideas may have found their way back into Germany and Cameralism, as there were, in the 1630s and 1640s, a lot of Swedish people (and people in the service of the Swedes) travelling across the German lands. Who would not have stood in awe looking at Gustavus Adolphus, the Lion from the North and champion of Protestantism, who would, according to an old prophecy, overcome the southern Eagle, represented by the Catholic Holy Roman Emperor? This was the myth which the Swedish kings built upon during 'Sweden's Age of Greatness' (Wennerlind) in the second half of the seventeenth century, when the Baltic had almost turned into a large, domestic Swedish lake.

Re-enter Reason and Order, the keywords of the age. At Hörnigk's time, the habit of 'efficiency' and 'productivity' accounting entered the scene – certainly not as stringently as these concepts would be taught and applied in today's microeconomics and management textbooks.[26] Since the 1680s, the habit of constructing 'National Accounts' and balance of trade calculations spread, usually directed at goals and strategies formulated within the political discourse of the day. In England and Ireland we find the first modern trade statistics, the *Inspector General's Ledgers of Imports and Exports*, in 1694-96; for Scotland, these statistics were first produced in 1755.[27] As early as the 1670s, a national balance of trade sheet was drawn up for Scotland. In 1700, one John Spreull published a pamphlet quantifying the several production branches of the Scottish economy and their contribution to overall exports and imports, drawn (presumably) from the Scottish customhouse or port books which became important for debates on Scotland's national wealth and economic health on the eve of the Union of the Kingdoms in 1707.[28] The 1720s and 1730s saw further efforts in statistical monitoring of select branches of trade and economy, both within and outside Scotland and England. In Saxony and Prussia during the 1720s and 1730s, modern economic administrative bodies were founded whose task it was to oversee the domestic economy, its performance (and tax base) and to implement economic improvement (growth and development). In Scotland, this struggle for development manifested itself inter alia in the so-called *Board of Trustees for the Fisheries and Manufactures*, established

---

26 Werner Sombart, *Der Moderne Kapitalismus. Historisch-systematische Darstellung des gesamteuropäischen Wirtschaftslebens von seinen Anfängen bis zur Gegenwart*, 3rd ed., vol. II, n. 1: *Das europäische Wirtschaftsleben im Zeitalter des Frühkapitalismus vornehmlich im 16., 17. und 18. Jahrhundert* (Munich and Leipzig: Duncker & Humblot, 1919) still contains fascinating insights.

27 Rössner, *Wake*, 117–27 for a full discussion.

28 John Spreull, *An Accompt Current Betwixt Scotland and England Ballanced* (1705). See the very apt discussion of these debates and circumstances in Richard Saville, *Bank of Scotland. A History 1695–1995* (Edinburgh: Edinburgh University Press, 1996), ch. 4.

in 1727, whose main point of attention would subsequently be the Scottish linen manufacture (which eventually managed a quite successful transition towards industrialization in the nascent cotton manufacture). The fallacy of contemporary statistical methods and techniques is obvious;[29] we should not forget that Gregory King (1688), the god-father of English political arithmetic, not only drew up a detailed national income account for England and Wales in 1688[30] but also was quite convinced that, by using state-of-the-art mathematics and statistical method, he would arrive at a reliable estimate of England's rabbit population. We should not forget, either, that an important step had been made, and that modern statistical knowledge emerged gradually over time until it reached the (superficial) state of perfection witnessed during the twentieth century.[31] In many ways, contemporaries were not too far-off the mark. What counted was their *desire* to measure the world, accordingly also commercial, monetary and economic flows. And this desire made them get better over time, although by the late seventeenth century, they were nowhere near where these techniques are today.

As has been noted, very often the drive towards statistical coverage was frequently derived from political goals – such as Scotland's survival as an independent nation and economy; or – in the present case of Philipp Wilhelm von Hörnigk's *Oesterreich über alles* – getting a reliable estimate of the wealth which France drew out of the Empire in return for exports (French manufactures imported into the countries of the Empire). This was a prime variable in the political processes of survival; of the Empire as a somewhat artificial, yet highly meaningful, political fiction and entity in the minds of the actors; or its smaller components, the small- and medium-sized states as independent economies. Nevertheless – and regardless how closely and inseparably-entangled politics and economics were (as they are usually nowadays) – a body of theoretical insights emerged and attained a shape which deserves to be called characteristic, and which in many ways represented the foundations of modern economic theory. This was an economics of rivalry and competition, of connectivity on world markets,[32] which was modelled and shaped by certain rules of the game that have become known by names such as 'Mercantilism', 'reason of state' or 'Cameralism'.

---

29 See for instance William Deringer, 'Finding the Money: Public Accounting, Political Arithmetic, and Probability in the 1690s', *Journal of British Studies* 52, no. 3 (2013), 638–68.

30 See, e.g. Peter Lindert and Jeffrey G. Williamson, 'Revising England's Social Tables 1688–1812', *Explorations in Economic History* 19 (1982), 385–408.

31 On the political history of modern national income accounting, see J. Adam Tooze, *Statistics and the German State, 1900–1945: The Making of Modern Economic Knowledge* (Cambridge; New York: Cambridge University Press, 2001); Philipp Lepenies, *Die Macht der einen Zahl: eine politische Geschichte des Bruttoinlandsprodukts* (Frankfurt: Suhrkamp, 2013).

32 Reinert, *Translating Empire*, ch. 1.

Chapter Three

CAMERALISM – *BAROQUE-O*-NOMICS

Cameralist Economic Theory

How successful the Cameralists and their theory were is indicated by the fact that 'by the time they had disappeared in the middle of the nineteenth century, they had amassed a collective bibliography of more than 14,000 items, according to Magdalene Humpert (1937).'[1] And from work currently in process by former Harvard University librarian Ken Carpenter, we know that hundreds of 'German' cameralist texts and textbooks found their way into other languages and scientific cultures, such as Swedish and Italian. On what Cameralism was, what it represented and what – or rather how much – it contributed to the emergence and evolution of modern economics there has been perhaps more controversy than unity. Mercantilism (and Cameralism) have suffered from a series of accusations, mainly by twentieth-century scholars, that are, upon hindsight, more a reflection of academic fashion and convention than deep insight. The main charges can be summarized as follows, at the risk of oversimplification inherent to any such exercise.

- Mercantilist economics lacked *theoretical foundation and epistemological stringency*. Even eminent Marxist economic historians spoke about the *theoretische Armseligkeit des Kameralismus* (here they shared common ground with the liberal interpretation),[2] or 'Mercantilism in the service of the feudal state' – 'Merkantilismus des deutschen Zwergstaates.' There was no Cameralist thinker, as the saying went in the Communist interpretation of the history of political economy, who would have matched the analytical level and rigour of the contemporary English Mercantilists. German theory remained as primitive and backword as the German economy throughout 1600–1900, it was said.[3] Both interpretations can be challenged on the basis of more recent research.
- It was likewise often maintained that Mercantilism/Cameralism represented no *'closed'* or *'unified' theory* (usually taken to mean a theory that explains everything, that is, all

---

1 Richard E. Wagner, 'The Cameralists: Fertile Source for a New Science of Public Finance', in Jürgen Georg Backhaus, ed. *Handbook of the History of Economic Thought. Insights on the Founders of Modern Economics* (Frankfurt: Springer, 2012), 123–36 (123).

2 Autorenkollektiv (Werner Krause, Hermann Lehmann, Günter Rudolph and Erich Sommerfeld), *Grundlinien des ökonomischen Denkens in Deutschland. Von den Anfängen bis zur Mitte des 19. Jahrhunderts* (Berlin/East: Akademie-Verlag, 1977), 186.

3 Fritz Behrens, *Grundriss der Geschichte der Politischen Ökonomie, I: Die politische Ökonomie der Bürgerlichen Klassik* (Berlin/East: Akademie–Verlag, 1962), 114–16.

types of possible economic fields and constellations, out of itself, such as Marxism or Keynesian economics).

- Perhaps the gravest of all charges may be the accusation that Cameralism (in the same way as Mercantilism) lacked *the potential to raise general economic welfare in a Pareto-optimal way*[4] if applied as an economic policy – as though such characteristics would either be necessary or represent *conditiones sine qua non*, in a sense of being ultimately relevant, for determining how good or useful one particular theory really is in terms of improving the economic fate of mankind. The latter is, following a common notion, one of the main aims of economics; we may adopt it as a benchmark for judging the success of a particular economic theory. All available evidence from Europe's Mercantilist world during the early modern age seems to suggest that what we call 'Mercantilist' or Cameralist economics in the German lands – there is still much scholarly controversy as to the usefulness of either term – seems to have done the trick quite well during the time when it flourished, circa 1500–1800. Contrary to a most recent dictum, it was neither creating a Nash-equilibrium (below the Pareto optimum) nor inept to effect sustained economic growth and development.[5] Quite the contrary, Mercantilist political economy, when applied wisely and effectively in the several regional economies of early modern Europe, seems to have laid the foundations for Europe's successful transition towards industrialization.[6]

Yet, even a most recent textbook in a widely acclaimed Princeton monograph series devotes less than two pages to Mercantilism, but still states that

---

4　Most recently, Mokyr, *Enlightened Economy*, ch. 4, or Robert E. Ekelund and Robert D. Tollison, *Mercantilism as a Rent-seeking Society: Economic Regulation in Historical Perspective* (College Station: Texas A&M University Press, 1981).

5　The most relevant studies on this topic include Birger P. Priddat, 'Kameralismus als paradoxe Konzeption der gleichzeitigen Stärkung von Markt und Staat. Komplexe Theorielagen im deutschen 18. Jahrhundert', *Berichte zur Wissenschaftsgeschichte* 31 (2008), 249–63; the relevant sections in Burkhardt and Priddat, eds *Geschichte der Ökonomie*. See also Keith Tribe, *Strategies of Economic Order. German Economic Discourse, 1750–1950* (Cambridge: Cambridge University Press, 1995), ch. 1; Bertram Schefold, 'Glückseligkeit und Wirtschaftspolitik: Zu Justis "Grundsätze der Policey-Wissenschaft"', in ibid., ed. *Vademecum zu einem Klassiker des Kameralismus: Johann Heinrich Gottlob von Justi, Grundsätze der Policey-Wissenschaft* (Düsseldorf: Verlag Wirtschaft und Finanzen, 1993); Ingomar Bog, 'Ist die Kameralistik eine untergegangene Wissenschaft?', *Berichte zur Wissenschaftsgeschichte* 4 (1981), 61–72; Cilly Böhle, *Die Idee der Wirtschaftsverfassung im deutschen Merkantilismus* (Jena: Gustav Fischer, 1940); Hans Joachim Röpke, 'Die Wachstumstheorie der deutschen Merkantilisten' (PhD diss. Marburg 1971); Lars Magnusson, *Mercantilism. The Shaping of an Economic Language* (London: Routledge 1994); id., ed. *Mercantilist Economics* (Boston, MA: Kluwer, 1993); id. *The Political Economy of Mercantilism* (London & New York: Routledge, 2015).

6　Lars Magnusson, *Nation, State and the Industrial Revolution: The Visible Hand* (London and New York: Routledge, 2009) does not go exactly as far as this but the evidence Magnusson provides on state involvement in the process of European economic growth and development, 1500–1900, does indeed suggest this. See Philipp Robinson Rössner, 'Heckscher Reloaded? Mercantilism, the State and Europe's Transition to Industrialization (1600–1900)', *The Historical Journal*, 58, no. 2 (2015), 663–83.

Mercantilism was above all a set of economic policy prescriptions for rulers whose aim was to promote their country's interests, its wealth, and power, relative to other nations. But the 'country' and 'nation' were in the world of the mercantilists the same as the state or the individuals in power; the time had not yet come when the interests of the country were to be identical with those of the people or the general public.[7]

Recent research suggests that this interpretation is skewed, based on a serious misunderstanding of Mercantilist texts as well as the dynamics of early modern political history and theory. The question is, on the one hand, one of value judgement (and thus ultimately unsolvable). On the other hand, it is one of definition. It hinges, for example, on whether the Cameralists' *Wohlfahrtsstaat* (welfare state) we know really was akin to what we see today as the welfare state, or whether the Cameralists weren't really after something else, for instance, economic growth and development. And then, can we compare such different times and locations as seventeenth- and eighteenth-century Germany with the economic (and material and cultural) constellations and problems of an industrialized world characteristic of the twentieth century, when 'Keynesian' economics (and other streams of the modern economic sciences) came to the fore, when material conditions, technological processes and the cultural outlook of people were certainly much different than three hundred years earlier? Historians have spilled much ink in recent times about the problem of time breaks, changes between historical periods or ages and the basic incomparability of different times, ages and societies. Much time and effort has also been spent on the truism that moral questions sometimes occupied a higher relevance than 'economic' ones in the 'models' of the Cameralists and proto-Mercantilists in the German lands since the times of Martin Luther and the Saxon pamphleteers of the 1530s.[8] More recent research on Cameralism has shifted attention to 'non-economic' aspects inherent in Cameralism, such as the spatial morphology,[9] the praxeology[10] or population theory in Cameralist texts.[11] A recent book by Sedlacek allows the conclusion that, however, that this does not mean that the Cameralists had no theory; they had a theory that was simply different from what our modern scientific paradigms, developed in the wake of the Newtonian Revolution and the Enlightenment *defined* as theory and model, that is, largely de-contextualized, time-space indifferent, axiomatic formulations or statements of opinion that became transformed into, and can still be found in many textbooks in international economics or straight micro- and macro-economics, as widely-acknowledged 'wisdoms' and 'truths'.[12] But this does not mean we cannot or should not

7   Agnar Sandmo, *Economics Evolving. A History of Economic Thought* (Princeton, NJ: Princeton University Press, 2011), 19.
8   Pribram, *Geschichte des ökonomischen Denkens*, 181–82.
9   Marcus Sandl, *Ökonomie des Raumes: der kameralwissenschaftliche Entwurf der Staatswirtschaft im 18. Jahrhundert* (Cologne: Böhlau, 1999).
10 Wakefield, *Disordered Police State*.
11 Nipperdey, *Die Erfindung der Bevölkerungspolitik*.
12 A provocative history of economics since the early beginnings of society is Tomáš Sedláček, *Economics of Good and Evil. The Quest for Economic Meaning from Gilgamesh to Wall Street* (Oxford: Oxford University Press, 2011).

study the Cameralists first and foremost through an economistic lens, using an economic focus. Economics is, after all, what their main passion or field of interest appears to have been. The field is all but settled; contrary to what is sometimes suggested by the mere amount of existing scholarship on the history of economics, we are still at the beginning of a more grounded and objective understanding of the true weight and place of Cameralism in the evolution of modern political economy.

Perhaps we need to turn modern economics on its head to get a better understanding of its evolution. It was Schumpeter, who wrote what would become the prime (yet in many ways illegible and nebulous) account of the history of economic doctrine in the twentieth century. Schumpeter did not like the Cameralists that much. But about Johann Gottlob Heinrich Justi he remarked,

> Of course, we must grant the professor a fair ration of ponderous triviality, and also allow for his way of arriving at common-sense conclusions by a circuitous route that leads through questionable political philosophies. An example will illustrate the latter point: freedom is absolute by virtue of natural law; only, as the professor has somewhere learnedly shown, it consists in freedom to obey the laws and the rulings of the bureaucracy; but the latter as taught by Justi is so very reasonable that after all we come out of the woods with the results to be presented in the text.[13]

Schumpeter at least cleared the Mercantilists of the general charge of having 'wrong' or incorrect models (as they had – in his opinion – none at all). As many others, including Marc Blaug,[14] Schumpeter understood economics and the history of political economy to be a science where development could be captured and analysed following the quest for *progress* – as though people's ideas always and by necessity *improve* over time. He considered most of the Mercantilist writings more or less useless for this purpose. Schumpeter was on a never-ending quest for 'mistakes' they had made in the light of the modern economic reasoning (and he found a lot). He repeatedly called them and their models 'primitive' and, by suggesting that they were after a 'planned economy' (*Planwirtschaft* in the original), he accused them of things and modernisms they could not possibly have had in mind.[15] That the Cameralists lacked, apart from 'good' models, a coherent set of axiomatic rules or a theory, another common blame by the likes of Schumpeter or Heckscher, was something Johann Gottlob von Justi himself had acknowledged. It was one of the reasons for him to come forward and develop what came as close as possible to a 'unified' Cameralist theory, so as to make up for this deficiency;[16] rather

13 Joseph A. Schumpeter, *History of Economic Analysis*, ed. E. Boody Schumpeter (London: Routledge pbk edition [1954] 1986), 170.

14 Mark Blaug, *Economic Theory in Retrospect* (Cambridge and New York: Cambridge University Press, 1985).

15 Schumpeter, *Geschichte der ökonomischen Analyse*, I, 423–72.

16 Keith Tribe, 'Polizei, Staat und die Staatswissenschaften bei J. H. G. von Justi', in Bertram Schefold, ed., *Vademecum zu einem Klassiker des Kameralismus: Johann Heinrich Gottlob von Justi, Grundsätze der Policey-Wissenschaft* (Verlag Wirtschaft und Finanzen, 1993), 107–140 (112–13).

than Seckendorff, it is for these reasons that Justi probably better deserves the label of 'Godfather of Cameralism'.[17]

But what exactly *was* Cameralism, then? It is quite correct, as earlier accounts have stressed, that 'at the outset, Kameralism [*sic*] was a combination of ideas, political, juristic, technical, and economic [...]'; that 'throughout its entire development Finance [*sic*] figured prominently in Kameralistic [*sic*] thought [...]' and that 'Kameralism [*sic*] became a study or discipline for training officials, largely for the work of remedying the economic evils which afflicted the German states in the sixteenth and seventeenth centuries. [...] In this situation, coupled with an undeveloped system of taxation, lay the roots of German Mercantilism.'[18] Others have stressed that, contrary to English or French Mercantilism, Cameralism was, early on, a subject that could be studied professionally at university level, but that the cameralist volumes would be 'no siempre inteligible'.[19] And yet Cameralism was much more, much larger. In fact, it was the overarching and only existing unified 'theory' or paradigm of economic growth and development in the pre-industrial age. Definitions can be treacherous, especially when it comes to labelling fashions, traditions or 'schools' in political economy and economic theory (it is not always easy to meaningfully disentangle the two). Modern assessments usually search for theoretical closeness or wholeness when awarding the seal of approval to a theory. Such a perspective comes across, for instance, in Streissler's introduction to the German companion volume (Vademecum) to Hörnigk (1997). Streissler is ready to acknowledge that there are many proto-Keynesian stances to be found in Hörnigk's text which were, however, not developed further by Hörnigk into anything that looks like Keynesian economics (but how could Hörnigk possibly be expected to do this?) and which would classify as a 'modern theory'. This is because, as Streissler goes on to state very correctly, Hörnigk neither had a grasp of modern economic principles nor modern theoretical requirements – because, as Streissler admits further, neither modern nor Keynesian economics could possibly have existed at the time when Hörnigk wrote his text.[20] Thus, we are left at square one again. This assessment seems as anachronistic as the other extreme, that is, the interpretation (by Bog and Blaich and others[21]) that Cameralism and Mercantilism could be classified as the *origin* of Keynesianism.

Cameralism was, was by the end of the eighteenth-century, a full-fledged and fully institutionalized academic science. In 1798, there were 23 chairs in Cameralist economics

17 Heinz Rieter, 'Justis Theorie der Wirtschaftspolitik', in Schefold, ed. *Vademecum zu einem Klassiker des Kameralismus: Johann Heinrich Gottlob von Justi*, 45–80 (51–54 and 69–70).

18 Lewis H. Haney, *History of Economic Thought. A Critical Account of the Origin and Development of the Economic Theories of the Leading Thinkers in the Leading Nations* (New York: Macmillan, 1915), 114, 115.

19 Manuel Agustin Aguirre, *Apuntes para el estudio de la historia del pensamiento económico* (Quito, Ecuador: [publisher not identified], [197-?]) (119).

20 See Erich Streissler and Monika W. Streissler, 'Philip Wilhelm von Hörnigk und die wirtschaftstheoretischen und – politischen Vorstellungen des Kameralismus', in Matis et al., eds *Vademecum zu einem Klassiker absolutistischer Wirtschaftspolitik*, 139–241.

21 See the relevant annotations in subsequent sections.

in the German-speaking lands. Cameral science was also taught at universities in Italy and Sweden, with Swedish 'Cameralist' Anders Berch holding the first university chair in economics ever to be established in Sweden in 1741. In Germany, the first two chairs in Cameralist economics had been founded in 1727. By contrast, the first chair in economics established in Britain was created in Oxford in 1826.[22] Prominent American sociologist Small's dictum that

> in a word, the cameralists were a series of German writers, from the middle of the sixteenth to the end of the eighteenth century, who approached civic problems from a common viewpoint, who proposed the same central question, and who developed a coherent civic theory, corresponding with the German system of administration at the same time in course of evolution. To the cameralists the central problem of science was the problem of the state. To them the object of all social theory was to show how the welfare of the state might be secured. They saw in the welfare of the state the source of all other welfare. Their key to the welfare of the state was revenue to supply the needs of the state. Their whole social theory radiated from the central task of furnishing the state with ready means,[23]

is, of course, out-dated now, but it also contained a few true elements. It was to be found in many a modern textbook until fairly recently. Zielenziger, who wrote a major treatise on Cameralism (*Die alten deutschen Kameralisten*) called it a German version of Mercantilism;[24] it was no closed theory, he maintained, but Cameralists were economists (*Volkswirte*). The main difference to English Mercantilists was that whilst the latter were usually merchants, the German Cameralists were administrators in the services of the prince or state. Not all German Mercantilists were Cameralists, Zielenziger maintains, implying that Cameralism was a special or peculiar version of Mercantilism and not the other way round (drawing the border along the question of employment for a particular prince, with Johann Joachim Becher often labelled 'Mercantilist'); but perhaps this is nit-picking. Certainly the needs of the fiscal state loomed large in the classical or mainstream Cameralist accounts. But, especially in the later works, we find that the Cameralists' main aim also was 'die geeinte Volkswirtschaft', that means an integrated national economy. They viewed the economy as a whole, as an organism that worked according to quite characteristic working mechanisms which needed an accordingly calibrated theory. Later on, Justi's theory would include the curbing of rent-seeking and the abolition of monopolies and other market distortions within the domestic economy, including those

22 Jürgen G. Backhaus, 'The German Economic Tradition: From Cameralism to the Verein für Sozialpolitik', in Manuela Albertone and Alberto Masoero, eds *Political Economy and National Realities: Papers presented at the Conference held at the Luigi Einaudi Foundation, Palazzo d'Azeglio, Turin, September 10–12, 1992* (Turin: Fondazione Luigi Einaudi, 1994), 329–56 (343).

23 Albion W. Small, *The Cameralists: The Pioneers of German Social Polity* (Chicago: University of Chicago Press, 1909), preface.

24 Zielenziger, *Die alten Kameralisten, passim*.

institutional rigidities that negatively influenced the property rights of the actors (*villainage* and serfdom) and reduced the privileges or 'freedoms'[25] of the native aristocracy. The latter were seen by the later Cameralists as the main hindrance towards national economic development. The Cameralists definitely were no mere fiscalists, but entertained the idea of a symbiotic relationship between economic development and a strong state or prince – not a subordinate relationship between the two (that would have put the state's health on top). They had similar ideas as we do nowadays relating to 'free' markets, meaning economic exchange free from asymmetry such as usury, arbitrage, speculation and rent-seeking – the main hindrances to 'good' market performance in modern economic theory.

In many ways, the ultimate goals of Cameralist economics or theory were quite close to the prime economic goals we cherish nowadays, especially including:

- economic growth and development;
- free markets and transparency in the economic process (price formation, market access);
- equitable conditions of exchange and economic freedom, as well as
- Pareto-optimal distribution of economic resources (that is, a scenario in which no one's economic condition can be improved unless at the cost of someone else's).

Simply the means to achieve this and the assumed preconditions – the real configurations of the economy and economic process – were different in the Cameralist-Mercantilist age. It is a well-known and almost trivially obvious fact that Cameralism originated and was based uponidiosyncratic features that were quite different from the conditions of time, space and sociology prevailing in, say seventeenth- and eighteenth-century France and England. They were quite characteristic of, but by no means limited to, the states and territories making up the political conglomerate that went by the name of *Holy Roman Empire* (of German Nations, as is sometimes added; usually called *Germany*), a confederation of states that had come into being around the eleventh century and which ceased to exist in 1806.[26] Most of the German states and territories that made up the early modern Empire were:

---

25 See Stephen R. Epstein, *Freedom and Growth. The Rise of States and Markets in Europe, 1300–1750* (London / New York: Routledge, 2000) on different notions of 'freedom' as 'freedoms' (*libertas*, liberty, freedom from privilege) entertained in medieval and early modern Europe.

26 There has been much debate about the Empire in the historical sciences; recent studies have 'rehabilitated' the Empire as a functional working mechanism (albeit there is still a lot of controversy as to what exactly the Holy Roman Empire was). Good recent state-of-the-art surveys include Barbara Stollberg-Rilinger, *Das Heilige Römische Reich Deutscher Nation: Vom Ende des Mittelalters bis 1806*; and the much-acclaimed two-volume study by Joachim Whaley, *Germany and the Holy Roman Empire*, 2 vols. (Oxford: Oxford University Press, 2012–13). See also the review by Christoph Kampmann, 'Einheit in der Vielfalt – Einheit für die Vielfalt. Eine neue Gesamtgeschichte des römisch-deutschen Reichs 1493 bis 1806', *Historische Zeitschrift* 299, no.3 (2014), 696–707.

- *small*, but politically independent;
- *open* (especially for foreign manufactures!) and *vulnerable* (to political invasion) economies;
- *landlocked* economies, lacking (mostly) access to either the North Sea or the Baltic;
- and, due to the geopolitical dynamics of the Empire, in almost constant potential *threat* of annexation and incorporation by bigger or rival states.
- These territories were usually also *internally, institutionally* and *geographically fragmented.* Very often they were made up of a conglomerate consisting of core territory, enclaves and exclaves spread across the map like blots of ink spilled by a toddler attempting to paint a picture. And usually there existed fragmented and competing claims to sovereignty within these mini- and medium-sized entities, including disputed claims on jurisdiction and the share of taxes, dues, tolls and other 'public' levies to be distributed between the ruler and the native aristocracy (who often claimed special legal and economic privileges and tax exemptions on top of this).
- Last but not least: these states were also frequently hampered by the economic, social and cultural consequences of the Thirty Years War, one of the biggest catastrophes in the political history of Europe. The search for order, for linear and straight-rectangular patterns coupled with the emerging drive towards stylistic opulence characteristic of the cultural and artistic expressions of the age of *Baroque* manifested itself in branches as different and divergent as architecture, gardening, dance and banqueting – and economics.[27] This search for order comes across clearly in Veit Ludwig von Seckendorff's sketch of the ideal and 'well- ordered Police state', the *Teutscher Fürsten Stat* (1655), which is more than just a vision of a reformed Christian state that is in good religious order. It is the vision of a new type of state, a new economy.[28]

This emphasis on order[29] may or may not have been a Germanic peculiarity. But in terms of its core features, German economic theory in the early modern age was not sufficiently different from other national branches of economic theory so as to warrant being called a 'German' *Sonderweg.* Surely the political geography of early modern Germany required a political economy and development strategy that was slightly different compared to the larger and geographically more unified territorial powers such as France or the naval power England, or the relatively more open or economically 'inclusive' Netherlands; but surely this was more a difference in terms of nuance and less so in terms of analysis.[30] Especially, the larger German states such as Bavaria, Saxony, or Brandenburg-Prussia faced constant threats of territorial erosion; usually when a dynastic succession was contested upon the regent's death (the major reason why wars were fought in pre-industrial Europe). Therefore, the prime 'reason of state' was, for most of

---

27 Heinz Schilling, *Höfe und Allianzen. Deutschland 1648–1763*, 1994 new ed. (Berlin: Siedler, 1994), 189–90.

28 The account in Wakefield, *Disordered Police State*, first chapter, is very different from the sections on Seckendorff in Reinert, *How Rich Countries Got Rich*, ch. 3.

29 Tribe, *Strategies of Economic Order.*

30 Arthur Weststeijn and Jan Hartman, 'An Empire of Trade: Commercial Reason of State in Seventeenth-Century Holland', in S. Reinert and Røge, eds *Political Economy of Empire*, 11–31.

the medium-sized and bigger territories (including the largest and most powerful, Austria or the Austrian Hereditary Lands), to survive under such adverse geopolitical conditions. And that meant, usually, either to pay a lot of money on diplomacy and the forging of mutual protective allegiances, or else to pay a major share of gross domestic product to raise and maintain large standing armies for self-defense (as in Brandenburg-Prussia). Many wars were fought as pre-emptive strikes. For instance in 1740, when Frederick II 'the Great' annexed Silesia without a cause (but only from a modern vantage point). Throughout his lifetime, Frederick maintained that if he had not struck first, Austria would have; with the inevitable consequence of Brandenburg-Prussia being reduced from a middle-ranking but emerging player into a small and low-ranking 'non-player' and bystander on the Central European political scene. In order to safeguard the mere existence of the state – and thus the economy – a much higher share of economic resources had to be devoted to political and strategic-military means. This was a world in which nothing could quite be taken for granted, a world in which the state's survival was under more or less constant, if only potential, threat.[31]

This explains, partly at least, the strong focus of Cameralist literature on state finance and the 'private chamber' (*Camera*) of the princes and states that proclaimed to be, yet never were, *absolutist*.[32] In eighteenth-century Prussia, up to four per cent of the population were permanently enlisted in the army; Prussia's cultural outlook became, in many ways, militarized (or is said to have become so) under Frederick II 'the Great' (reigned (r.) 1740–1784).[33] His father had been even worse; but only under Frederick did Prussia rise to become one of the more militarized states of her time. Others were doing the same thing. A lot of resources and state money was put into the creation of an army in Saxony under Johann Georg III (1680–91).[34] The Hessian Landgraves acquired a proverbial reputation for hiring out their army, which had grown to a prodigious size by the 1680s, to foreign powers and their conflicts fought out overseas, most prominently perhaps during the War of American Independence (1776–83), when Hessian soldiers fought for the British cause on North American soil, as shown in the movie *Sleepy Hollow* with the

---

31 Schilling, *Höfe und Allianzen*, 90–91.
32 There has been a long scholarly controversy on whether or not the term 'Absolutism' would be an accurate description of the political landscape of post-1648 continental Europe; modern convention has it that this is not the case. See Ronald G. Asch and Heinz Duchardt, eds *Der Absolutismus – ein Mythos? Strukturwandel monarchischer Herrschaft in West- und Mitteleuropa (ca. 1550–1700* (Cologne: Böhlau, 1996); Nicholas Henshall, *The Myth of Absolutism. Change and Continuity in Early Modern European Monarchy* (London and New York: Longman, 2001); Heinz Duchardt, *Barock und Aufklärung* 4th ed. (Munich: Oldenbourg, 2007); Peter Baumgart, 'Absolutismus ein Mythos? Aufgeklärter Absolutismus ein Widerspruch? Reflexionen zu einem kontroversen Thema gegenwärtiger Frühneuzeitforschung', *Zeitschrift für Historische Forschung*, 27 (2000), 573–89, as well as Dagmar Freist, *Absolutismus* (Darmstadt: Wissenschaftliche Buchgesellschaft, 2008).
33 An up-to-date panorama of state-of-the-art historical research on Frederician Prussia can be found in Bernd Sösemann and Gregor Vogt-Spira, *Friedrich der Grosse in Europa: Geschichte einer wechselvollen Beziehung*, 2 vols. (Stuttgart: Franz Steiner, 2012).
34 Schilling, *Höfe und Allianzen*, 164.

headless Hessian mercenary played by Christopher Walken. Under Landgrave Frederick II (1760–85) more than 19,000 Hessians were deployed in the Americas. Proverbial is the *Uriasbrief* (which may or may not have been written by the Landgrave) lamenting the death of 'only' 1,465 of his subjects in the American war (Britain paid more for dead soldiers than for those that were only wounded or crippled).[35]

Similar conditions applied to the empire as a whole. Many contemporaries such as Samuel Pufendorf, in a 1667 fictitious account (*De statu Imperii Germanici*), expressed their stylized amazement at the very fact that the Empire survived – the crisis of the Thirty Years War, the French Sun King's appetite for expansion, the Turkish threat from the southeast, and the centrifugal powers from within this loose and amorphous confederation of states itself (of which Voltaire used to remark that it was neither holy nor Roman nor an empire).[36] Since the days of the Reformation in the 1520s and 1530s, there remained, curiously enough – and in spite of all 'federalist' (or centrifugal) forces within the empire – the notion that in certain regards, as in imperial military defence and monetary policy, all member states of the empire should pull the same string. This empire of the minds existed on paper until 1806. But it was in many ways a paper tiger and quite incomparable to other, more modern notions of either empire or state. Yet, it remained a firm unit to be reckoned with, at least *in the minds* of the political actors (monetary policy and integration were quite ineffective on the imperial level, though[37]).

Mercantilism, which could be found as a political moment and economic discourse in most German territories in some form or another during the sixteenth to nineteenth century, was also operative on the higher level, where it was located within a tension field and two conflicting goals: on the one hand to keep the Empire intact (imperial Mercantilism as a policy in the 1670s and 1680s) and to hold France in check, and at the same time to curb the expansive thirst and keep in check the political aspirations of the emerging big players within, mainly Austria (with the Emperor remaining *primus inter pares* amongst the imperial actors) and, later, Brandenburg-Prussia (the centrifugal forces). Accordingly, be that on the state level or the imperial stage, the share of public funds that could be allocated to what we would now call 'economic development' was, after deduction for the funds necessary to *create*, consolidate and perpetuate the state, rather humble. It was included as an item on the overall balance of the *ragion di stato* – thus *economic reason of state*. The military issue was entangled with the question of development.

Contrary to another common fallacy, Mercantilist economics were generally in favour of trade and exchange. None of the contemporary authors would ever be as fully or

35 Charles W. Ingrao, *The Hessian Mercenary State: Ideas, Institutions, and Reform under Frederick II, 1760–1785* (Cambridge and New York: Cambridge University Press, 1987), 1–3.

36 Schilling, *Höfe und Allianzen*, 94 (for the Pufendorf dictum); see the two-volume account by Whaley, *Germany and the Holy Roman Empire*.

37 Philipp Robinson Rössner, 'Monetary Instability, Lack of Integration and the Curse of a Commodity Money Standard. The German Lands, circa 1400–1900 AD', *Credit and Capital Markets*, 47, no. 2 (2014), 297–340.

die-hard protectionist as has often been claimed in modern textbooks. Cameralism was perhaps, above all else, about circulation. Cameralist economists entertained a clear vision of the economy as a living organism which, if methods were applied wisely, could not only be brought to flourish but also be made to grow, akin to a human individual who develops from toddler into a mature, middle-aged, full-strength human being if nourished wisely, brought up well and educated carefully. No one would expect the toddler to act like and be as wise and informed as a middle-aged individual. This has some implications regarding the development of modern free-trade discourse versus the older protectionist theory and Listian 'Erziehungszölle' – an age-old debate amongst historians and economists ever since the days of Adam Smith and James Steuart. Metaphors of the economy as a living organism are to be found all over the place in the Cameralists' (and many English Mercantilists') texts on the *politische Körper*, Body politick and so on. We find the idea of circulation – money as the 'blood' of this organism – in Becher's *Discurs* (1688), as well as Hörnigk's works (gold and silver – *unser bestes Geblueth*); as well as in in many an anonymous pamphlet, such as the one printed at Leipzig in 1702, of which the author is unknown but which is believed to have circulated widely.[38] Frequently, these models were based on or verging upon alchemy[39]; a topic which has been immortalized in Johann Wolfgang von Goethe's *Faust*, both parts of the magnum opus. The second one, which is clearly more esoteric than the first, is said to represent a sketch of the unfolding 'New Economy' based upon industrialization and the introduction of machines, as well as infinite monetary expansion by the creation of a paper currency.[40] This Faustian strategy of monetary expansion (or, to use a modernism, 'quantitative easing') would occupy a core position in the economic discourses of the Hartlib Circle in mid-seventeenth-century England.[41] Alchemy, rather than irrational-occult reasoning, was the core of the Faustian zeal to discover what held the world together (*was die Welt im innersten zusammenhält*). It was the search for the quintessence, *Urelement, spiritus universalis* and not uncharacteristic of the so-called earlier 'Austrian' Cameralists of the second half of the seventeenth century.[42] As late as 1778, Johann Friedrich von Pfeiffer (1718–1787), sometime professor in Cameral sciences at the University of Mainz, wrote in his *Grundriß der wahren und falschen Staatskunst*, vol. I (Berlin, 1778) that society was represented by individuals connected with each other through a system of pipes or arteries (*Röhren* or, *Communikationskanäle*, […] *theils physisch,*

38 See the anonymous pamphlet *Die ietzt florirende Kauffmannschafft in Teutschland und andern Europäischen Reichen* (Leipzig: Andreas Zeidler, 1702), 1–2.

39 Zielenziger, *Die alten Kameralisten*, 108; also Keith Tribe, 'Die Wirtschaftssemantik der Frühen Neuzeit', in Matis et al., eds *Vademecum zu einem Klassiker absolutistischer Wirtschaftspolitik*, 245–89, at 278–79; Pamela H. Smith, *The Business of Alchemy: Science and Culture in the Holy Roman Empire* (Princeton, NJ: Princeton University Press, 1994).

40 Hans Christoph Binswanger, *Geld und Magie: Deutung und Kritik der modernen Wirtschaft anhand von Goethes Faust* (Stuttgart: Edition Weitbrecht, 1985).

41 Wennerlind, 'Money: Hartlibian Political Economy and the New Culture of Credit'.

42 Wilhelm Roscher, 'Die österreichische Nationalökonomik unter Kaiser Leopold I', *Jahrbücher für Nationalökonomie und Statistik* (1864), 25–59 and 105–22; Louise Sommer, *Die österreichischen Kameralisten. In dogmengeschichtlicher Darstellung*, 2 vols. (Vienna: Konegen, 1920/25), I, 60, 62–63.

theils moralisch (p. 10). Hörnigk's text, however, remained free of alchemistic reasoning, which makes him somewhat distinct from the Cameralist mainstream of his day.[43]

Trade − foreign trade or external commerce − was important as an agent for cultural exchange, as well as knowledge and technology transfer by learning and emulation. Connectivity and firm trading relations with the outside world were central, even indispensable, for economic growth in Cameralist thought. As Johann Heinrich Justi would write later, in his *Chimäre des Gleichgewichts der Handlung und Schiffahrt:*[44]

Allein aus dem vorhergehenden ist leicht einzusehen, daß eine Nation, die der andern die Handlungsbilanz bezahlen muß, und die folglich mit Schaden handelt, diesen Schaden nicht der andern Nation, mit der sie handelt, beymäßigen kann, sondern daß die Ursache davon lediglich in dem Mangel der natürlichen Vorteile ihres Landes, oder in der geringern Arbeitsamkeit und Geschicklichkeit zu suchen ist, die ihre Bürger haben. Ja! wenn man genau gehen will; so ist dieser Schade allemal ihr selbst zuzuschreiben. Es ist fast nie ein Boden so unfruchtbar, der nicht durch Arbeitsamkeit und Geschicklichkeit ersetzet werden könnte; und wenn auch dieses unmöglich wäre; so kann eine jede Nation allemal die Handlungsbilanz gleich machen und ihre Verarmung verhindern, wenn sie den Gebrauch der fremden Waren, das ist, ihren Aufwand einschränket. Die Landesproducte, die eine jede Nation jährlich ausführet, das sind ihre eigentlichen Einkünfte, wenn sie sich nicht nach ihrer innerlichen Haushaltung, sondern nach ihrem Verhältniß und Zusammenhang mit andern Völkern betrachtet; und dasjenige, was sie jährlich an fremden Waaren verbrauchet, das ist ihr Aufwand. Gleichwie nun die Vernunft einem jeden Haushalter saget, daß der Aufwand, den er mache, seinen Einkünften gleich seyn muß, wenn er nicht verarmen will; so befiehlt ihm eben diese gesunde Vernunft, wenn er seinen Aufwand höher, als seine Einkünfte befindet, daß er entweder seine Einkünfte vermehren, oder im Fall der Unmöglichkeit, seinen Aufwand einschränken muß. Sollte aber ein Staat die allererste Regel der Haushaltung nicht in der höchsten Maaße ausüben, er, der die oberste Haushaltung so vieler Menschen führet, und dessen Wirthschaft von rechtswegen das vortrefflichste Beyspiel und Muster vor alle Privathaushaltungen seyn sollte? Wenn demnach ein Volk den schädlichen Zustand seiner Handlung lediglich sich selbst beyzumässen hat; so kann es auch nicht die geringste Ursache haben, dasjenige Volk zu beneiden und anzufeinden, an welches es die Handlungsbilanz bezahlen muß. Dieses Verfahren würde eben so niederträchtig seyn, als wenn ein durch Verschwendung verarmter Edelmann diejenigen Kaufleut, auf das äußerste hassen wollte, die ihm auf sein Verlangen die Waaren zu seiner Verschwendung geliefert haben. Nicht diese Kaufleute, sondern seine unbesonnene Haushaltung hat er Ursache zu hassen.[45]

[From the preceding it is eminently clear that the nation or country with a negative balance of payment (which is detrimental economically) cannot blame the other country for this but

43 Ernst Stabreit, *Philipp Wilhelm von Hörnigk: Ein Vorkämpfer einer nationalen Wirtschaftspolitik in Deutschland am Ausgang des 17. Jahrhunderts* (Berlin: Blanke, 1921), 20–21.

44 *Die Chimäre des Gleichgewichts der Handlung und Schiffahrt: Oder: Ungrund und Nichtigkeit einiger neuerlich geäußerten Meynungen von denen Maaßregeln der freyen Mächte gegen die zu befürchtende Herrschaft und Obermacht zur See, wobey zugleich Neue und wichtige Betrachtungen über die Handlung und Schiffahrt der Völker, und über den höchsten Punkt der daraus entstehenden Macht und Glückseligkeit beygebracht warden* (Altona: Iversen, 1759).

45 Justi, *Chimäre* (1759), 17.

has to look for the reasons and origins of this within her own domestic economy, some sort of natural disadvantage, sloth and laziness and lack of skill amongst her domestic population. Never is a piece of soil so completely barren and infertile that it cannot be made to yield at least modestly by diligent labour and care and even if this cannot be made to happen the nation can even out her negative trade balance by curbing the desire of her citizens for foreign imports. The products of the land that this nation exports year after year are the source of her wealth if seen against and in connection with the surrounding nations which she choses to connect with by means of trade. In the same way as the prudent housekeeper will know how to even out his income and expenses lest he becomes impoverished, his ratio will tell him that in case his expenses exceed his income he will need to either crank down on expenses or else raise more income. Should not the state, the house-holder for the whole nation, be the first and foremost leading example keeping this good rule of oeconomy and thus set a good example for all citizens and households? If it is the case that a bad state of commerce (a negative balance of trade/payment) is entirely the fault of the respective nation, there can be no reason to be envious and hostile to the other country from which she imports more than sending back in return. In fact this would be as hideous as the impoverished nobleman who blames for his state of poverty the very same merchants that procured the wares for him and for which he became indebted in the first place. He should not despise these merchants but rather his bad and inconsiderate oeconomy.]

This was the economic programme of the Mercantilists and mainstream political economy formulated in a nutshell. Sophus Reinert has stressed the symbiotic relationship between economic connectivity and protectionism in European political economy discourse since the Renaissance.[46] *Arbeit* – productive labour, as well as *Gewerbefleiß* or industriousness were central in the process of generating wealth and added value in manufacturing. Agrarian economies were rather static; something the Cameralist textbooks didn't like very much. Not surprisingly then, a lot of the pages in Cameralist textbooks were devoted to the question of dynamics, circulation and economic development.

Configuring the Free Market: *Homo imperfectabilis*

The main problem to be tackled in Cameralist economics was rather philosophical. It was the ubiquitous divergence between intention and reality (similar to Schopenhauer's *World as Will and Representation*). In order for a market economy to flourish, even to function, the economy had to be *created* first. It had to be made to work. We have, in the previous section, seen how the German territorial state had to be created by maintaining an army (that safeguarded its geographical borders). But there was also a lot of work to be done on the *inside*. And that meant the configuration of a state and reliable government institutions, including what we cherish today as the so-called 'Free Market'. This almost goes without saying: good or inclusive institutions require strong and proactive states.[47] But things were, unfortunately, not as easy as they looked on paper. According

---

46 Reinert, *Translating Empire*; id., 'Rivalry'.
47 Douglass C. North, John Joseph Wallis and Barry R. Weingast, *Violence and Social Orders: A Conceptual Framework for Interpreting Recorded Human History* (Cambridge and New York: Cambridge

to Sommer, another major scholar, Cameralist economics were marked by the desire to strengthen the absolutist state. This was, of course, not an accomplishable goal at the time; truly absolutist rulers are not to be found on the historical record prior to Hitler or Stalin. Connected to this was the creation of free markets and integrated national economies. Mercantilist policies represented, therefore, both aims and goals at the same time.[48] Sommer, of course, erred in her assessment that Mercantilism was the prime tool of the absolutist state, first because there never existed, in European history, anything like absolute monarchs and absolutist states (Absolutism was a discursive concept, both now and then); secondly, because the prime example of a truly Mercantilist state that managed to accomplish successful long-term economic development was, of course, post-1688 England, a state that can by no means be labelled absolutist.[49]

These obvious divergences between (Cameralist) theory and (Cameralist) reality have led to a refreshing growth of new scholarly models in recent decades. According to Tribe and Wakefield, we may call Cameralism a discursive-linguistic or praxeological strategy of selling a product and eliminating competitors competing for the same job. The Cameralists' main purpose and principle, after all, was to get a job by cultivating a body of expert knowledge, sometimes bordering upon the occult (e.g. alchemy) which would secure permanent employment with a prince and *Staatenlenker* interested in lifting the wealth of the country. Such certainly was neither the sole nor main aim of English economic pamphleteers, who shared otherwise many convictions with the writers who have come to be known as Cameralists.[50]

German economist Priddat has made another important point in this regard, in a sense taking the debate from the totally overdrawn view of the Communists ('Die "gemeinsame Glückseligkeit", die die Staatswirtschaft fördern soll, ist die "Glückseligkeit" des seinen Zwergstaat aussaugenden deutschen Landesfürsten",[51] a dictum that was shared implicitly by most of the modern, including 'bourgeois', interpretations of Cameralism as 'German Mercantilism') much further. The conception of human nature entertained by the Cameralists was somewhat distinct – the *homo imperfectabilis* with her often conflicting or antagonistic and childish desires and neither an understanding of nor care for the needs of the developmental state. Such subjects needed the strong hand of a caring autocrat – the Prince – to steer the economy, akin to a big household, into a better schedule of resource allocation. Markets clearing spontaneously to the best outcome (we would say Pareto-optimal resource allocation) were as unknown to this conception

---

University Press, 2009), and Daron Acemoglu and James A. Robinson, *Why Nations Fail: The Origins of Power, Prosperity, and Poverty* (New York: Crown, 2012) are prominent works that do not always explicitly stress this aspect.

48 Sommer, *Die österreichischen Kameralisten*, I, 48–56, quote on 55.
49 Prasannan Parthasarathi, *Why Europe Grew Rich and Asia Did Not. Global Economic Divergence, 1600–1850* (Cambridge: Cambridge University Press, 2011), and Ha-Joon Chang, *Kicking Away the Ladder: Development Strategy in Historical Perspective* (London: Anthem, 2003) on the economic development of the British economy under a Mercantilist umbrella.
50 Tribe, 'Die Wirtschaftssemantik der Frühen Neuzeit', in Schefold (ed.), Vademecum.
51 Behrens, *Grundriss*, 121.

as the idea of an economy that would have functioned independently from the state and would be a *mechanism* that was governed by its own *laws* of demand and supply and allocation. One important conclusion derived from this was: 'Free markets' as we known them (and as pre-classical thinkers knew them) had to be created first and foremost, by the will and initiative of the ruler – very much a product of Enlightenment thought coupled with a somewhat pessimistic outlook toward the idiosyncratic features of seventeenth- and eighteenth-century political, social and legal reality in the continental feudal economies.[52]

Recent accounts have considerably modified a somewhat binary 'Whiggish' model of developed north-west Atlantic versus primitive and unfree central-eastern European economies or the old and very stylized division between the west Elbian market-friendly agrarian regime versus the east Elbian *villainage* and serfdom.[53] There was much more agency and flexibility within the eastern continental agrarian production regimes (of Prussia, Bohemia, Poland-Lithuania, Russia) than previously thought, even when it came to the more extreme versions such as serfdom (hereditary bondage or *Erbuntertänigkeit/ Leibeigenschaft*). But nevertheless, until well after the end of the Ancien Règime and the Napoleonic Wars and reforms, the native nobility entertained a huge set of economic privileges – both east as well as west of the River Elbe – which were incompatible with notions of a 'free market' according to the pre-classical as well as our modern notion, meaning a market with equalized chances of access; and usury, rent-seeking and other market distortions (arbitrage, speculation) reduced to a minimum (ideally they would have been totally absent, but that was an utopia, both then and now). And the eighteenth-century Cameralists *were* aware of that and all were adamant about abolishing it. So the Cameralist conception of the *homo imperfectabilis* was less an inherently primitive axiomatic or epistemological conception as such, but rather an idiosyncratic version of the modern free market idea, contingent upon the peculiar conditions prevailing in situ in the German and other regions east and west of the River Elbe.

We should stress at this point – with more emphasis than expended in the works by Tribe, Priddat or Wakefield – that the idea of the free market has a prehistory that is much older than usually thought.[54] Small's dictum that '[a]ccording to the Cameralist conception then, the state was a magnified family with a big farm as its property'[55] is ill-conceived, if not plain wrong, if seen from the modern vantage point, especially in

---

52 Priddat, 'Paradoxe Konzeption'.

53 Markus Cerman, *Villagers and Lords in Eastern Europe, 1300–1800* (Houndmills, Basingstoke and New York: Palgrave Macmillan, 2012); William W. Hagen, *Ordinary Prussians: Brandenburg Junkers and Villagers, 1500–1840* (New York: Cambridge University Press, 2002), 184–279 (184, 278–79).

54 Even Harcourt, *Illusion of Free Markets*, only commences his analysis in the mid-eighteenth century, which is far too late – the free market problem and discourse have medieval origins. See Philipp Robinson Rössner, 'Freie Märkte? Zur Konzeption von Konnektivität, Wettbewerb und Markt im vorklassischen Wirtschaftsdenken und die Lektionen aus der Geschichte', *Historische Zeitschrift* 303 (2016), 349–92.

55 Quoted after Zielenziger, *Die alten Kameralisten*, 96.

the light of more recent research into the intellectual and legal history pertaining to the discursive figure of 'free markets'.[56] In the Cameralist model the relationship between market and state was, actually, very different. More importantly, Wakefield has made yet another departure on the topic which deserves consideration in the present context, as it belongs to the problem of how the Cameralists 'created' and then designed their reality based on a very specific model. In an extremely well-written account of *The Disordered Police State* (2009), Wakefield has set himself the task to de-bunk the myth of the Cameralists by focusing on what may perhaps – for want of a better term, using a modernism – be called their *praxeology*. Cameralists, Wakefield argues, were habitual vagabonds, travelling from court to court; trained in a science that has gotten lost and which ranged between things we may call, using modern anachronisms, 'fiscal sociology', 'development economics', or 'public finance'. Cameralists, with their voluminous textbooks – from Veit Ludwig von Seckendorff's *Teutscher Fürsten Stat* (first ed. 1655; nine editions were printed; Seckendorff was read until the end of the eighteenth century!) to Johann Heinrich von Justi's *Staatswirthschaft* (*Principles of Economics*, 1755) – sketched an idealized version of the economy. This vision couldn't possibly be translated into practice, Wakefield argues. It was too good to be true. Cameralists captured an absurdly wide-ranging panoptical array of topics, ranging from agriculture, horticulture, mining, forestry, chemistry, animal husbandry; mineralogy, geology, botany to public finance and fiscal sociology. Here the Cameralists seem near to the Hartlibian economists studied by Wennerlind and others. Around mid-seventeenth century, a learned circle of natural scientists and economists with an inclination towards alchemy (which was not at all unusual at the time) had formed in England around Prussian émigré Samuel Hartlib, who believed that infinite economic growth and advancement were principally possible using the tools of empiricism and scientific reasoning in uncovering the hidden working mechanisms of nature's panoptical world of goods and endowment.[57] Parallels with similar developments on the continent are obvious, topically as well as geographically (with Hartlib being from Prussia). While around 1600, much of German economics had focused on thoroughly agrarian household management issues (*Hausväterliteratur*) – the characteristic economics genre resting between medieval neo-Aristotelianism or Scholastic economics and mainstream Mercantilism – by the later 1600s, economic growth and development of the national economy (as opposed to the singular household or *oikos*) now occupied a centre stage in Cameralist economic theory. The transition from *oiko*-nomics to economics (a science studying the national economy as a whole) had been completed by the seventeenth century.[58]

But the Cameralists would, Wakefield argues, serve two conflicting interests. One was to fill the coffers of the prince. The other was to promote public welfare. These

---

56   Nicely summarized in Harcourt, *Illusion of Free Markets*.

57   Wennerlind, 'Money: Hartlibian Political Economy and the New Culture of Credit'.

58   On the Hausväterliteratur see Tribe, *German Economic Discourse*, and the relevant sections in Burkhardt and Priddat, *Geschichte der Ökonomie*.

two goals were mutually exclusive. If you furthered the wealth of the prince, you would have to take away something from the public via additional taxes and levies; if you chose to promote public welfare, this would mean that the prince (or state) could not take as much out of the economy as they would want to. A sound fiscal policy and development were, as it appears, mutually exclusive, at least when seen in the empirical practice in seventeenth- and eighteenth-century German states. Cameralists were cunning, scheming, strategic, smooth operators. We should not 'conflate Seckendorff's model police state with an actually existing principality'. Rather, Wakefield concludes that '[o]nly in the well-ordered worlds of his imagination was Justi sovereign. He escaped there by candlelight, safe from the tortures of everyday failure and frustration.'[59]

But such an assessment is slightly anachronistic, judging the Cameralist achievement from a theoretical stance developed in the modern social sciences, that is, developed long after the Cameralists had gone. Were the two goals – raising the Prince's finances and promoting economic growth and development – really mutually exclusive? The available evidence suggests that they weren't. True, Cameralist texts and pamphlets look as though Cameralism was more about discourse and the purpose of selling oneself so as to get a job. But if you think twice about it, they also sound, in many places, quite like the somewhat idealized, and in many ways surreal, models that can be found in modern economics textbooks. Cameralist textbooks *did* sketch an ideal world, starting with Seckendorff's *Teutscher Fürsten Stat* (1655) that was a model of the ideal princely state (see later in the chapter). Re-reading Wakefield in the light of recent research, we may conclude that the Cameralists actually *had* a theory. They *had* a clear set of axiomatic principles on how markets should work; how exchange should be governed and put on fair grounds, and how an economy could be developed towards a more effective production frontier. Some of their key principles shared common ground with what has been called 'Mercantilist' economics. Many of their ideas about 'free' markets (in a sense of 'just' or 'fair' exchange) have found their way into modern neoclassical and liberal theory – and, as an authority with no apparent tendentious inclination has demonstrated, not always with expressive acknowledgement.[60]

We can safely say that the modern economic sciences firmly rest on the shoulders of Mercantilism and Cameralism, but that some of the foundations were reformulated and modified, sometimes even distorted and misrepresented, replacing some of the basic epistemological foundations of what 'free' markets are and how freedom in the market is to be created with notions of spontaneous or 'natural order' in the market, which appear, in the light of recent studies, quite unrealistic.[61] Modern assessments of Cameralism have therefore ranged from firm scepticism as to Cameralism's nature as a 'theory',[62] to

---

59 Wakefield, *Disordered Police State*, 143–44. This discussion and the following paragraph are based on Rössner, 'Heckscher Reloaded?'.
60 Grampp, 'An Appreciation of Mercantilism' is a most apt and relevant study.
61 Harcourt, *Illusion of Free Markets*.
62 See Tribe, *Strategies of Economic Order*, 12.

a somewhat compromise or in-between assessment: a theory of free markets according to early modern contingencies à la Priddat (2008),[63] or the stressing of its idiosyncratic nature as a science developed for small landlocked competing states.[64] Earlier, mainly German-speaking economists and historians had been, during the 1950s and 1960s, much more positive.

According to Bog and Blaich, two eminent historians of Cameralist discourse and practice,

- Mercantilism was a full and distinct economic theory in the modern sense. This was marked for instance by Johann Joachim Becher's conception of the economy as a composite being made up of variables that interact with each other according to 'functional relationships' which could be modelled and analysed using scientific reasoning.[65] We find such expressions of theoretical aspiration as an epistemological foundation in Zincke's (1746) dictum that economic analysis must be based on theoretical principles, so as to derive, from a given set of empirical facts and observations, principles that are either invisible on the surface or as yet unknown.[66] This theorization is based upon constant empirical observation of reality; it attempts to reduce complexity by modelling functional relationships that can be observed from economic reality by distilling them into ideal types. It is hard to see where modern economic and social sciences should take issue with this, apart from the fact that, in many ways, modern economics and econometrics have given up analysis of reality in favour of complexity reduction by suggesting that the economy could be conceived as and studied using sets of never-ending mathematical equations and quite fictive assumptions.
- Mercantilist theory contained crucial elements inherent to modern economic theory, including its foundations, addressing 'modern' problems and issues through a 'modern' lens or looking glass. Perhaps the parallels with Keynesian economics invoked by many a scholar since the 1940s[67] (issues of underemployment of resources, mainly capital and labour), which some have seen as recurring repeatedly in history, for example, after the end of the Thirty Years War (1648) or the Great Depression (1929–32) are a bit too anachronistic for the historian's liking.[68] But if we consider that the goals of the Cameralists (and many Mercantilists) included, inter alia,

63 Priddat, 'Paradoxe Kombination'; id., 'Kameralistisches Menschenbild: homo imperfectabilis und die Vervollkommnung des Menschen durch Ordnung', in Andrea Grisold, Luise Gubitzer and Reinhard Pirker, eds *Das Menschenbild in der Ökonomie: Eine verschwiegene Voraussetzung* (Vienna: Löcker, 2007), 75–104; see also Tribe, *Strategies of Economic Order*, ch. 1.

64 Jürgen G. Backhaus, 'From Wolff to Justi', in id., ed *The Beginnings of Political Economy: Johann Heinrich Gottlob von Justi* (Boston, MA: Springer, 2009), 1–18 (4).

65 Bog, *Reichsmerkantilismus*, 7.

66 Sommer, *Die österreichischen Kameralisten*, I, 80.

67 Böhle, *Die Idee der Wirtschaftsverfassung*; Röpke, 'Wachstumstheorie'; and the relevant passages in Fritz Blaich, *Die Wirtschaftspolitik des Reichstags im Heiligen Römischen Reich: ein Beitrag zur Problemgeschichte wirtschaftlichen Gestaltens* (Stuttgart: Fischer, 1970).

68 Ingomar Bog, 'Ist die Kameralistik eine untergegangene Wissenschaft?', *Berichte zur Wissenschaftsgeschichte* 4 (1981), 61–72.

- Economic growth and development;
- Full employment;
- Price level stability;
- Economic freedom of individual actors ('free markets');
- Equalized distributions of income; preventing poverty and destitution amongst the lower strata of society (A. Sen's capability approach!);
- Introduction of welfare systems for those unable to work (unemployed, chronically ill, old age). We find these notions most clearly perhaps in the works by J. G. H. Justi, and, occasionally, also natural philosopher Christian Wolff's *Grundsätze des Natur- und Völkerrechts* (Halle: Renger, 1754)[69];
- Market integration (by the goal to create a national economy)[70]

We yet again see how 'modern' and close to modern economics Cameralist theory really was.[71] Cameralism also had a focus on manufacturing (economies of scale; demand elasticities higher for manufactures than raw materials). It stressed the role of the state in the economy's development. Empirical/experience-based *Erfahrungswissenschaft* was fundamental. Further elements were that culture matters; overarching circumstances: '*Struk turzusammenhänge* – structural coherence and connections – among economic factors and between the economy and the rest of society were not only obvious; but to understand such connections is also most important for both economic theory and policy (E. Reinert). Context and idiosyncrasy are crucial variables determining both the epistemological foundations and the outcome of mercantile economic policy. With import substitution and modest tariff protection, the Cameralists also prefigured key concepts of modern development economics. With their somewhat dirigiste approach to market governance and the abolition of guilds and other forms of market distortion (usury, rent-seeking and so forth), manifested in their call for a strong prince or 'state' and their conception of a *homo imperfectibilis* (B. Priddat), especially the later Cameralists (Sonnenfels, Justi) were firmly vested within the contingencies and accordingly calibrated epistemology of the seventeenth- and eighteenth-century continental European world.[72] But – and this needs emphasizing – they were essentially formulating the same goals to be found in modern (contemporary) economics textbooks. A strong state was needed for free markets to proliferate; as Priddat notes, this would be somewhat different from modern conceptions of how the economy is organized.[73]

---

69 Backhaus, 'The German Economic Tradition', 341.
70 Hans Kretschmar, *Die Einheit der Volkswirtschaft in den älteren deutschen Wirtschaftslehren* (Jena: Gustav Fischer, 1930), ch. 4.
71 See also Gerhard Kolb, *Geschichte der Volkswirtschaftslehre. Dogmenhistorische Positionen des ökonomischen Denkens* (Munich: Vahlen, 1997), 29–31; in the German tradition Cameralism and Mercantilism seem to have been treated slightly more favourably, even in the more recent textbooks on the history of political economy.
72 Priddat, 'Zur paradoxen Konzeption'.
73 Ibid., 285.

- Some would even classify Cameralism as the overarching theory. Cameralist economics, in the words of Blaich, comprised a larger area or field of economic action than Mercantilism ('in fact, it completely includes Mercantilist economic theory').[74] Traditionalist accounts have seen it exactly the other way round, as for instance reflected in Raeff's dictum that 'it is usually and quite correctly asserted that Mercantilism, by whatever definition, inspired the economic theory and practice of cameralism [...].'[75] Much of the history of European political economy has become rather skewed and biased, in consequence of this quite peculiar viewpoint, as with Cameralist economics we seem to have lost the possibility and will to formulate a holistic model of economics – which included, at times (and for a reason!) amongst others, public administration, public finance, public sector management, accounting and statistics, but also pigs, geese and hens. The latter was the heritage of the German *Hausväter*-literature.[76]

The problem hinges, of course, precisely upon how we define and assess what a modern theory is. It is quite a moot point to search for either 'modern' or 'theory' in Cameralism and Mercantilism, as even the more recent economic theories have been subject to more divergence and diversity than unity in paradigm sufficient for them to be called 'paradigmatic'; both a consensual definition of what would classify as 'modern' as well as 'theory' is lacking, when recent developments in the history of political economy and economics are taken into account.

We may conclude this line of thought by stating expressively what Cameralism was not:

- It was not simply a variant of Mercantilist theory; in fact, it seems as though it was the other way round. English and French Mercantilism may have been a side strand of a much larger continental theory we may, for want of a better term, label 'Cameralism' or 'economic reason of state';
- Cameralism did not represent a peculiarly German *Sonderweg*.[77] In fact, we find Cameralism all over the place; from Sweden to Italy[78];
- Cameralism was not a random set of principles extending across the entire spectrum of economic activity – from raising pigs, horticulture, to building up a manufacturing industry and financing a standing army, subject to the overall strategic goal of filling the

---

74 Blaich, quoted after Bog, 'Ist die Kameralistik eine untergegangene Wissenschaft?', 63. On the theoretical achievements of the Mercantilists and their pedigree in modern liberal and neoclassical theory, see previous notes, as well as Jürgen G. Backhaus, 'From Wolff to Justi', and Helge Peukert, 'Justi's Concept of Moral Economics and the Good Society', in Backhaus, ed. *The Beginnings of Political Economy*, 117–32.

75 Marc Raeff, *The Well-Ordered Police State. Social and Institutional Change through Law in the Germanies and Russia, 1600–1800* (New Haven and London: Yale University Press, 1983), 92.

76 Backhaus, 'The German Economic Tradition', 343; Wakefield, *Disordered Police State*. Andre Wakefield communicated this idea to me in a face-to-face conversation at the University of Leipzig in July 2014.

77 E.g. Dittrich, *Die deutschen und österreichischen Kameralisten*, 1, 16.

78 Ernest Lluch, 'Cameralism Beyond the Germanic World: A Note on Tribe', in *History of Economic Ideas*, V (2) (1991), 85–99.

state's coffers. It was a full-blown economic theory and as 'closed' or unified as some of the prime examples of modern economic theory.

Late eighteenth-century Cameralists such as Sonnenfels were quite specific. Cameralism was first about economic growth and development; state power came second.[79] Scholars have for a long time stressed, alongside the Cameralist and Mercantilist pedigree in Keynesianism, the applicability of Mercantilist theory for modern under- or less developed countries. Mercantilist theories were direct precursors of modern growth and development economics.[80] We should therefore give up the somewhat antiquated notion entertained by many twentieth-century scholars, that Mercantilism and Cameralism were unscientific, astringent, un-modern and non-theoretical. The reverse is true. We should simply read the old texts more carefully.

Development into Underdevelopment or the Shadow of the Great War

The Cameralists stood in the ashes of the Thirty Years War, a war that decisively changed Europe's political and cultural landscape. After the Treaty of Westphalia had been signed in 1648, things would never be the same again.[81] It has been suggested that the Thirty Years War was the prime cause for Germany's subsequent economic backwardness well into mid-nineteenth century.[82] But we must, before proceeding with the analysis, bear in mind two things. First, the productivity gap in manufacturing visible in many a German manufacturing industry of the later seventeenth century (compared especially with

---

79 J. v. Sonnenfels, *Grundsätze der Polizey, Handlung und Finanzwissenschaft*, 2 Theil (Vienna 1771), 4, quoted after Röpke, 'Wachstumstheorie', 7 ('Auch als das Mittel, das Vermögen des Staates zu vergrößern, wird die Handlung betrachtet. Der vergrößerte Reichtum des Staats ist eine beständige Folge der Handlung, nicht aber in Ansehen des Staates der Endzweck, dem der Reichtum ohne Bürger unnütz seyn würde.').

80 G. Baumbach, 'Wirtschaftswachstum', in *Handwörterbuch der Staatswissenschaften* 12, 765 as quoted in Blaich, *Wirtschaftspolitik des Reichstags*, 183; see also ibid., 183–84; and most recently Reinert, *How Rich Countries Got Rich*.

81 On the political and military history, see the excellent studies by Peter H. Wilson, *Europe's Tragedy: A History of the Thirty Years War* (London: Allen Lane, 2009), and Peter Englund, *Ofredsår*; I have used the new German edition: *Verwüstung: Eine Geschichte des Dreißigjährigen Krieges* (Reinbek bei Hamburg: Rowohlt-Taschenbuch-Verlag, 2013). Further Herfried Münkler, *Der Dreißigjährige Krieg: Europäische Katastrophe, deutsches Trauma 1618–1648*, 5th ed. (Berlin: Rowohlt, 2017); Georg Schmidt, *Die Reiter der Apokalypse: Geschichte des Dreißigjährigen Krieges* (Munich: C. H. Beck, 2018); Heinz Duchardt, ed. *Der Westfälische Friede. – Diplomatie – politische Zäsur – kulturelles Umfeld – Rezeptionsgeschichte* (Munich: Oldenbourg, 1998), and Heinrich Lutz, *Reformation und Gegenreformation*, 5th ed. (Munich: Oldenbourg, 2002), 97–111, and 181–91, with further literature.

82 Friedrich-Wilhelm Henning, *Landwirtschaft und ländliche Gesellschaft in Deutschland*, vol. 1, *800 bis 1750*, 3rd ed. (Paderborn, Munich and Vienna: F. Schöningh, 1996), 224. But see, more recently (and with updated data), Ulrich Pfister, 'The Timing and Pattern of Real Wage Divergence in Pre-industrial Europe: Evidence from Germany, c. 1500–1850,' *Economic History Review*, Second Series, 70:3 (2017), 701–29.

France and the Netherlands) had been commented on by contemporaries long before the War. As early as the the later sixteenth century, there are written documents lamenting a lack of competitiveness, and accordingly, problems with export sales, of some German manufacturing industries. These were usually related to rising costs for wages, inputs and raw materials in the age of the 'Price Revolution' that were not met with a concomitant rise in the artisans' incomes and profit. The consequence was frequently that the quality of the product deteriorated.[83] Many branches of industrial production – such as textile weaving and bleaching at Ulm, the number of new admissions to the Nuremberg Citizenship, the number of new admissions to the Nuremberg textile guilds, the number of active blacksmiths and metalworkers and many more – had been in decline during the two decades *preceding* the war, since about 1600 (or earlier).[84] Secondly, war, conflict and crisis hit the different regional economies very differently. There were many regions on the continent that suffered greatly during and in direct consequence of the war, others that didn't so much, and others – including certain people, usually magnates – that flourished.[85]

The Great War, however, surely made things much worse where they had not been so good before – especially in the central German areas around Saxony and Thuringia and further south, that witnessed the brunt of the campaigns fought out between the Swedes and the imperial troops under Wallenstein. In this area, Veit Ludwig von Seckendorff's *Teutscher Fürsten Stat* originated, a Cameralist *Ur*-Text (it was not entirely without good reason that American sociologist Albion Small would call Seckendorff the 'Adam Smith of Cameralism'). This war was, as many have noted, not so much about total destruction (as twentieth-century wars were), but frequently followed a strategy of 'controlled' bleeding-out of the adversaries' military and economic resources.[86] The war caused much economic dislocation and disintegration of markets, especially by the dissolution of the previously thriving commercial and economic networks controlled by

---

83 Blaich, *Die Wirtschaftspolitik des Reichstags*; see also Ingomar Bog, 'Wachstumsprobleme der oberdeutschen Wirtschaft 1540–1618', *Jahrbücher für Nationalökonomie und Statistik* 179, no. 6 (1966), 493–537 (527–28).

84 Bog, 'Wachstumsprobleme', 432–537, graphs.

85 For an excellent survey especially of Central Europe, see e.g. Cerman, *Villagers and Lords*, Hagen, *Ordinary Prussians*, 184–279; Erich Landsteiner, 'Wiederaufbau oder Transformation? Niederösterreich vor, während und nach dem Dreißigjährigen Krieg', in: Walter Leitsch and Stanisław Trawkowski, eds *Polen und Österreich im 17. Jahrhundert* (Vienna/Cologne/ Weimar: Böhlau, 1999), 133–203, id. and Andreas Weigl, "Sonsten finden wir die Sachen sehr übel aufm Landt beschaffen". Krieg und lokale Gesellschaft in Niederösterreich (1618– 1621)', in Benigna von Krusenstjern and Hans Medick, eds *Zwischen Alltag und Katastrophe. Der Dreißigjährige Krieg aus der Nähe* (Göttingen: Vandenhoeck & Ruprecht, 1999), 229–72; or Miroslav Hroch and Josef Petráň, *Das 17. Jahrhundert–Krise der Feudalgesellschaft?* (Hamburg: Hoffmann & Campe, 1981), especially 83–99.

86 Still a useful overview is Frank Tallett, *War and Society in Early-Modern Europe: 1495–1715* (London, New York: Routledge, 1992); and Geoffrey Parker, *The Military Revolution: Military Innovation and the Rise of the West, 1500–1800* (Cambridge and New York: Cambridge University Press, 1988).

the rich merchant-bankers of the export-oriented industrial cities, particularly in Upper Germany.[87] But in the immediate vicinity of armies and battle sites it could cause, at least according to contemporary reports, much havoc and disorder, so much in fact that peasants and entire villages sometimes took the law into their own hands, lynching those unlucky soldiers who happened to lose track of their regiments upon their armies' retreat. Pillaging and moving troops across the country were as important moves as actual battles and campaigns (due to the logistic problems of supplying large armies, frequently numbering into the 40,000 – 50,000s, armies *had* to move constantly). Armies lived off the surrounding countryside. War financed war.

Therefore, by the late 1640s, three decades of campaigning had left their blood toll on the German lands. Population levels were much reduced in those areas that had been touched by the campaigns; many agricultural lands had been laid waste. Markets were cut down to a fraction of their former size. Some areas experienced only very moderate losses; others lost up to 90 per cent of their pre-war population. The War was not only drawn-out over time, but also changed its locations, as the war years and armies moved on, hither and thither, often playing cat-and-mouse.[88] For a whole generation or two, death, murder and slaughtering and pillaging would have represented normal experiences for the majority of the population (something the average twenty-first-century Northern European observer only knows very indirectly, mostly from the TV daily news). Pomerania, Brandenburg, Bohemia and most of the Central German lands in the Thuringian-Saxonian borderland, as well as the Upper and Southwest German lands, were heavily hit. The Duchy of Württemberg was reduced from about 400,000 to 50,000 inhabitants during 1618–48; the smallish County (*Grafschaft*) of Henneberg went from 60,000 to 16,000. In the Palatinate town of Frankenthal, the population collapsed from 18,000 to 324. Some areas in Mecklenburg and Thuringia were reduced to less than ten per cent of the pre-war population.[89] Overall, Germany's population may have declined by 40 to 50 per cent, from somewhere between 13 and 14 million at the beginning of the War to around seven million in the 1650s (although 'German' is a thoroughly meaningless economic and demographic category for the time; estimates that are based on sample data from certain regions and territories within the Holy Roman Empire vary considerably).[90] The size of the armies that moved across the Empire sometimes reached into the 100,000s, to which provisioning merchants, canteen proprietors, whores and relatives of the soldiers must be counted. All in all, it has been reckoned that

---

87 Röpke, 'Wachstumstheorie'. Friedrich Lütge, *Deutsche Wirtschafts- und Sozialgeschichte*, 3rd ed. (Berlin etc.: Springer, 1966), especially 321–343, is outdated in terms of its over-interpretation of the absolutist state, but useful for the economic framework after 1648.

88 Englund, *Verwüstung*, passim.

89 Friedrich-Wilhelm Henning, *Das vorindustrielle Deutschland 800–1800*, 5th ed. (Paderborn: Schöningh, 1996), 236–37; id., *Landwirtschaft und ländliche Gesellschaft*, I, 3rd ed., 225–27.

90 Christian Pfister, *Bevölkerungsgeschichte und historische Demographie 1500–1800* (Munich: Oldenbourg, 1994), and a most recent survey in: Geoffrey Parker, *Global Crisis: War, Climate Change and Catastrophe in the Seventeenth Century* (New Haven: Yale University Press, 2013).

at its peak about one million people, out of a total population anywhere between seven and thirteen million, were constantly on the move during the war. That would have been five to ten per cent of the total German population.[91]

One major result of the war was the considerable destruction of productive capital. Within agrarian economies with a low fixed capital stock and, accordingly, a small share of gross domestic capital formation in total national economic activity, productive capital extended mainly to circulating capital assets, such as cattle that were confiscated and slaughtered, and the loss of manure; farmsteads that were burned; grain reserves that were taken and which would have provided the basis for next year's seed and so on. The amount of arable land under the plough declined by at least a third compared to pre-war capacities. This was bound to have negative consequences on agrarian productivity (even though marginal yields would have increased in consequence).[92] There was not much difference between Swedish and the allied or imperial troops; the latter usually were as bad as the Swedes. The siege and bleeding-out of Magdeburg by Tilly's army (later called either *Magdeburg Wedding* or *Magdeburg Sacrifice*) became proverbial for the act later called '*madgeburgizing*' (Figure 1). The contributions extracted in Lower Saxony amounted to two million Thalers; in one year, the Imperial City of Goslar had to pay 544,000 Thalers in ransom money.[93] Harvest shortfalls and hunger were the result. Grain was left to rot, and barns were set on fire. The Black Death and other diseases thrived where armies came through and battles were fought. In those areas where battles and actual campaigns had been fought, the immediate consequences may have caused more destitution than elsewhere. The disintegration of regional economies led to a capping of town-country economic relations, which were important in an age where much of industrial production – the main sector being woollen and linen textiles – was de-centralized and organized under the putting-out system where textile entrepreneurs bought the finished product from individual producers dispersed across the countryside (and to whom they usually advanced the raw material such as linen yarn).[94] Coin debasement rates absurdly high rates during the so-called Kipper- and Wipper-Inflation (1618–23), which was the worst hyperinflation in Germany's recorded monetary history between 1459 and 1923.[95] In order to finance the war effort, many rulers and princes of the German lands resorted to minting copper pennies and small change currencies that contained no silver (or gold). As the circulating currencies were based on silver (and the general understanding was that coins' material or intrinsic value should reflect their purchasing power – usually called a 'commodity theory' or standard of money), the progressive reduction of the silver content of the circulating pennies and other small-change coins

---

91 Henning, *Das vorindustrielle Deutschland*, 5th ed., 235.

92 Henning, *Landwirtschaft und ländliche Gesellschaft*, I, 3rd ed., 224–25.

93 Henning, *Das vorindustrielle Deutschland*, 5th ed., 238.

94 A vivid description of the war and its consequences is to be found in Englund, *Verwüstung*, *passim*.

95 A concise recent account of the crisis may be found in Martha White Paas, John Roger Paas and George C. Schofield, *Kipper Und Wipper Inflation, 1619–23 – An Economic History with Contemporary German Broadsheets* (New Haven: Yale University Press, 2012).

Figure 1 The Siege of Magdeburg, after Matthäus Merian
Source: Wikipedia – commons.

(the full-bodied silver coins were not reduced so much in terms of intrinsic content) led
to a rapid depreciation of these coins' purchasing power on the market. People ceased
to use them as money. This led to the appreciation of the 'good' florin money to several
thousands of pennies per gulden, from initial, that is nominal, coin exchange or 'spot
rates' at 288 pennies to the Gulden.[96] There were, of course, also regions and cities that
flourished during and in direct consequence of the War. Hamburg, a protestant and Free
Imperial City, remained neutral and even turned into the biggest commercial hub of the
German North (its Age of Greatness, however, came after the 1780s). It not only handled
a large branch of German seaborne imports and exports but also an increasing amount
of finance and payments, especially state loans to the Swedish Crown (but, of course, also
to the Swedish adversaries). Hamburg experienced a century of commercial slump after
the War, between the mid-1670s and 1765, while at the same time the fortunes of the big

---

96 Different currency systems existed in Germany at the time, and the number of coin types used
    ranged into several hundreds. See Michael North, *Das Geld und seine Geschichte. Vom Mittelalter
    bis zur Gegenwart* (Munich: Beck, 1994), and ibid., *Kleine Geschichte des Geldes. Vom Mittelalter bis
    heute* (Munich: Beck, 2009). For the sixteenth century, see Philipp Robinson Rössner, *Deflation –
    Devaluation – Rebellion. Geld im Zeitalter der Reformation* (Stuttgart: Franz Steiner, 2012).

entrepôts of Amsterdam and London went to ever-increasing heights.[97] But during the War, Hamburg did comparatively well.

Moreover, the seventeenth century is usually held to have been a period of *general*, that is pan-European, even global crisis.[98] There were only three out of a hundred years that were completely peaceful (in a sense that no war was fought upon European soil). War, plague and other diseases were endemic. Winters became harsher and summers wetter, as a general climatic deterioration had set in, with beginnings in the later sixteenth century – the 'Little Ice Age'.[99] It reached its low point in the so-called Maunder minimum, the climatic trough of the 1680s; which was yet to come.[100] After a peak in the 1610s, the European price series for bread grains and most other products began to decline, setting in motion a period of secular deflation which lasted, different from country to country, well into the 1720s and 1730s. This crisis led, on top of the raging war, to a further depopulation of marginal soils, agrarian areas which, given the new macroeconomic parameters of the time, would prove too difficult or unprofitable to cultivate. After the sixteenth-century inflation and expansion, the European population growth came to a halt. This stagnation lasted, in most areas, into the eighteenth century. Only the developing and highly productive and innovative economy of the Netherlands continued to grow at rates well above the European average, compounding a process that had begun by the early 1500s at latest – the unfolding of the 'Dutch Economic Miracle'.[101] In the German lands, the Thirty Years War cast a long shadow that would prevail well into the eighteenth century. Only after the 1720s do we find the first and precariously slender signs of economic improvement (see later in this chapter).

---

97 Michael North, *Kommunikation, Handel, Geld und Banken in der frühen Neuzeit* (Munich: Oldenbourg, 2000), 8; Matthias Asche, 'Krieg, Militär und Migration in der Frühen Neuzeit – einleitende Beobachtungen zum Verhältnis von horizontaler und vertikaler Mobilität in der kriegsgeprägten Gesellschaft Alteuropas im 17. Jahrhundert', in id. et al., eds *Krieg, Militär und Migration in der Frühen Neuzeit* (Berlin: LIT, 2008), 11–36 (32–34). On financial integration, see Markus A. Denzel, 'Die Integration Deutschlands in das internationale Zahlungsverkehrssystem im 17. und 18. Jahrhundert', in Eckart Schremmer, ed. *Wirtschaftliche und soziale Integration in historischer Sicht: Arbeitstagung der Gesellschaft für Sozial- und Wirtschaftsgeschichte in Marburg 1995* (Stuttgart: Franz Steiner, 1996), 58–109 (76–80). Figures for Hamburg's trade in Rössner, 'Structural Change in European Economy and Commerce, 1660–1800', and Karin Newman, 'Hamburg in the European Economy, 1660–1750', *Journal of European Economic History*, XIV, 1 (1985), 57–93. Details on Hamburg's import trades after 1733 may be found in Schneider, Krawehl and Denzel, eds *Statistik*, as well as more recently Markus A. Denzel, 'Der seewärtige Einfuhrhandel Hamburgs nach den Admiralitäts- und Convoygeld-Einnahmebüchern (1733–1798)', *Vierteljahrschrift für Sozial- und Wirtschaftsgeschichte* 102 (2015), 131–60.

98 Parker, *Global Crisis*.

99 Geoffrey Parker and Lesley M. Smith, eds, *The General Crisis of the 17th century*, 2nd ed. (London and New York: Routledge, 1997).

100 John A. Eddy, 'The Maunder Minimum'. Sunspots and Climate in the Age of Louis XIV, in Parker and Smith, eds *General Crisis*, 266–301.

101 Jan de Vries and Ad van der Woude, *The First Modern Economy: Success, Failure, and Perseverance of the Dutch Economy, 1500–1815* (Cambridge and New York: Cambridge University Press,

Around mid-century, the central German lands, which are said to have been the place where Cameralism saw the light of day, faced an acute situation of relative poverty and underdevelopment vis-à-vis those countries that were more productive or had stayed more or less out of and had remained unscathed by the Great War. Moreover, one of the more manifest consequences would have been that France now surpassed the Holy Roman Empire as the largest state, measured in terms of population numbers as well as land mass (if we exclude Russia) – *economic potential* (P. Kennedy; see earlier in the chapter) being the most important economic and political-military resource of the day, determining relative economic wealth in early modern Europe.[102] The post-war campaigns of Louis XIV and the Swedish Wars after the war led to further reductions of population in areas such as Lotharingia, the Palatinate, Mecklenburg or Brandenburg. The actual process of underdevelopment vis-à-vis the more dynamically growing export economies of the Atlantic Fringe had certainly commenced during the sixteenth century; but the income and productivity gap between the German/Central European lands and the richer Atlantic Southwest had become more pronounced after the Great War and more decisive for the pattern of European development for the centuries to come. Some of the crucial branches of German manufacture may already have been less competitive prior to the war (see earlier in this chapter); some aspects of demand were also clearly dependent upon consumer preference and individual taste. As early as 1566, German woollen cloth producers complained that even day labourers and peasants would prefer English, French and Italian clothes to native German production.[103] Martin Luther had spoken, in his Table Talk *Italian Clothing is Better than German* (1538), about multiplier effects of the spending on manufactures, to use modern language, that were foregone when spent on imports – and a lot was spent, according to Luther, on foreign manufactures and imports.[104] Linen, yarn and woollen cloth exports were much reduced after the war, as were iron production and mining output. After the war, Germany exported mostly workers, such as seasonal migrants to the Netherlands (so-called *Hollandgänger* – 'seasonal cross-country commuters to Holland'). Many agrarian areas and farms lay or had been laid waste; the Swedes had cleared large branches of the northwest German forests and exported the timber to Dutch ports (they also took away libraries, see earlier in this book). The number of cattle and draught animals had been greatly reduced, which had a negative impact not only upon agrarian productivity (see earlier in this chapter), but also meat production and consumption, as well as the availability of carting facilities and transport services, a much needed input for a market economy. Other branches of manufacturing flourished quite early on again, that is, the 1660s and 1670s, such as the Essen rifle manufactory or the Aachen pin and needle manufacture.[105] Thus, generalizations should be

---

1997); Marten R. Prak, *The Dutch Republic in the Seventeenth Century: The Golden Age* (Cambridge and New York: Cambridge University Press, 2005).

102 Lütge, *Deutsche Wirtschafts- und Sozialgeschichte*, 333.

103 After Blaich, *Wirtschaftspolitik des Reichstags*, 84.

104 *Luther's Works*, ed. Hartmut Lehmann, vol. 54, *Table Talk*, ed. Theodore G. Tappert 1967, Nr. 3956, 298.

105 Blaich, *Wirtschaftspolitik*, 80.

avoided, in the same way as for the immediate war-period (see earlier). But generally, it is safe to state that the Great War had drastically reduced the productive and consumptive potential of the German regional economies. These developments were also reflected in real wages and prices. Rye prices, according to the most recent calculations, declined by about 35 per cent in real terms (1625–75); the purchasing power of urban construction workers (16 German cities), which was inversely correlated with grain prices if we assume that bread grain was their main item of consumption, may have increased by up to 140 per cent during the same time.[106] Some improvement in agrarian techniques and productivity can be asserted for the German lands around 1700, leading after the 1730s into an agrarian boom with a rise in prices, with some improvement in the agrarian sector, and perhaps about ten per cent agrarian productivity output growth between late seventeenth and mid-eighteenth century.[107]

This is the backdrop against which Cameralism – and the present *Oesterreich über alles* by Philip(p) Wilhelm von Hörnigk – needs to be viewed.[108] It was a very different starting point compared to the seventeenth-century Anglophone Mercantilist writers, who would have had a more commercialized, a stabler and sometimes more flourishing economy before their eyes; an economy moreover, that was not without its wars and problems, as marked by the great Civil War (1642–52) which had spread into Ireland and Scotland, but which had clearly not experienced the same level of interruption as (some) German lands had during the 1630s and 1640s.[109] Most economic historians would nowadays agree that English per capita income was significantly higher than Germany's around 1650, which was not only a direct consequence of differential affection by war and military campaigns, but also due to different total factor productivity levels and differences in stages of economic development that had originated long before the great war. Certainly the destitute situation in the export-orientated industries of Germany would have perpetuated a high propensity to import (especially manufactures), which would have precipitated a decline of domestic export industries and productivity levels after the 1640s, when the war raged. These problems of comparative disadvantage in manufacturing were crucial and stood at the heart of the early Cameralist economics, as borne out by the texts written during the second half of the seventeenth century by Johann Joachim Becher, Wilhelm von Schröder or our Philipp Wilhelm von Hörnigk. Based on these given parameters, the Cameralists formulated something that came very, very close to a modern theory of growth and development.[110]

106 Ulrich Pfister, 'Consumer Prices and Wages in Germany, 1500–1850', WWU Münster, CQE Working Paper 2010, no. 15, p. 17, 37 f. (col. 5).

107 Id., 'German Economic Growth, circa 1500–1850', unpublished paper, XVth World Economic History Congress, Utrecht, August 3–7, 2009, 13.

108 Most clearly in Reinert, *How Rich Countries Got Rich*, esp. ch. 3.

109 Michael Braddick, *God's Fury, England's Fire: A New History of the English Civil Wars* (London: Penguin, 2011); Barry Coward, *The Stuart Age* (London: Longman, 1994); id., *The Stuart Age: England, 1603–1714* (Harlow: Pearson Education, 2003).

110 Röpke, 'Wachstumstheorie', 31–47, 128–29 et passim; Reinert, *How Rich Countries Got Rich*.

Cameralism and Its Place in Modern Economics

Two canons or types of economics had developed since the Renaissance. One was production-based, with an emphasis on innovation, a holistic conception of economy embedded within society; the other one a rather sterile view, conceiving of the economy as a rather abstract and almost antiseptic mechanism, with its own working laws. In the latter, all activities are very much alike. It became focused on truck and barter, left little room for human creativity, invention and knowledge and, eventually, after centuries and much variation and refinement, turned into what has become known in vulgar nomenclature as the 'neoclassical' paradigm.[111] Cameralism belonged to the former 'canon'. It is a moot point to speculate about 'good' or 'bad' in economics or to determine which of the two theories was (or is, or would be) the 'better' canon. Rather the question is about applicability and practical usefulness, that is, how realistic one particular theory can and ought to be and how helpful it is in solving actual problems. There is always a trade-off between complexity-reduction (abstract reasoning; deductive reasoning) and realistic yet, due to the complexity of the real-life world, ultimately incomplete (and thus inaccurate) description of economic problems. Economics is, at least to an extent, idiosyncratic, or in Backhaus' words: 'Although [...] the core of economic theory has to be identical across cultures, nations and centuries, I do insist that national economic realities are different and that for this reason both theoretical emphases and to an even larger degree the practical work of economists will be different in reflecting the different national realities these economists are confronted with.'[112] Nowadays, mainstream undergraduate textbooks in introductory micro- and macroeconomics suggest the contrary, and the existence of a rather homologous 'world economics', which is roughly equal to what is usually portrayed as 'neoclassical', containing an eclectic mixture of Keynesianism, Monetarism, Post-Keynesianism and many more streams of theory and ideas, but which does not leave, as Noble Laureate Paul Krugman once remarked, much space for geography and, as others would add, (national) culture(s) as crucial variables.[113] The contrary conception (i.e. that idiosyncrasy does not matter for the evolution and applicability of economic theory, something that has often been invoked, if implicitly, in the modern economic sciences) seems to have been connected to the widely shared assumption that there was progress in economic reasoning over time.[114] Both assumptions have faced increased scepticism by scholars in recent decades.

As has been noted above, the free market – a fully transparent market with equal access, absence of rent-seeking behaviour including monopoly, speculation, arbitrage and forestalling and other forms of usurious behaviour – had to be *created*. It *wasn't* simply there.

---

111 Erik S. Reinert, 'German Economics as Development Economics: From the Thirty Years War to World War II', in K. S. Jomo and Erik S. Reinert, eds *Origins of Development Economics* (London: Zed Publications/New Delhi: Tulika Books, 2005), 48–68.

112 Backhaus, 'The German Economic Tradition', 329–56 (329).

113 See, e.g., Paul Krugman, *Geography and Trade* (Leuven: Leuven University Press; Cambridge, MA and London: MIT Press, 1991).

114 Backhaus, 'The German Economic Tradition'.

It had to be designed from scratch sometimes, steered, and proactively managed if it was to function and continue to function. The idea had been there for a long time; in a very rudimentary form it can be found in medieval Scholastic theory about 'just' exchange. Only, that reality was very different. The late medieval and early modern world was full of what modern economic theory would define and usually condemn as either market distortions, leading to or creating market failures, or rent-seeking behaviour (amounting to a similar effect). Usurious merchants trying to reap a gain at the expense of someone else by charging unduly high prices, artificially limiting supply, creating shortages (especially of food) and driving up prices in order to increase their profit, were ubiquitous in early modern European economic discourse. A whole body of textual evidence and specific legislation, known in German as *Gute Policey*, dealt with bad market performance and lack of justice in the market place. Edicts and ordinances regulating market behaviour and market times, prohibiting forestalling and other usurious manipulations were numerous for the hundreds of territories and mini-states making up the German lands in the late Middle Ages and Early Modern Period.[115] Throughout the continental lands, there were noblemen, aristocrats and other privileged people that enjoyed peculiar rights, prerogatives and special privileges that limited the market and capability of others to participate in the market equally (or equitably). Craft and merchant guilds usually held control over the markets for their goods; they limited access to the market by keeping a strict ceiling on new admissions to a particular trade; they frequently regulated quality, and usually also the quantity, of supply so as to stabilize prices and profits for those that were 'members of the club', that is, the incorporated craftsmen and traders.

Above all, there prevailed a very peculiar system of resource allocation (labour and product) in European agriculture known by the slight misnomer and now rather outdated concept of *Feudalism*.[116] In its more extreme variant, which could be found especially, but by no means exclusively, east of the River Elbe, this could mean that the lords of the land – the owners – had control over the major share of their tenants, the 'possessors' or renters of the soil, their lifetime allocation of time, labour and product output – up to the point that lords sometimes had a say about the tenant's decision about marriage, inheritance, relocation and other issues which modern social theory would

---

115   See Andrea Iseli, *Gute Policey. Öffentliche Ordnung in der frühen Neuzeit* (Stuttgart: Ulmer, 2009); Thomas Simon, *"Gute Policey": Ordnungsleitbilder und Zielvorstellungen politischen Handelns in der Frühen Neuzeit* (Frankfurt: Klostermann, 2004); the introduction in Karl Härter and Michael Stolleis, eds *Repertorium der Policeyordnungen der Frühen Neuzeit*, vol. 1 (Frankfurt: Klostermann, 1996), 1–36; Karl Härter, *Policey und frühneuzeitliche Gesellschaft* (Frankfurt, 2000); Achim Landwehr, *Policey im Alltag: die Implementation frühneuzeitlicher Policeyordnungen in Leonberg* (Frankfurt: Klostermann, 2000); Peter Blickle, *Gute Policey als Politik im 16. Jahrhundert: die Entstehung des öffentlichen Raumes in Oberdeutschland* (Frankfurt: Klostermann, 2003); Karl Härter, ed. *Policey und frühneuzeitliche Gesellschaft* (Frankfurt: Klostermann, 2000). For a European comparison, see Michael Stolleis et al., eds *Policey im Europa der Frühen Neuzeit* (Frankfurt, 1996).

116   See the old work by Marc Bloch, *Feudal Society* (London etc.: Routledge 2014), a work that originally appeared in French 1939/40. Most recently, German, *Villagers and Lords*.

classify as private and belonging to the individual – to the innermost part of the individual that is. But while the more extreme variants of feudalism – such as *villainage* and *serfdom* (*Erbuntertänigkeit, Leibeigenschaft*) – have often been likened by historians to forms of slavery, this would certainly be an extreme and unjust comparison, especially when applied to seventeenth- to nineteenth-century practices and systems of slave economy in the Caribbean and the American South. New research has convincingly demonstrated that there was much more 'agency', even within the East Elbian manorial systems than previously or usually acknowledged.[117] As always, there seems to be a grain of truth in the notion. A system in which the lord had a statutory claim (however effectively realized) to up to five working days labour or carrying services to be performed by his tenants on the lordly manor or demesne (corvée) cannot be called particularly free or inclusive as an institutional system peculiarly apt to safeguard stable economic development. Nevertheless, the most recent comparative study on this topic has come to the conclusion that – contrary to a much-popularized version of 'backwards Eastern Europe' versus 'progressive West' – there was much more agency and flexibility within the so called restrictive East Elbian manorial economy. These systems worked better than their reputation with modern econometricians and Institutional Economists would seem since North and Thomas published their path-breaking economic model of *The Rise of the West* (1973). In many cases, the manorial economies could boast productivity and efficiency levels that compared well with the high-powered and more inclusive agrarian regimes of the North-West (in Holland and South-east England) so that we should give up the somewhat simplistic dichotomous notion of 'developed west' versus 'primitive east'. But the density and number of privileges and special freedoms enjoyed by individuals was, in continental Europe during the Early Modern Period, quite considerable – both east and west of the invisible curtain marked by the River Elbe. Thus, what we would define as freedom in the market – equitable conditions of access, perfect competition of demand and supply – had to be created, sometimes from scratch. It was a condition that was known *in principle* but which, more often than not, did not yet exist *in situ*. It had to be managed. In the continental economic literature of the period, this achievement of free markets (equitable access and absence of usurious behaviour and other market distortions) could only be done by the hands of the ruler. No self-respecting Cameralist or Mercantilist would possibly have entertained the notion that freedom in the market would originate spontaneously, that is, exclusively as the result of individual decisions by individual actors, without external coordination or coercion. As we have seen above, their *Menschenbild*, their anthropology and 'image of man' was the *homo imperfectabilis* (Priddat), who had constantly to be guarded and watched by the state because if left to herself *homo*

117　Cerman, *Villagers and Lords*, is excellent and provides an up-to-date survey of the modern secondary literature available on the topic, especially in the Slavic languages. The latter have been usually unavailable to Western scholars, often leading to quite grotesque binary portraits of Western/Atlantic Europe as 'progressive' and East Central Europe as 'backward', as for instance in Daron Acemoglu, Simon Johnson and James A. Robinson, 'The Rise of Europe: Atlantic Trade, Institutional Change, and Economic Growth', *American Economic Review* 95, no. 3 (2005), 546–79.

imperfectabilis would do, in sum, more harm than good to others, if unintended; frequently making 'wrong', naïve or even consciously bad decisions to another man's detriment.[118]

If we consider the density of modern supervision and regulation in modern markets – even the most 'perfect' ones, such as the Chicago Wheat Exchange or the New York Stock Exchange – we realise that we have not come much further since. Rules and regulations banning 'unfair' trading in the market nowadays number into the millions, differentiated according to product and market[119]; and the European Union, as well as most of its member states, has attained a proverbially infamous reputation for 'overregulating' its denizens. Homo sapiens today is as *imperfectabilis* and unknowledgeable as he was three hundred years ago. Accordingly, in the Mercantilist-Cameralist model, the state – incarnated and personified by the ruler, Prince or king – had to strengthen the national economy by raising domestic employment, exports, competitiveness and productivity, as well as to raise the powers of the state. The two goals were linked symbiotically; one could not function without the other. In isolation, they would each be meaningless. Derived from this was the strengthening of manufacturing and export-orientated industries, something we find early on in Europe's textual history, visible in the continental literature since the works of Giovanni Botero and Antonio Serra. Since Botero (at latest) this model was based upon the idea of a productivity difference between cities and countryside; accordingly, workers had to be relocated into cities that offered higher wages and increasing returns to scale. Labour and capital input in agriculture soon reached into the zone or area of the productive function (where the x-axis denotes input and the y-axis output) known in business economics as 'declining marginal returns'. Arable landmass was limited geographically, as were the number of farms and peasant households (as claims to natural resources such as land). The latter was not only contingent upon deliberations of economic and ecological sustainability but also upon legal traditions and prevailing institutions, such as inherited claims towards usage of the commons within the village, and so forth. Cities on the other hand – which stayed outside the peculiar socio-economic configurations delineated by 'feudal' agrarian regimes – knew virtually no limits to the extension of inhabitants or the number and size of crafts and industries to be located within the city walls. The anonymous *Bedencken von Manufacturen* (1683) usually ascribed to Johann Daniel Crafft or Krafft – a seventeenth-century Saxon 'project-maker', whom Hörnigk knew and met several times and on whose work *Oesterreich über alles* (1684) drew, reiterated this topos: 'where cities decline and become desolate, the surrounding countryside will decline as well; but where cities are populous, peasants will be rich', Crafft wrote (Figure 2).[120]

The higher the final or sales value of a product the higher the value added. The income and employment multipliers of a newly-established manufactory of silk stockings would be innumerably higher than an additionally-founded farmstead or other venture

---

118 Priddat, 'Kameralismus als paradoxe Konzeption'.
119 Harcourt, *Illusion of Free Markets*.
120 [Johann Daniel Crafft/Krafft], *Bedencken von Manufacturen in Deutschland* [Jena: Bauhofer, 1683), 3–4.

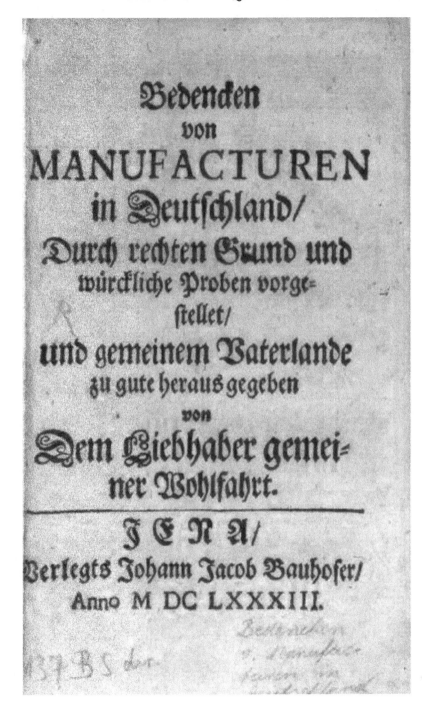

Figure 2 Johann Daniel Crafft, *Bedencken von Manufacturen* (1683), Frontispiece
Bayerische Staatsbibliothek / MDZ (http://reader.digitale-sammlungen.de/de/fs1/object/display/bsb10304381_00007.html)

in agrarian or semi-manufactured production (such as tobacco rolling). The processes of silk production – from the cultivation of the mulberry plants and the silkworms, the harvesting of the raw silk up to final weaving of silk – involved a larger and longer supply and commodity chain than for instance the production of one ell of coarse linen. No wonder that the manufacture of high-end or luxury textiles (silk, cotton and fine woollen stuffs) featured prominently in the texts and models of seventeenth-century Mercantilists, not only in the German-speaking lands. Hörnigk's text is a fine example of this tradition and focus in economics.

Crucial to Cameralist economics was the conception of *Glückseligkeit* – a term that does not translate well from German English and which has had little place in modern economics (we may perhaps translate it as 'The Good Life'[121] but amongst modern historians of ideas it has also been known as 'Public Happiness' and *Eudaimonia* discourse). It was based upon the preconceived right of the monarch to rule a country, which automatically translated into the *duty* to develop it, and not primarily in order to raise taxes and state finance, but initially to raise the general wealth and welfare of the *bonum commune*. Clearly this type of 'development dictatorship'[122] looks strange to the modern eye. Democratic societies are built upon the idea that everyone knows what is best for them. The perverts, criminals and usurers who exploit someone else's weaknesses in a harmful way to reap a benefit for themselves will be held in check by the punishing executive. They represent aberrations and statistical outliers from a mass of individuals who are held to think and act as good and self-respecting non-psychopaths do (but new empirical studies have shown that psychopaths, who represent not more than about one per cent of the total population, are overrepresented amongst business executives; that is, far more businessmen and executives are psychopaths than the average or expected value of one per cent for the total population would predict). It reflected a characteristic and very peculiar economic anthropology. It assumed a highly imperfect world, fragmented institutions and rent-seeking. Cameralists entertained a conception of the individual as 'psycho-physiological'[123]; mankind was composed of matter *and* mentality; pleasure *and* pain; reason *and* madness, rationality *and* irrationality; desires *and* needs; ratio *and* feeling. Both were equally important. The one could not possibly exist without the other. Mankind was fundamentally driven by its animalist characteristics and instincts – including sentiments and feelings[124] – which had to be tamed, in the same way as her ability to abstract to the sublime and discover Godly

---

121 Robert Skidelsky and Edward Skidelsky, *How Much is Enough? The Love of Money, and the Case for the Good Life* (New York: Other Press, 2012).

122 Erik S. Reinert, *Warum manche Länder reich und andere arm sind: Wie der Westen seine Geschichte ignoriert und deshalb seine Wirtschaftsmacht verliert* (Stuttgart: Schäffer-Poeschel, 2014), 46

123 A term coined by R. C. Bowler, 'Menschenbild und Wirtschaftsordnung: Der Menschenbegriff im Kameralismus und in der Nationalökonomie', *Berichte zur Wissenschaftsgeschichte*, 25, no. 4 (2002), 283–99.

124 Emma Rothschild, *Economic Sentiments: Adam Smith, Condorcet, and the Enlightenment* (Cambridge, MA: Harvard University Press, 2001), has studied this more culturalist branch of political economy.

ethical principles of boundless love and tolerance (modern economics seems to have tended towards catering to the latter and discarding the possibility that the former could be equally important in a human's choices and preferences). Mankind was individualistic; and, for the reasons given earlier, incalculable. One of the fundamental conclusions derived from this peculiar anthropology was the need for regulation, state and order in certain realms of human action and interaction.[125] This is how Cameralism evolved out of the psycho-geographical landscape of the day.

Thus, the Cameralists had a model. For this model, let us return to the *Ur-Cameralist* or 'Adam Smith of German Cameralism' (with all due caveats relating to this label, referenced earlier in the chapter), Veit Ludwig von Seckendorff (1626–1692), who was active in the services of Duke Ernest 'the Pious' I of Saxony-Gotha, first as *Hof- und Justizrat*, from 1656, *Geheimer Hof und Kammerrat* and from 1663, chancellor, before he moved on into the services of Duke Moritz of Saxony-Zeitz. In Gotha, on Friedenstein, the first baroque castle built in the central German lands after the Thirty Years War, Seckendorff was witness and in a sense intellectual father of the physical and economic processes of reconstruction. The model of a well-ordered police state, which he sketched in his best-selling book on *Teutscher Fürsten Stat*, went through at least thirteen editions between 1656, when it first appeared, and 1754, nearly matching Hörnigk's work in terms of popularity and longevity.[126] The following principles are evident from the 1720 edition and preface to the 1656 edition. They deserve special consideration as they shed much light upon the present task of placing Cameralism's achievement, and also Hörnigk's *Oesterreich über alles*, in the history of European political economy and economics as a scientific discipline:

- The text employed an idealized concept of 'reason' (pure reason), manifested in the model of the fully enlightened prince. That this was a model which we should not take literally, in a sense of representing actual circumstances, comes across clearly from a comparison of the text and the historical reality, aptly analysed in the recent work by Wakefield.[127] But we must stress that Seckendorff (and arguably none of the other Cameralists) never purported or claimed to *describe* reality. Quite to the contrary; he formulated an economic *model*.

- In order to arrive at a reliable description of the 'muster state', Seckendorff studied what he called the 'middle course' or *Mittelstrasse*. Modifications had to be made to this middle course, according to special cases and particular examples of actual states. Seckendorff considered such analytical modifications 'easy' (*unschwer*). The *Fürstenstaat* was based on the *Erbfürstentümer* (meaning, in the German context, the medium-sized Duchies, Electorates and Counties governed by princes that followed a pattern of

---

125 Bowler, 'Menschenbild und Wirtschaftsordnung'.
126 Erik S. Reinert and Ken Carpenter, 'German Language Economic Bestsellers before 1850, with Two Chapters on a Common Reference Point of Cameralism and Mercantilism', in Rössner, ed. *Economic Growth and the Origins of Modern Political Economy*.
127 Pointed yet stimulating: Wakefield, *Disordered Police State*, chs. 1 and 6.

dynastic succession, which we would identify, from the modern vantage point, as proper 'states'). But it could be easily modified so as to include *Stiffts=capitel* (church principalities such as archbishoprics, bishoprics and abbeys with landed possessions) and other principalities as well. By using the title *Landesfürst* or 'territorial prince' Seckendorff simplified his general model without suggesting either exclusivity or one-to-one applicability of his model. He wrote, in the first chapter on the descriptive nature of states, of a *General-modell* and *unverfaenglich Modell oder Art, wornach die materialische Beschreibung eines jeden Lands eingerichtet werden koente, daran wir jedoch keinen binden* (§6), a general-purpose model apt to describe the basic common features of the 'well-ordered' police states without purporting an actual 100 per cent overlap between model and reality.[128]

- Seckendorff favoured a 'free floating consecutive discourse' over 'short and dark, clouded sentences' (meaning abstract principles), especially in order for his treatise to be grasped by non-academics also – which places his model into the scientific tradition of the visual-intuitive continental Cameralist tradition (which continued into the nineteenth-century Historical School) that chose to analyse and model reality economics by 'thick description' rather than analytical reduction.

- Seckendorff was quite clear about the fantastical nature of what he described. Modern social science may call this 'theoretical' or 'model'. Reality in German principalities was much different (see earlier).

- Based on these premises, Seckendorff explored a general model of Cameralism based on the following principles:

  - All economic steering and development begins with the prince (replace, if more suitable or comfortable, with 'the state': princes, abbots, dukes etc. *were* the early modern German state).

  - The prime or superordinate welfare goal of economic policy was to raise *Glückseligkeit* – as seen earlier, a rather difficult to translate term for anyone unused to the German language and not accustomed to Enlightenment uses of the term '(Public) Happiness'. Modern economics usually speak of Pareto-optimal allocation results in the market place and utility functions that drive the economic behaviour of individual actors who, according to a long-cherished paradigm, either maximize their benefit (with a given set of resources) or, alternatively, minimize their expenses (with a given goal or end zeal, *telos*). This has been known as the *homo oeconomicus* principle (which most economists would nowadays agree does not accurately describe economic psychology). *Glückseligkeit* – the 'Good Life', in the Cameralist conception, went far beyond modern welfare measures such as gross domestic product per capita, including happiness and tranquillity, law and order, but also a pious and good Christian life guided by a well-ordered confessional landscape.[129]

---

128 Veit Ludwig von Seckendorff, *Teutscher Fürsten-Stat*, 5th ed. (Frankfurt and Leipzig: Meyer, 1687), *Vorrede* (preface), p. 3 and *passim*.

129 Johann Heinrich Gottlob von Justi, *Staatswirthschaft oder Systematische Abhandlung aller Oekonomischen und Cameral-Wissenschaften, die zur Regierung eines Landes erfodert [sic!] werden*, 2 vols. 2nd ed. (Leipzig: Breitkopf, 1758).

We find perhaps the clearest formulation of what *Glückseeligkeit* meant, and why it was important, in the later works by Johann Gottlob Heinrich Justi (1717–1771), one of the most prominent figures in Austro-German Cameralism. Justi (1720–1771), who had studied law and Cameralist sciences at Jena, Wittenberg and Leipzig between 1742 and 1744 and became overseer of the Prussian glass works and other manufactories in the 1760s. Justi formulated one of the most concise and widely-read textbooks in the eighteenth century.[130] The main goal of political economy according to him was *Glückseligkeit*, something which 'happiness' would be far too imprecise a translation for. We may perhaps call it the 'good life'[131] of the subjects. This goal was to be achieved by promoting 'circulation' (of goods and money), commerce, industry and stable property rights.[132] Only a monarchical state, Justi argued, impersonated by an enlightened despot (the King), could coordinate economic resources and promote economic well-being effectively and achieve maximum distributional efficiency by eliminating particular interests and actually curbing, rather than enforcing, rent-seeking: by abolishing monopolies. Without this degree of coordination and regulation, Justi argued, powerful rent-seeking interests would gain the upper hand and act to the detriment of society.[133]

This reasoning turns the Smithian or neoclassical 'modern' conception of free market and rent-seeking behaviour on its head. Rather than completely freeing the market forces by abolishing control altogether, one needed, Justi maintained, a strong hand of the state to promote equality and even development. This was an idiosyncratic recipe specifically calibrated to circumstances that were particular to Prussia (and most German states), where the nobility had a much firmer grip on the people and their individual freedoms than in northwest Europe. Markets should be regulated where appropriate, especially for labour (wages) and essentials. Quality controls should be applied across the board, so as to protect the consumer. Immigration, especially of experts and master craftsmen and cultural exchange, knowledge and technology transfer should be encouraged. These principles were widely-known and shared in the period, not only in Frederician Prussia.[134]

Justi's ideas, however, were not new. About the 'Good Life', Seckendorff had remarked, in his *Fürsten-Stat*, 5th ed. (1687), that the pure eternal wisdom needed 'to act to the ultimate good of the country' and raise the nation's *Glückseligkeit* was something only to be derived from God.[135] It was something sublime, indescribably pure, shining as bright as the brightest of suns. In other words, principles of the highest abstraction – to be applied wisely on the ground by careful reflection, rigorous

130 Most recently, Wakefield, *Disordered Police State*.
131 Skidelsky/Skidelsky, *How Much is Enough?*; Sedlacek, *Economics of Good and Evil*.
132 Johann Heinrich Gottlob von Justi, *Grundsätze der Policeywissenschaft* (Göttingen: W. Vandenhoek, 1782, 3rd ed. [1756]), 219, 222.
133 Ibid., 227.
134 Sandl, *Ökonomie des Raumes*.
135 'Weißheit / durch welche die Königreiche / Fürstenthuemer und Lande / glückselig regieret werden / ist / ihrem Ursprung nach Göttlich / an sich selbst herzlich und unvergleichlich / und begreiffet in ihrer Weite und Allgemeinheit alles das jenige / waß in andern Wissenschafften Stückweise sich befindet.' Seckendorff, *Fürsten-Stat* (5th ed. 1687, dedication, no p.).

deliberation and sheer ratio. And welfare – *Wohlfahrt* – he defined as a *Paradise*: ever green, ever blossoming with the most beautiful and useful plants of human virtue and good order.[136] And so on.

Sure, his language and style were picturesque to say the least; meandering, elaborate and complicated at the same time, in many cases unbeknown and unfathomable to the modern reader, based on what an eminent historian of economic thought has labelled the 'Goethe Barrier'.[137] Modern German linguistic use and stylistic conventions are largely based on classicism; the pre-classical linguistic heritage is sometimes difficult to interpret; at least it does not sound as conversant, understandable and familiar – in terms of the feelings, emotions and associations conveyed by the text – to the modern ear as Goethe's and Schiller's texts for instance do. If we read Seckendorff with a twenty-first century looking glass, he sounds very much akin to a heart- and lifeless world of Foucauldian imprisonment and punishment, law and order, restrictive social order. We must acknowledge, however, the heritage of the two Totalitarian Orders of the twentieth century: Fascism and Communism, especially Stalinism. With these political perversions in mind and an ex-post viewpoint of totalitarian, perhaps even Orwellian states (consider what states can do nowadays in terms of supervision and surveillances compared to the pre-modern world), which Seckendorff and the early modern Cameralists could not possibly have conceived of, Cameralist texts and ideas do sound alienating, obscure. But that is because ideas of order, mainly relating to order in the market place (interaction of individuals in the processes of demand and supply) became perverted during the political excesses of the twentieth century and its totalitarian *Zwangsgesellschaften* (social-political and ideological *Gleichschaltung*; economic *Planwirtschaft*); moreover, the idiosyncratic location points (time, space, sociology) were notably different around 1650 compared to, say, 1900 or 1940 or 2000 AD. Seckendorff's method was, apparently, one of abstraction clouded in idiosyncratic formulations and axiomatics and something we have lost touch with. We can unearth it only very carefully, but should certainly give up any teleological ex-post judgement. Seckendorff's model state was based on taxation, and raising the funds of the princely chamber, including *Gute Policey* – that is, the regulation of certain branches of social life and economic activity (however successful in practice). It sketched a regulative, almost *dirigiste* economy. The model was based on a hands-on approach with historical examples (which we should not always take literally; a lot of what Seckendorff and others interpreted as 'historical' was more akin to 'being made-up'). Experience, case studies, tradition and custom mattered. History mattered – something from which modern economists may learn.[138] Seckendorff's

---

136 This was an 'immer grünendes Paradieß von allen schönsten und nützlichsten Pflantzen der Tugenden und guten Ordnungen; Stralen dieser hell=leuchtenden Sonnen / einige Tropffen aus diesem grossen Meer / und etliche Früchte aus solchem allgemeinen Welt=Garten / zusammen fassen.' Ibid.

137 Schefold, 'Glückseligkeit und Wirtschaftspolitik'.

138 Acemoglu and Robinson, *Why Nations Fail*.

preface to the *Fürsten-Stat* (1656 ed.) gives away the epistemological and methodological rationale of Cameralism:

> Solte jemand gedencken / daß nach der Art / wie die Beschreibung erfordert / vielleicht wenig / oder keine Länder in Teutschland regieret werden / und ich doch hierinnen nicht Regal=mäßig / sondern nach der Geschicht und Beschaffenheit schreiben wollen / der wolle unbeschwert erwegen / daß es viel nützlicher sey / das Gute als das Böse aus jedem Dinge zu wissen und anzumercken.[139]

> [Should anyone intervene and tell me that no country was known that was governed exactly according to these principles and that I should, rather than formulating some abstract rules and theories, tell about things as they really are, I would urge him to consider: would it not be much more useful to *know* about the good rather than evil of things and to analyse it carefully?]

We should ask, is that not a very modern stance – the idea that you can formulate economics as a model-based and axiomatic discipline? More importantly:

> Der Allmächtige GOTT / der Beherrscher des Erdbodens / und oberster Regent aller hohen Häupter und Obrigkeiten / wolle mit seiner göttlichen Gnade ihme das Höchste Haupt / und die fürtrefflichen Glieder unseres Teutschen Vaterlandes / befohlen seyn lassen sie zu immerwährendem kräfftigen *Wachsthum* in erwünschter Zusammenstimmung erhalten. (emphasis added)

> [GOD the Almighty, ruler of the earth and supreme king of all kings, may come with his grace upon our German fatherland and its limbs – meaning the individual rulers and territories – and incense them to permanent sustained increase in the desired harmonious order.]

Seckendorff would be taught and read and re-edited a hundred years later. In the 1737 ed. by Andreas Simson von Biechling, the preface emphasized that to promote 'harmony, happiness, true wealth and welfare' of the population would have to be considered the supreme goal of the state ('H a r m o n i e, Glückseligkeit, wahren Wohlstand und Glückseligkeit ihrer höchsten und hohen Häuser, ja aller getreuen Unterthanen, allenthalben herstellen und täglich vermehren, diejenigen, so am Ruder sitzen, mit wahrer Klugheit und ungeheuchelter Tugend ausrüsten, allesamt aber zu Erlangung dieses Endzwecks mit seiner Weißheit so lange begnadigen wolle, bis dereinst alle Fürstenthümer und Herrschafften ein Ende haben werden).

Just contrast this with Sir James Steuart, the author of *An Enquiry into the Principles of Political Œconomy* (1767), one of the most-widely read economists in eighteenth-century Britain and Europe – prior to Adam Smith.[140] Steuart had spent time on the continent as an exile, among others in the poor, destitute mud hole Tübingen, where he completed

---

139 Seckendorff, *Fürsten-Stat* (1656, identical in 5th ed., 1687), *Vorrede* (with minor divergences in terms of capitalization of letters).

140 On Steuart, see, e.g. Ramon Tortajada, ed. *The Economics of James Steuart* (New York: Routledge, 1999); S. R. Sen, *The Economics of Sir James Steuart* (Cambridge, MA: Harvard University Press, 1957); Hong-Seok Yang, *The Political Economy of Trade and Growth: An Analytical Interpretation of Sir*

Part I and II of his *Political Oeconomy* and where he would have extensively read Justi's work. On the ruler or 'statesman' – his abstract concept of the state as a regulating and guarding authority – Steuart said, very much akin to Justi:

> He who fits at the head of this operation, is called the statesman. I suppose him to be constantly awake, attentive to his employment, able and uncorrupted, tender in his love for the society he governs, impartially just in his indulgence for every class of inhabitants, and disregardful of the interest of individuals, when that regard is inconsistent with the general welfare. (1767, Book I, p. 149)

And:

> In all compositions of this kind, two things are principally requisite. The first is, to represent such ideas as are abstract, clearly, simply, and uncompounded. This part resembles the forging out the links of a chain. The second is, to dispose those ideas in a proper order; that is, according to their most immediate relations. When such a composition is laid before a good understanding, memory finishes the work, by cementing the links together; and providing any one of them can be retained, the whole will follow of course. (1767, Book II, p. 162)

Hardly could a model be formulated in more abstract terms. This is the epistemological foundation upon which modern economic and social theory still rests. Cameralism laid the foundation of what we know as modern free market economics. We should pay more attention to prefaces as a literary genre.

James Steuart's Inquiry (Aldershot, Hants, England and Brookfield, VT: E. Elgar, 1994); Andrew Skinner, 'Steuart: Author of a System, *Scottish Journal of Political Economy*, 28, no. 1 (1981), 20–42; the essays by Skinner and others on Steuart in Douglas Mair, ed *The Scottish Contribution to Modern Economic Thought* (Aberdeen: Aberdeen University Press, 1990), as well as the essays in Terence W. Hutchinson, Andrew Skinner et al., *Sir James Steuart und seine "Principles of political oeconomy"* (Düsseldorf: Verlag Wirtschaft und Finanzen, 1993), and the analytical introductions in Andrew Skinner, Noboru Kobayashi and Hiroshi Mizuta, eds *Sir James Steuart's Principles of Political Oeconomy* (Brookfield, VT: Pickering & Chatto, 1998).

Chapter Four

EXTREMIS MORBIS EXTREMA REMEDIA – ANALYTICAL SUMMARY OF HÖRNIGK'S *OESTERREICH ÜBER ALLES* (1684)

Hörnigk's Theoretical Achievement

Hörnigk's book was a product of the mainstream – Cameralist-Mercantilist economics as it emerged to perfection between 1650 and 1750. But in many ways, with his Nine Principles or 'Rules' of Economic Development (see later in this chapter), Hörnigk was the one who would set the tone for years to come.[1] Even Ekelund and Tollison, who portrayed Mercantilist theory and practice in a rather bizarre way, took Hörnigk's Nine Rules of economic development as representing Mercantilist thought in a nutshell (interestingly, they did not bother too much about Cameralism; while getting Hörnigk's first rule wrong).[2] On the one hand, Hörnigk put into words what many others thought in his day. Economics was symbiotically linked with the big political issues of his day. We must not forget that anti-French publications and discourses reached a climax towards the beginning of the 1680s in the German territories.[3] This had to do with the expansionist, and at times openly aggressive, policies of Louis XIV, the great French Sun King, who strove to turn France into the most powerful state in Europe. For this goal, he was admired and feared at the same time by his contemporaries. Alliances and allegiances were fluid and kept changing; in German politics pro- and anti-French stances were to be found coexisting and alternating sometimes within the same territory. Politics were not quite as ideological yet as they would be in later centuries, especially the twentieth century. Political stances and diplomatic connections could vary in the blink of an eye, with the death of a prince or a new bribe. They were in more or less constant flux throughout the 1660s and 1670s in the territories of the empire[4] – especially as so many of these mini-states existed in the heart of Europe, which increased the demand for, as well as the supply of, itinerant messengers, ambassadors, negotiators and other diplomats, a new

---

1   John Fred Bell, *A History of Economic Thought* (New York: The Ronald Press Company, 1953), 111–13.
2   Robert B. Ekelund Jr and Robert F. Hébert, *A History of Economic Theory and Method*, 3rd ed. (New York: McGraw Hill, 1990), 43–44.
3   Schilling, *Höfe und Allianzen*, 242.
4   Schilling, *Höfe und Allianzen*, 147–252 is a detailed and quite masterful account of the political developments within the German territories during the second half of the seventeenth century.

class of individuals that made politics and lobbyism increasingly their main business. Very often, especially towards the earlier modern period, it would have been merchants whose main occupation was to travel large distances; people who would enter the service of a prince or king to carry out diplomatic tasks alongside their main occupation. But since the end of the Thirty Years War, diplomacy increasingly emerged as an occupation of its own. It was one of the long-lasting achievements of the processes of unstable political equilibrium reached after the Peace of Westphalia in 1648: the rise of European diplomacy as a political technique, cultural style and praxeology. Often the diplomatic world of 'absolutist' Europe post-1648 has been described as a huge theatrical stage, and the rules and rituals of political negotiation were as formalized and regulated as the complicated moves and patterns in Baroque music and dance. As we have seen above, Hörnigk was part of this world. During his travels through the German lands of the Empire in the services of Cardinal Lamberg, the imperial legate, as well as Bishop Royas in the 1670s and 1680s, he became an integral part of this world of high diplomacy (see Chapter One).

But more often than not, the main task was perceived to be holding in check the emerging economic and political super-power of the day: France. Hörnigk had been born in the later phase of the Thirty Years War, with an Anti-Habsburg coalition in the making. *Francophobia* was, in fact, and quite unfortunately so, a common, vulgar and typical discourse of the day. It had emerged no later than 1600 in the German lands.[5] A growing and quite primitive sensibility of what it meant to be 'German' (by whatever definition) had emerged. Perceived 'German' virtues were propagated in the texts from the seventeenth century; such as sobriety and hard work; French luxury culture was often depicted as effeminate in contrast. These discourses were usually economically framed. In fact it is, especially in this early period, hard to disentangle the 'economic' from the cultural, political, even the religious – especially since during the seventeenth century the discourse on superfluity, luxury imports and excess still usually carried a moral, sometimes even religious undertone and connotation – something we find in many underdeveloped societies, and as late as 1740s in Scotland, where the luxury discourse featured prominently in the early issues of the *Scots Magazine* (founded 1739) in the 1740s, until the debate stopped at the end of the decade, towards 1750. France was not only the biggest economy of the day, in terms of absolute GDP – as it was the biggest country of the age. France had had around 18 million inhabitants in 1600; the Holy Roman Empire between 16 and 18; by the end of the war, Germany's population had crumbled down to somewhere between ten and 13 million inhabitants (scholars have put forth varying estimates). France had a higher per capita income than the German lands; she had a larger population – also, but by no means exclusively, a consequence of the Big War – and she had by far the biggest army of the age, with up to 400,000 men under arms towards the end of the century (when the War of the Spanish Succession broke out). Moreover, France was the leading

---

5   E.g. Georg Schmidt, *Wandel durch Vernunft: Deutschland 1715–1806* (Munich: C. H. Beck, 2009), 95; Achim Landwehr, *Geburt der Gegenwart: Eine Geschichte der Zeit im 17. Jahrhundert* (Frankfurt: Fischer, 2014).

producer of luxury manufactures, fine woollen and silk cloth, ribbons, laces, shoes, à-la-modes and many more – something the ladies desired and contemporary economic writers feared. France set the trends in luxury consumption and production well into the nineteenth century (and, apparently, in many ways today still does, especially with regards to high-end clothing and fashion). No wonder, then, that in that age, calls for autarky were heard, vis-à-vis a politically, as well as economically, very powerful French (export) economy. Yet another danger came from the southeast, marked by the advances of the Ottoman Empire. On 17 July 1683 – more or less one year before *Oesterreich über alles* came out – Vienna was besieged by an Ottoman army, something the city had last witnessed in 1529.[6] The Ottoman army was defeated in battle on 12 September the same year, which substantiated the myth of Emperor Leopold as a 'liberator' of the Christian world. It was almost like the age of the crusades had returned. To an extent therefore, *Oesterreich über alles* must be called a political treatise.

But of course – and this is the main reason for the longevity of the work – *Oesterreich über alles* was manifestly an economic book. The Austrian lands had been comparatively spared by the vagaries of the Thirty Years War. But Austria had had a stronger industry before the 1680s, large branches of which seem to have vanished by the second half of the century, if contemporary pamphlets and statistics are to be believed.[7] Philipp Wilhelm Hörnigk was part of the seventeenth-century triumvirate of Germanic economic writers, together with Becher, Schröder, who have sometimes been labelled 'Old Austrian School', or 'Older Mercantilists', 'Older Cameralists', or practical-progressive economists (Roscher).[8] Hörnigk would have been in many ways ahead of his time (and in others more conservative), especially inasmuch as he valued much higher the national economy than the *Cameralökonomie* – that is, the fiscal element or state finance.[9] In fact, as Mombert has stressed, Hörnigk was amongst the first economists arguing for a national economic policy,[10] that is, a theory that saw the economy as a whole, as a system. This was an important abstraction from older economic concepts that saw either the Prince (Camera; state finance), or the household as the subject of analysis. These men were prone to reform, 'reformfreudig' (Stabreit), because they had to be, if things were to change in a positive way for Austria.[11] Even though in many ways Hörnigk was quite restrictive, especially in his protectionist ideas (most of the Cameralists, especially of the eighteenth century, would usually advocate modest or graded import tariffs, where Hörnigk argued for prohibitive duties or complete prohibition of imports), he still developed a quite systematic view of the national economy as an organism that was more than the sum of its parts; the latter were connected and related to each other in a functional relationship.[12]

---

6 Harm Klueting, *Das Reich und Österreich 1648–1740* (Münster: Lit, 1999), 73.

7 See the introduction by Horst Knapp, in ibid. et al., eds '*Österreich über alles', wann es nur will*, 22–23.

8 Roscher, 'Die österreichische Nationalökonomik unter Kaiser Leopold I', 30.

9 Roscher, *Geschichte*, 292.

10 Paul Mombert, *Geschichte der Nationalökonomie* (Jena: Gustav Fischer, 1927), 168–69.

11 Stabreit, *Philipp Wilhelm von Hörnigk*, 9. Stabreit errs on many counts, such as the date of birth (which he gives as 1636) as well as Hörnigk's (never-obtained) doctoral degree.

12 Ibid., 42–52.

In Knapp's words, Hörnigk was obsolete in terms of theory, but not practice, which sounds rather odd ('obsoleten Wirtschaftstheorie – wenn auch keineswegs ebenso obsoleten Wirtschaftspolitik')[13]; but Knapp also expressed his admiration for Hörnigk's rather holistic view of the economy – 'a standard work concerning the close relationship between macro-economic theory and micro-economic practice: would it be conceivable nowadays that a major proponent of supply-side economics also deals with problems of industrial training and the education of specific individuals within the same work'[14]? Inama-Sternegg, on the other hand, praised *Oesterreich über alles*, in a similar over-drawn manner, as being 'always the most precise and serene version of German Mercantilism, with lasting effect and value for subsequent economic analysis, including its errors and mistakes.'[15] The great American sociologist Albion Small did not discuss Hörnigk in his big work on Cameralism at all; Zielenziger, in his magnum opus on *Die Alten Kameralisten* (1914) called his work a 'prime example of contemporary Mercantilisms with all its strengths and weaknesses'.[16] Sommer, in her two-volume study on Austrian Cameralist theory (1920/25), said that, with his political focus, Hörnigk extended the realm of analysis beyond what was to be found in Becher's and Sonnenfels' writings. Schumpeter called his insights interesting and solid, but lacking any analytical depth (which was a charge Schumpeter (alas!) levied against almost every other economist, dead or alive).[17]

We should be careful not to earmark Hörnigk's work as 'Austrian'. Upon hindsight, this was a pan-European, if not global strategy. Most editions of it appeared outside the Austrian lands, in 'Germany' (this was mainly for reasons of censorship[18]). It was formulated developing a set of general principles as a blueprint which could, upon careful consideration and modification, be applied in a much wider geographical as well as historical context. Hörnigk's 1684 treatise therefore is, if formulated pointedly, a treatise on general economic development. His idea of equilibrium as formulated in the text referred to the equilibrium between Austria on the one hand and the rest of Europe on the other; manifest in the work is the dependency idea.[19] But if we abstract from the political and economic conditions idiosyncratic to the Austrian situation around 1680, we may explain the long-lasting popularity of his work. Many of the ideas presented are, in fact, quite timeless.

At the usual risk of over-simplification, we may subsume these ideas as follows, before a brief summary of the text will be presented.

---

13 See Knapp's introduction in ibid., et al., eds '*Österreich über alles', wann es nur will*, 16.

14 Ibid., 14; also Karl Brandt, *Geschichte der deutschen Volkswirtschaftslehre, Vol. I: Von der Scholastik bis zur klassischen Nationalökonomie* (Freiburg i. B.: Rudolf Haufe, 1992), 68.

15 Karl Theodor von Inama-Sternegg, 'Ueber Philipp Wilhelm von Hörnigk', *Jahrbücher für Nationalökonomie und Statistik*, NF 2 (1881), 194–200, (200), quoted after Amman, 70.

16 Zielenziger, *Die alten Kameralisten*, 278.

17 Schumpeter, *History of Economic Analysis*.

18 Freudenberger, *Lost Momentum*, 90.

19 Sommer, *Die österreichischen Kameralisten*, II, esp. 124–149. Pribram, *Geschichte des ökonomischen Denkens*.

- Hörnigk calls for a revaluation of manufacturing as honourable productivity-enhancing and value generating strategy (economies of scale) – something which would have been eminently obvious to any economic writer since the days of Giovanni Botero, but which had been neglected in recent times, as Hörnigk never ceases to state.
- He focuses on value added (*wertschöpfungsorientiert*) activities as the main way to increase welfare and national income.
- In order to raise productivity and general efficiency, and thus to achieve sustained economic growth, the factor endowment of a country with raw materials does not matter so much; rather it is what people *do* with what they have at their hands, how they combine resources, skill and knowledge so as to transform the productive landscape towards a growth-orientated production frontier. Culture, knowledge, psychology and mentality enter the equation (but are absent from most of the modern economics models).
- The role of the ruler (Prince) is obvious, in terms of curbing of monopoly, usury, cartels and rent-seeking (Justi; Priddat). The key to growth is a more just economy and society.
- A positive balance of trade represents a boost to political as well as economic power. Hörnigk argues for quite a peculiar sequence, first, to diminish imports, then to raise exports. This is somewhat different from later Cameralism (especially Justi) and has sometimes earned Hörnigk the label or classification as 'primitive' or die-hard protectionist.
- There is a focus on precious metals – for several reasons that are quite understandable upon hindsight and rational from a contemporary viewpoint. Precious metals represented the basis for the monetary stock and main monetary material (currency); the amount of money was positively correlated with the amount of silver available in the economy. Whenever silver and currency declined, so did general welfare and social, as well as economic, equilibrium. One example is coin debasement: a persistent pressure upon the balance of payments frequently led to an appreciation of silver in price, which meant that coins had to be debased. The frequent coexistence of 'good' (that is, relatively stable high value money, such as Gulden or florins) and 'bad', or debased small change, led to persistent disequilibrium in payments, especially when made on the spot or in cash. The lack of suitable substitutes (that is, paper money, banknotes) would leave especially the common people without alternatives; it increased transaction costs and often led to riots and other forms of social unrest.[20]
- Circulation is imperative, as is the practice of raising money's velocity, for instance, by preventing the population from hoarding money.
- Hörnigk's model is focused on economic growth; it is dynamic.
- Hörnigk acknowledges that the world is *connected* and the economic fate of Austria is not exclusively dependent upon factors that are peculiar or exclusive to Austria. However, one of the main goals is to achieve 'independency'. But that means, above

---

20 Rössner, *Deflation – Devaluation – Rebellion*, esp. ch. IV; id., 'Mercantilism as an Effective Resource Management Strategy: Money in the German Empire, circa 1500–1800', in Moritz Isenmann, ed. *Merkantilismus. Wiederaufnahme einer Debatte* (Stuttgart: Franz Steiner, 2014), 39–64.

all, independency from foreign manufactured imports, which must by no means be conflated with economic *autarky*.

- His view is based on the assumption that population increase is a desiderate in its own right (third rule of development; (*Bevölkerungspolitik*)[21] – this will increase not just the country's military prowess as well as fiscal standing or tax base, but also enlarge the domestic market (demand for manufactures). Modern research would emphasize the role of human capital. The larger the population, the larger chance that one 'genius' (nowadays: potential Noble Prize winner) will emerge out of it.

'*Oesterreich über alles*', Wann es Nur Will

Hörnigk states at the outset that his work applies to the Austrian Hereditary Lands or monarchy, including the Kingdom of Hungary; but as has been seen above, what he really meant to represent was the 'imperial' zeal. His programme applied to any other of the German countries making up the Holy Roman Empire (and, as we have seen previously, his 'strategy' is a very general one, if we abstract from the Austrian context and terminology: on this strategy, England became the first industrial nation of the world). Hörnigk says that the chief goal of analysis, framed in modern terms, would be an abundance of goods and commodities, as well as ample stocks of specie (*Uberfluß menschlicher Nothdurften und Bequemlichkeiten / in specie, Goldes und Silbers*). Knowledge of 'good' economics and principles is one thing, he says; their translation into practice is another. The latter is in God's hand alone, or – if the right measures were chosen – in Austria's power. But right now there is every reason to believe that people have not yet chosen the right path (I[22]). He cites the negative example of Germany (the Holy Roman Empire, excluding the Austrian dominions), a country that loses specie in return for French imports day after day. A similar *topos* had been heard as early as 1524, in Martin Luther's *Treatise on Commerce and Usury*;[23] in the writings of the Humanists of the early 1520s;[24] the Saxon currency dispute of 1530–31, as well as the first Cameralist treatises of Saxon jurist Melchior Osse.[25] In fact, Hörnigk specifically quotes Luther's major economic treatise 'On Commerce and Usury', 1524 (*Von Kauffshandlung vnd Wucher*) at a later stage in his text. However, the explicitly anti-French stance was something characteristic of the later seventeenth century. We know from contemporary discourse that French *À-la-mode* and luxury imports were as popular amongst the upper classes as they were frowned upon by contemporary economists.[26] They feature most prominently in J. J. Becher's *Politischer Discurs* (1688),

---

21 Most recently, Nipperdey, *Die Erfindung der Bevölkerungspolitik*.

22 These numbers follow the original chapter headings in the 1684 text by Hörnigk, rendered in the English translation in the appendix.

23 Philipp Robinson Rössner, *Martin Luther on Commerce and Usury* (London and New York: Anthem, 2015).

24 Id., 'Luther – Ein tüchtiger Ökonom? Über die monetären Ursprünge der Deutschen Reformation', *Zeitschrift für Historische Forschung*, 42, no.1 (2015), 37–74.

25 Zielenziger, *Die alten Kameralisten*, 88.

26 Landwehr, *Geburt der Gegenwart*.

which contains a host of anti-French passages that come across in a very vicious style, which has to be seen against the literary as well as general academic conventions of the day. Most of the economic writings were studies in over-egging the pudding using drastic and explicit language, endless sentences as well as grotesque exaggerations. There was, so to speak, nothing explicitly anti-French in Becher's or Hörnigk's text. It simply was the way someone nailed down a point in a text those days. Hörnigk laments over the hopelessness of imperial measures (Imperial Mercantilism); that hardly a German prince existed comparable to Johann Philipp von Schönborn, Archbishop of Mainz who had been patron of his father, Ludwig von Hörnigk (1600–1667). The prime goal was to raise manufacturing (*des Gewerbs und der Manufacturen*, their 'Thunlichkeit'). This included entrepreneurial profit, as well as societal benefit through imitation and emulation: a core element of Cameralist economic thought and by no means something reserved to spontaneous generation of 'useful knowledge', according to a common recent neoclassical interpretation of the eighteenth-century 'Enlightened Economy'.[27]

To Hörnigk, it was clear that no country other than Austria would be in a better position to prove the guiding example. The Austrian lands were united under one sovereign (the countries of the Empire weren't); Austria represented *einen einigen natuerlichen Leib* ('one natural body politick'). It even bore the possibility of achieving autarky. Whether or not such a thing was a desirable thing per se is another question. But given the circumstances of the day, political as well as economical, this concept of autarky is different from what the common notion would suggest. Austria is such a big and multifaceted country, endowed with such a variety of different resources, according to Hörnigk, that what it lacks in one place is available over-abundantly in another (II). At the time he wrote, a lack of money (due mainly to war efforts) called for a rational and effective *Landesoeconomie*, a strategy of growth and development. At times of war, social and political dislocation, upheaval and confusion, people will be more inclined to subscribe to a new strategy, a 'New Deal', than when times are good. Silk, woollen, linen and 'French' goods should be banned as long as is necessary for them to be fully substituted by domestic production. Silesian, Moravia and Bohemia provide abundant sources of cloth that is as good as anywhere else. Silesia, Upper Austrian and other native linens should be substituted for Indian bombasin and 'pestilentious' French clothes (*pestilentialische Frantzoesische Mode=Waaren*), Hörnigk insists. In order to achieve this goal, one did not need an army, unaffordable sums of capital or peculiar, complex and elaborate models (*Rath= und Anschlaege*). All one needed was *Federn und Dinte*, ink and a quill and a basic dose of human reason. It was there before one's eyes, but Hörnigk made sure to explain this solution in writing so that no one could say it wasn't there for everybody to grasp. If kept to the strategy Hörnigk was going to unfold, this plan would yield the Emperor an additional kingdom and a 'Peruvian Potosí' – a silver mine that is.[28]

---

27 Mokyr, *Enlightened Economy*.

28 The silver mines of the Cerro Rico near Potosí turned into the world's largest silver source in the early modern period. See Earl J. Hamilton, *American Treasure and the Price Revolution in Spain, 1501–1650* (New York: Octagon, 1934); John H. Munro, 'The Monetary Origins of the "Price Revolution"', in Dennis O. Flynn, Arturo Giráldez and Richard von Glahn, eds *Global*

Hörnigk then invokes Rome, France and the independent Netherlands, which, in the last century or so, had experienced considerable economic development based on the rise of commerce and industry (III). Here Hörnigk's assessment is entirely in line with recent research in comparative European economic history regarding the 'Dutch Economic Miracle'. Historians have paid a little less attention to France, mainly because, according to recent cliometric models and quantitative economic evidence on national income accounts, France was not performing above the North-west European average in terms of per capita GDP.[29] Good ideas in *Lands=oeconomie* (national economics) had been and were promulgated within the empire for some time during Hörnigk's days, but with mixed success. That does not necessarily mean the ideas were bad. But they would have to be modified according to context. Hörnigk attacks merchants who are frequently reluctant to buy and support domestic manufactures, thus decreasing the common wealth (IV). But he was not generally negative about merchants; in fact, as Hörnigk also says, merchants are the perfect instrument to make a good *Landes=Oeconomie* work. (Justi would have been slightly more positive concerning merchants later on. Within a laissez-faire or market economy, in the way Justi had it in mind, there is no point in ordering the merchants to do as the Prince or benevolent statesman would like them to act: that is, buy domestic goods and sell them to foreigners. If the domestic economy does not provide enough attractive or price-competitive goods for the domestic market, the merchant is forced to rely upon foreign imports. It is the productive landscape and production function that has to be changed – not the merchant). Hörnigk distinguishes between merchants who *decrease* the common wealth and those who contribute to its *increase*, for instance by exporting only manufactured goods, keeping raw materials within the country (except from those that can only be put to use in the raw stage). Re-exporting contributes to the latter (increase of national wealth). Hörnigk refers to the example of the Dutch, who do this all the time and all over Europe and India, with goods that hardly ever touch Dutch soil, nor originate within the Dutch economy. What originates within Holland is skill, know-how and transport infrastructure that allow the Dutch to maintain their status as the 'carrier of the world' (but they would, ironically or not, *not* turn into the 'workshop of the world' – that would be England, of course, post-1800). Imports of raw materials that are processed and transformed into manufactures within the country, thus keeping money within the domestic economy, are also welcome activities by merchants.

Connections and Monetary History, 1470–1800 (Aldershot and Burlington: Ashgate, 2003), 1–34, as well as Jan de Vries, 'Connecting Europe and Asia: A Quantitative Analysis of the Cape-route Trade, 1497–1797', in ibid., 35–106.

29 The traditional account remains A. Maddison, *The World Economy: A Millennial Perspective* (Paris, France: Development Centre of the Organisation for Economic Co-operation and Development, 2001, reprint 2006), and id., *Contours of the World Economy, 1–2030 AD. Essays in Macro-economic History* (Oxford and New York: Oxford University Press, 2007). The 'Maddison Database' is constantly being updated by ongoing and new research results, see http://www.ggdc.net/maddison/maddison-project/home.htm (last accessed 22 January 2015). J. Bolt and J. L. van Zanden, 'The Maddison Project: Collaborative Research on Historical National Accounts, *The Economic History Review*, Second Series, 67, no. 3 (2014), 627–51.

But those merchants who import foreign manufactures or only deal in foreign goods will decrease the net wealth of the country (V). There are too many divergent individual interests in the country which have led, from ancient times, to the state taking the first step, as in the example of Henry IV of France, who introduced the manufacturing of silk into his country (VI). This example corresponds to later and more refined conceptions of the absolutist state, for example, by Justi. But it is also a familiar problem in modern development studies, public choice theory and institutional economics – it is the question in whose interest it is to develop a nation's resources (and to whom these resources chiefly belong) so as to make the entire country or economy flourish, rather than benefiting just a very limited range of private entrepreneurs, aristo- and kleptocrats. Hörnigk further invokes the habit of the ancestors to stick to reliable if simple forms of wealth, embodied for instance in heavy gold and silver chalices or heavy pelts and felts, as well as woollens and muslins manufactured domestically – they had not been corrupted by the fallacious desire for the latest fashion and French à-la-modes, such as linen rags that will last for half a year until the fashion turns again. Hörnigk finds this a good thing; he is here at variance with the empirical economic history of Europe, which has seen luxury demand and the consumer revolution (or 'industrious revolution') at the heart of the series of transformations after mid-seventeenth century, which finally created the world of goods and patterns known as industrialization.[30] Hörnigk then makes a most interesting statement. He says

> Dann wo heutigen Tags eine Nation mächtig und reich sey oder nicht / hangt nicht ab der Menge oder Wenigkeit ihrer Kräffte oder Reichthum / sondern fürnehmlich ab deme / ob ihre Nachbarn deren mehr oder weniger / als sie / besitzen. Dann mächtig und reich zu seyn / ist zu einem Relativo worden / gegen diejenige / so schwächer und ärmer seynd. Waren nun vor anderthalb hundert oder mer Jahren / Franckreich / Engelland / Holland und andere / weit nicht so reich und mächtig / als jetzo: da konte sich Teutschland gegen sie starck und wohlhäbig preisen / und unsere Voreltern mit ihrem Zustand billig zufrieden seyn. Indeme nun aber unsere Nachbarn uns / *und gleichsam sich selbst* (my Italics) / so unvergleich überstiegen und angewachsen; so will uns wenigst / wann wir rechtschaffene Leute seynd / und unser Verfahren künfftig zu verantworten gedencken / gebühren / es auch nicht bey dem Alten bleiben zu lassen / sondern darob zu seyn / daß wir in Gegenhaltung unserer Nachbahrn wieder *auf den alten Fuß* / das ist / *wenigst auf einen mit der Wohlfahrt unserer Nachbahrn gleichen* / wo nicht höheren Grad kommen. (Hörnigk 1684, 20)

> [The wealth of today's countries does not depend upon their affluence or lack of powers and wealth as such, but above all from what their neighbours possess in terms of power and wealth. Wealth and power have turned into relative variables, compared to those who are weaker and poorer. About a hundred and fifty or more years ago France, England, Holland and others were by no means as rich and wealthy as they are today; and Germany could praise itself strong and affluent compared to the others; our forefathers could be quite content with their situation. But as our neighbours have in the meantime surpassed us – as well as themselves – and grown so considerably over time in terms of wealth this should give us

---

30 Jan de Vries, *The Industrious Revolution: Consumer Behavior and the Household Economy, 1650 to the Present* (Cambridge and New York: Cambridge University Press, 2008).

occasion to rethink where we are and, provided we are respectable to ourselves considering our future chances, not to let the matter rest as it stands, but to take all measures necessary to attain at least the same level of wealth as our neighbouring countries and thus move back to where we used to be, if not much further ahead.]

Hörnigk here uses the term *Wohlfahrt* (literally 'welfare'), which we may translate, with as much historical sensibility, as well as the audacity, to use anachronisms as a means to drive home a point, as 'national economic wealth'. Economists would be undecided: does Hörnigk mean GDP or GDP per capita? But of course the question is somewhat ana-chronistically phrased – where and when the notion of GDP did not yet exist, it would be futile to look for it. Hörnigk's formulation *und gleichsam sich selbst* is more interesting here, as he develops, if in a rudimentary stage, the concept of economic growth and national economic wealth, which clearly transcends the philosophical concept of the Common Good / *bonum commune*, which the Scholastic theologian-economists had known since the fourteenth century or earlier.[31] We may compare Hörnigk's descriptive account with the most recent figures on economic growth and development established by economists for pre-modern Europe, which confirm that, by about 1700 AD, the Netherlands were six or seven times as urbanized as the Holy Roman Empire and Austria measured in terms of the share of population living in cities over 10,000 inhabitants, and that German and Austrian 'real wages' were, on average, at least forty per cent lower usually than in Dutch and Southeast English cities. In other words, there were considerable gaps in terms of wealth and development prevailing across Europe, with the Atlantic fringe con-siderably richer than Central Europe. According to recent studies, this gap had widened during the sixteenth century and stabilized during the seventeenth century. The Thirty Years War played a part in this, but the basic features that accounted for this 'Small Divergence' were older than that. Hörnigk describes this 'Small Divergence' quite accur-ately. He apparently assumed that growth rate differentials existed both over time and across space. With the admonition that Austria should come *wieder auf den alten Fuß / das ist / wenigst auf einen mit der Wohlfahrt unserer Nachbahrn gleichen / wo nicht höheren Grad kommen* ('to return to the previous level, that is, at least of wealth that is equal, if not higher, than that of our neighbours') Hörnigk developed as clear an understanding of economic development and international national income disparities as possible at his time. He entertained the belief that these disparities could be changed, if only the right political economy was chosen. Fifty years before, things had not been as bad, but now the taste for French goods has corrupted manners; Hörnigk said that (Austrians) should not simply stick to the principle 'do as we have always done, as our forefathers have done', but rather adapt the good principles of our ancestors and discard those that prove, under given circumstances, unhelpful (VII).

Hörnigk then goes on to separate between gold and silver (money) on the one hand and clothing (manufacturing), subsistence (*Nahrung*, primary), *Wohnung* (rental property, shelter) and everything else necessary for human survival. From this, he derived the

---

31 A very good account is Wood, *Medieval Economic Thought*.

important conclusion that a land abundant in gold and silver could be called rich but not quite as rich as if it had a competitive domestic industry that dumped a considerable share of output on foreign markets. He differentiated between money and real wealth as clearly as any of the early Cameralists and Mercantilists could have, leaving us with enough evidence to repel once again the old myth of the Midas Fallacy introduced by Adam Smith into the historical discourse about pre-classical political economy.[32] What mattered in Hörnigk's model was dependency (*dependentz*) upon others. One means of overcoming current economic problems (mainly penetration with foreign imports of manufactures) was to achieve independency. Modern language has coined the term *import substitution* for the processes and strategy behind it. Even states completely without native gold and silver supplies, such as Genoa or the Netherlands, may develop a flourishing domestic manufacturing and export business, Hörnigk says, but still remain dependent upon other countries' goodwill to provide the necessary raw material inputs they need for their domestic production to flourish. He speaks about the Dutch and Genoese *Industrie oder Emsigkeit* strategy – the de Vriesian industrious revolution comes to mind.[33] So what a healthy economy also needs is a critical supply of raw materials. He illustrates this by an economic comparison between England and the Netherlands. The latter may be more successful commercially. But England's economy is sounder, because England has got raw materials to process whilst the Dutch have to procure everything – raw materials as well as foodstuffs – from outside. The Dutch 'economic miracle' represents a mixed blessing, therefore. England has got a lower trade volume or turnover of goods (imports plus exports) than Holland does. But she enjoys a larger net-balance, as she does not have as strong a propensity to import as Holland does, especially in terms of raw materials. Hörnigk comes to the interesting conclusion that England keeps the money earned from foreigners 'better than the Dutch do' (meaning in the country). No country can ever be fully independent, that is, autarkic – except, perhaps, for China, he says. But relative factor endowment, including precious metals, determines a country's position on the world market. It is neither geography nor skill alone; geography and the right economic strategy both matter.

Then, Hörnigk makes an interesting analytical separation between what modern usage would call economic 'sectors'. He speaks about three types of economic activity or production (*Pflege der Gueter*); first, agriculture (farming, pastoral, *Bau= und Pflantzung, Zucht und Fahung*), including minerals (*Gewinnung und zu Tagbringung*; modern usage is ambiguous, as minerals and mining are sometimes assigned to primary activity, sometimes to the secondary sector); secondly, manufacturing, or *Formgebung roher Gueter* (*Manufacturen*) and, finally, *rechtmaessiger Anwerdung so in= als ausser Landes* (transportation and distribution, both domestic and foreign trade). Like Johann Gottlob Heinrich Justi, Hörnigk sees a symbiotic relationship between manufacturing and commerce; between secondary and tertiary

---

32 A very useful synopsis can be found in the chapters in Stern and Wennerlind, eds *Mercantilism Reimagined*, as well as the paper by Lars Magnusson, 'Is Mercantilism a Useful Concept Still?', in Isenmann, ed. *Merkantilismus*, 18–39.

33 De Vries, *Industrious Revolution*.

sectors (VIII). He then formulates his famous 'Nine Rules of Economics', which are often taken to represent the core element of his economics. These rules are:

(1) All corners of the land, both above the earth and sub-terranean, should be surveyed carefully and put to productive use (also ch. XVI);

(2) all raw materials that cannot be used or consumed domestically should be worked-up (processed) into manufactures domestically because the value added by manufacturing surpasses their initial value *zwey / drey / zehen / zwantzig / auch wol hundertfach*. Hörnigk speaks of a transformation or transmutation [… *Inländischer rohen Güter oder deren Verwandelung in Manufacturen*]; he explicitly mentioned quicksilver that in Venice and Amsterdam was worked into *sublimat, praecipitat und Zinober*, as well as some other chemicals; or Pilsen wool that was processed in Saxony (Vogtland) and the Palatinate into proper woollen stuffs; or Annaberg and Dutch *Spitzen* (laces), made from Silesian yarn, with value that had increased by more than 100 times;

(3) there should be as large a population as possible under given constraints of incomes and living standards. Idleness should be taken care of and abolished. Technology transfer should be encouraged by hiring foreign expert manufacturers and getting foreign artisans to settle within the country;

(4) all native precious metal reserves should be mined, dug up, and brought into circulation; no unnecessary exportation of money should be spent on unnecessary imports;

(5) foreign imports should be minimized and limited to the absolute minimum necessary;

(6) if imports from abroad were to take place, they should be made in return for exports of goods; exports of specie in payment for imports should be avoided at all cost;

(7) imports of foreign semi-processed goods should be finished at home;

(8) exports should be encouraged and maximized, especially of manufactures;

(9) no goods must be imported that can be produced domestically. It would be better to spend two thalers on a domestically made good, Hörnigk says, that is lesser in terms of quality than to spend one thaler for importing a better substitute.

These rules were 'no invention of a speculative mind'; the nature of things is self-evident to everyone who is in their right mind (IX). Hörnigk continued with an extended account that was intended to prove his point; listing *ad nauseam* the commodities and things with which Austria was endowed over-abundantly. Austria is full of silver, he maintained; not only to be found at Schwaz in Tyrol (where the Falkenstein mines had yielded spectacular amounts in the 1480s and 1490s and into the 1520s and 1530s, providing the emperors with ample sources of state finance: Tyrolean silver yields were used as a collateral for debts incurred with German financiers such as the Fugger and Welser merchants from Augsburg). The same applied to salt, bread, corn (rye), wheat and barley, oats, vegetables, legumes, fruit, cattle, sheep, pigs, fowl, game – you name it. Wine, beer, brandy – all these things are there in great superfluity. Then wool, linen, hides, stuffs – or textiles in the wider sense of which Bohemia, Moravia and the Hereditary Lands can be proud. Base metals, iron, copper, tin, lead – even quicksilver, minerals and chemicals, such as saltpetre and other chemicals that can be used for making colours and dyes, bees and beeswax, horn, glass: all to be found somewhere within Austrian borders (X). Then he goes on to list what was lacking (*abgehen*): dry fish as the Nordic Countries have; Indian spices, foreign fruit, vegetables and confectionary (such as limes, oil, raisins, olives, capers, tobacco, chocolate, tea, coffee) and all other types of foreign grocery; fur products (sable), cotton, silk, Pernambuco wood, ivory and so on (XI). But the latter things are mere superfluities. He condemns the taste for East Indian spices, for the Nordic dry fish just mentioned, and for silk; there is hardly any need for silk in the cold continental climate of Austria! (We may take issue with all this). Anything that comes from the West Indies rather than the East Indies, such as sugar, and so forth, is much more bearable than East India goods. The former are paid with manufacturing exports; the latter in specie. Several times, we find a reference to Swedish matters and topics, such as the Swedish diplomat Peter (Julius) Coyet and his statement that whoever wants to indulge in Indian spices should have an Indian stomach – standard Mercantilist lingo. Hörnigk advocates import substitution across the board; for instance by replacing silk and 'bombazine' (a fine silk stuff that could later on also include or be made of cotton and merino wool) by fine linens and woollen stuffs made in Austria (XII). Any country that is as rich as Austria and which will have as much to sell and as little to buy from abroad will have to flourish; otherwise it must be doing something wrong (XIII). Then Hörnigk deals with possible arguments against his view, insists that it is human ingenuity in resource management that will decide whether Austria will be rich or poor (XIV).

Hörnigk stressed that a good standard of manufacturing had been achieved in Austria already prior to the Thirty Years War (for two centuries, he says) by careful observation of the first rule; especially in the woollen and linen sector. It is unlikely that this loss would have been due to a loss of ingenuity, industriousness, or lack of knowledge and skill, or a change in climatic conditions. Wrong policy, bad practice, and neglect of good rules of economics lay at the heart of that problem. He formulates a principle of protectionism and import substitution that sounds similar to List's *Erziehungszoll* (XV). Much is to be desired in terms of putting his Nine Rules into good practice. Again, he refers to the Netherlands and how the Dutch constantly rip land away from the sea by careful dyke management and hydraulic engineering; at the same time, he complains about mining works that have been given up and laid to waste in Austria. Precise empirical observation, surveying and measurement are the crucial techniques that come at the beginning of the process of economic development. Woad, saffron, aloe, potatoes – even such plants that are non-native can be made useful through careful importing, monitoring, empirical study, planning and resource management. Tobacco has been introduced in Hungary, Turkey, Poland. Some of the best wool is yielded from soils that are comparatively poor and unpromising on the surface, Hörnigk says, referring to Saxony (which, however, has some of the best soils in Europe, as modern geologists have proven). The same applies to animal husbandry and breeding. If mining output declines and silver mines decay, knowledge will be lost. Mines that had been flourishing in previous centuries, such as the gold mines at Ilowa/Eylau/Eule (near Prague) and which yielded at record peaks about 1.6 million Ducats per year, now lay waste. These mines lay waste in 1784 still, as noted by Franz Hermann in his much-amended edition of Hörnigk's *Oesterreich über Alles*, but must have been reopened some time thereafter.[34] But now, when the geological and geographical knowledge is lost, nature calls out, Hörnigk says, to deliver this offspring out of her pregnant womb (XVI).

Hörnigk then discusses the second rule, that is, the transformation of domestic raw materials within the realm of the domestic economy. He says Austria exports way too much unprocessed wool, flax, tin plates, raw hides and so forth, elsewhere. The foreign countries send these goods back in the shape of manufactures (cloths, fabrics, stockings, plates and so forth), to the detriment of Austria's economic health. In this way, the money lent to the outer world, in payment for raw material exports, is drawn out of Austria again, three times, six times, ten times – and in the case of laces and other high value textile manufactures, even a hundred times. Austrian quicksilver is transformed, in Venice and Amsterdam, into cinnabar; Austrian copper is turned into verdigris (copper acetate) in Montpellier (needed for manufacturing green colours). Raw wool is manufactured into cloth in the Saxon Vogtland (near Erz Mountains) and the Palatinate. He calls this cycle worse than 'Jewish usury' as it completely ruins the country. Keeping these manufactures in the country would give employment to the domestic poor and paupers, especially as the will and knowledge are there – if only the domestic working population would be educated properly towards manufacturing. He mentions two branches of manufacturing specifically, which had been important in the Bohemian lands before the Reformation, the manufacture of tin and blue colours or Smalta,[35] and which have now been relocated to the Saxon lands. Meissen in Saxony now has a monopoly on glass manufacture; Austria even supplies the timber and fuel needed in the Meissen lands to fire the hearths there. Hörnigk says that with the exception of Lower Austria (with the Turkish siege and the Battle of Vienna fought on 11 – 12 September 1683) the Hereditary Lands had not been ravaged by war for the last 24 years, but still look as bare, bleak and destitute as they did a quarter century ago. No development had taken place because the core elements or economic rules were disobeyed. Hörnigk says that the Reformation led to considerable migration of skilled people across Europe and some outmigration from the Austrian lands, but it should not be too difficult to attract skilled workers back into the country, (XVII). Hörnigk is in a somewhat complicated position. Being a Catholic convert, he opposes the Lutheran Reformation in principle, while at the same time he must, if indirectly, acknowledge that the forced outmigration from the Austrian lands would have created a dangerous 'brain drain' on Austrian society and economy, as among the refugees there were many skilled workers and craftsmen. This process he now seeks to

---

34 A traveller's handbook from the 1790s reiterates this number, possibly quoting from Hörnigk, mentioning that recently the mines had been reopened and were looking promising, see Ludwig Wilhelm Gilbert, *Handbuch für Reisende durch Deutschland*, I (Leipzig: im Schwickerschen Verlage, 1791), 167–68. See also Herrmann, *Herrn Horneks Bemerkungen*, 31.

35 A cobalt-based dyestuff produced in Saxony, used for glazing and producing violet colourings, see Johann Hübner, *Curieuses und Reales Natur=Kunst=Berg=Gewerck= und Handlungs=Lexicon* (Leipzig: Gleditschen, 1722), col. 1725, and Johann Gottfried Jugel, *Sehr geheim gehaltene, und nunmehro frey entdeckte experimentirte Kunst-Stücke, die schönsten und raresten Farben zu verfertigen* 3 vols., 3rd ed. (Zittau and Leipzig: Schöps, 1762), 258–59.

redress by promoting the immigration of skilled foreign workers and manufacturers. The other, more tolerant rulers of the age clearly benefited from this forced outmigration, by allowing religious refugees into the country (the Huguenot refugees from France that were attracted into Prussia were a prime example).

Hörnigk's other rules were also more or less constantly violated, as the text complains in chapter XVIII. In fact, much of Hörnigk's pamphlet is about lamenting the non-compliance with 'good economics' as manifested in his Nine Rules. The money that comes in for raw material exports flows out twice as much or more. Indian spices, northern fish and French clothes are paid in ready money. It is clear that the import bill for foreign manufactures is much larger than the export bill for raw materials. This will greatly decrease the domestic monetary stocks, even though some gold and silver still come out of Austria's mountains and mines. And while it is neither entirely feasible nor possible to completely curb foreign imports (such as stock fish, oil) woollen, linen and cotton cloth imports (such as bombazines) should be avoided at all costs, and must be substituted by domestic manufactures. He provides a detailed list of such high-value luxury manufactures, including tools and scissors, powder, coaches, knives. He complains about French fashion and the Germanic taste for foreign à-la-modes, a much lamented Mercantilist *topos*, especially in the early days of Mercantilist political economy. Many women would be convinced that French needles and French yarns are better than anything else – a must-have so to speak. French fashion is a study in persuasion; and Hörnigk gets all poetic about it. The sixth rule – to pay as little for imports as possible in cash – as well as the seventh rule, that is, to transform as many foreign imports at home, are clear, he says, discussing the Dutch cloth manufacture at Leiden in some detail. Here, Hörnigk reckons that more than 37,000 pieces of cloth are manufactured and brought to the Cloth Hall each year, yielding the town about 1.5 million Reichsthalers annually. But the Leiden cloth manufacture amounts to only a third of total cloth production there. All in all, Leiden's manufacture should be worth somewhere near five million thalers each year, and the putters-out would be able to put up a 100 per cent mark-up on the whole. And this is merely one city, Hörnigk says, suggesting the enormous multiplier effect of cloth manufacturing if implemented across the board in Austria. Too little effort is made to aggressively market domestic goods to foreign customers (rule number eight), and of course, the ninth rule – to principally favour domestic goods over foreign imports of comparable quality – is constantly being violated. He specifically refers to Indigo – the Devil's Plant –, which could, and should, be substituted, using domestic woad (a blue colour of similar type, but apparently lesser quality than indigo).[36] About a million thalers would leave the Empire for imports of indigo; also export sales from woad are gravely reduced. He refers to the 'patriotic author' of the *Bedencken ueber die Manufacturen in Teutschland* (Jena 1683), Daniel Krafft or Crafft (whom Hörnigk would have met at Dresden in 1683–84, see earlier), who said that Saxon imports of indigo alone amounted to close to 15,000 thalers each year.

---

36 A new study on indigo is now available: Anja Timmermann, *Indigo: Die Analyse eines ökonomischen Wissensbestandes im 18. Jahrhundert* (Stuttgart: Franz Steiner, 2014).

But all these rules are violated, Hörnigk says. If only one was kept and adhered to according to good practice, it would automatically follow that all the others would, too. It is a miracle, given these violations of good Mercantilist practice, that Austria has not completely decayed. In chapter XIX, Hörnigk complains about being the prophet who has no audience in his own country. In chapter XX, he says that the initiative needs to come from above, from princes, kings and the Emperor. The domestic merchants are unlikely candidates – frequently, they know nothing about domestic production processes and buy their goods from middlemen; all they care about is profits and sales. Eminent Germano-Austrian Cameralist Johann Heinrich Justi (see earlier in the chapter) said similar things in his theory about development, but was much less negatively inclined towards merchants as agents handling commodity and financial flows. In the eighteenth century, merchants would suddenly attain a much more positive connotation in economic discourse – as middlemen that created, that 'made' the market (and economic exchange possible).[37] Hörnigk was much more careful.

Chapter XXI of *Oesterreich über alles* turns out to be almost Listian in nature. Hörnigk says that if he were in the position to put the process of development into motion, he would start with the fifth rule, or

the inhabitants should make every effort to be satisfied with their domestic products,[38]

regardless of how bad or deficient domestic products are, so long as it is necessary to improve and build up what modern usage would call 'comparative advantage'. Once one rule was implemented as a general strategy, other branches of the economy would follow automatically; setting in motion a synergetic process and virtuous circle, with spill-overs from one sector into other branches of the economy– chain of events is so obvious to Hörnigk that he does not spill much ink explaining why (the idea goes back to Giovanni Botero). Everybody would be forced – with love, Hörnigk maintains – to lay their hands on domestic materials. Then, the second rule,

All commodities found in a country, which cannot be used in their natural state, should be worked up within the country,

would be translated into practice. Foreigners would observe that they couldn't obtain Austria's raw materials any more. If they wanted Austria's goods, they would have to immigrate, settle in the country and firmly establish themselves within the Austrian productive landscape, thus contributing not to theirs but to Austria's gross domestic product (as we would say), thus making the third rule come true,

attention should be given to the population, that it may be as large as the country can support.

---

37 Rothschild, *Economic Sentiments*.
38 This and the following quotes are based on the translation by Arthur E. Monroe.

This would automatically also reduce Austria's propensity to import foreign manufactures, implementing the fourth rule,

gold and silver, once in the country, are under no circumstances to be taken out for any purpose.

It is clear that some imports would have to remain in place, for instance for East India Goods, but the sixth rule could be applied with ease:

foreign goods should be obtained not for gold or silver, but in exchange for other domestic wares.

This would raise general welfare and consumption levels and sales for the domestic industry, putting rule number eight into practice, or

opportunities should be sought night and day for selling the country's superfluous goods to these foreigners in manufactured form.

So much money would flow in and circulate within the economy, raising economic activity, gross domestic product and entrepreneurial spirits of the people that rule number one would be increasingly applied, that is, to survey with more effort and care those economic and productive possibilities and productive factors of the country that are still un- or underemployed. This in turn would lead to a better implementation of the seventh, the third, the sixth and all the other rules. Especially rules number one, three, and eight are crucial to relieve Austria of its present state of underdevelopment vis-à-vis the others. Hörnigk also maintained that, if only Austria's manufactures were well-developed and competitive, a lessening of the strict prohibitions may be feasible and prohibition replaced by protective duties, which is again similar to List's argumentation.

What Hörnigk sketches out here, therefore, is an active programme of development, with synergies between the economic sectors and several branches of manufacturing, the importance of useful knowledge, of culture (including religion and education) and prospecting of the entire country's physical and economic geography, constant monitoring and conscientious resource management. He sees the proactive state at the centre of his model and strategy, as the economic interests of the individual actors, especially the merchants, more often than not, run contrary to the national economic interest (*Volkswirtschaft*). Import substitution and the building up of manufacturing and processing are crucial tools. In this way, Hörnigk is very close to the model of development designed by Friedrich List (1789–1846) about 150 years later. With regard to the fifth rule (import substitution), Hörnigk specifically named the woollen, linen and silk industry, and French manufactures in general. These branches were to be tackled first and foremost, so as to make his import substitution strategy work. Woollen cloth imports alone come to seven million thalers each year, he maintains; and yet again he quotes the pamphlet by Johann Daniel Crafft, who says that Saxony loses nine hundred thousand thalers each year for silk imports alone. If these manufactures would be brought to flourish, the entire *Körper* or body politick would begin to stir, move and become lively again (XXII). Hörnigk is a strict opponent to a more modest version of protectionism that was known during his time (not all Mercantilist authors of his time were strictly protectionist[39]). He maintains that such measures ('weak' protectionism) would only hinder the effective implementation of his strategy. They would weaken the mental inclination of the Austrian patient to get well again using the body's own defences as a cure to the Austrian Disease. France can afford a moderate customs policy (moderate protectionism); Austria cannot, unless she had as much export revenue and as little money flowing out for foreign imports as the French economy. But right now, extreme diseases call for extreme cures. Luxury demand would only be fuelled if foreign imports were not prohibited, but rather the duties on imports increased. Even if taxed at high, prohibitive rates, the rich and wealthy would be delighted, and certainly not disinclined, to consume something that was increased in price by a raised level of import duty. Quite to the contrary, this would only substantiate the product's character as an item of conspicuous consumption and social distinction: higher duties may even *stimulate* these goods' consumption. Hörnigk knew the argument of the emerging consensus amongst the late seventeenth-century 'moderate Mercantilists' that no import should be prohibited, but import tarriffs should be graded; moderate for those items that were 'necessary', and comparatively higher for those that were 'unnecessary' without forbidding imports of these goods altogether (and Justi would, in the eighteenth century, also argue for a sort of 'temperate' Mercantilism with graded protective duties, but without outright protectionism or force). But his stance is an extreme one: foreign manufactures must be prohibited so as to set the Hörnigkian Pandora's Box to work. To make domestic manufactures flourish, the foreign ones must be completely banned – and not the other way round. A more competitive export or domestic manufacturing economy will price out foreign competitors of the market eventually, using the mechanism of the market. But the carrot only works in tandem with the stick. That this process needs force, enforcement, is obvious. Hörnigk relates the gruesome example of how the King of France got hold of a servant who, in fun, extinguished one of the Paris street lanterns at night, as yobs do. The king had this poor fellow beheaded, so as to set an example and enforce public safety and security, reducing the incidence of crimes at night. The violation of the legislation about the prohibition of foreign manufactures and of the Nine Rules of good economic development should be treated as high treason, Hörnigk says. *Extremis morbis extrema veniant remedi* (**XXIII**).

Hörnigk maintains that the country would be able to make do without foreign woollen and linen cloth entirely. Austria possesses all the powers, materials, productivity and entrepreneurial and inventive spirit to craft them herself. Of course, processing industries that draw upon foreign imports, for instance, of raw silk, may incur some costs in the short run, due to the lack of reliable domestic substitutes. But these costs will be more than made up for by the economic proceeds once the import substitution processes have been successfully completed. This is, again, very much a Listian strategy of development. Those foreign manufactures that are still within the country at the time of the

---

39 Pribram, *Geschichte des ökonomischen Denkens*, 73–181, has a very differentiated analysis on the evolution of Mercantilist economic thought since the sixteenth century.

Hörnigk Strategy will find ready sale, with the customers knowing that these will be the last ones to be legally disposed of; one should therefore keep an eye on the merchants and the prices they charge. Foreign manufactures may as well be burned, as Queen Elizabeth did with the superfluous wool supplies that had remained in England unsold upon the implementation of the protectionist Tudor legislation since the later fifteenth century. And those merchants specializing in foreign manufactures may as well perish, Hörnigk says. Their peril will be to the good of the country in the long run. It will be more than balanced by the country's gain received from the relocation of the manufacturing process into the Austrian lands. Foreign products should be substituted by any means for domestic ones. 'Madame Fashion' must be sent back to her father, The Devil, Hörnigk says. Even if initially there may be a slow-down of production, the potential and know-how are there to produce goods that are as good as those produced by the French – and enjoyed by their customers.

Hörnigk calls this process of learning and technology transfer necessary to implement this import substitution strategy, *Æmulation* (emulation). He leaves no doubt that the state plays a crucial part in it. He mentions the fairs as places where native silver is chucked out of the country, quoting Luther's Sermon *On Commerce and Usury* (1524)[40] on the Frankfurt Trade fairs that draw liquid funds out of the Empire, as do the big fairs and markets of Braunschweig, Leipzig, Hamburg, and, interestingly, Magdeburg (XXIV). It is interesting that Luther – the Great German Reformer – is amongst the few sources from which Hörnigk quotes longer passages verbatim, with Hörnigk being a converted and somewhat die-hard Catholic. Then Hörnigk describes how useful knowledge will spill over from sector to sector, for example, from lace making to silk manufacture, which will allow building up a competitive edge in the four manufactures earmarked earlier for protection (XXV). The woollen manufacture, including the preparatory stages, such as combing and so forth, as well as flax spinning, will be sufficient to nourish whole armies of people and populate wide stretches of land in Bohemia, Moravia, Silesia and so forth. He relates the story of a poor Dutch spinster who had settled at a small town near Vienna recently and, for as little as a 'piece of bread' had created employment for more than 100 female spinsters. These spinsters now create, according to Hörnigk, a yarn that easily passes for Dutch, meaning it is extremely high in quality, and which would match the best and most expensive foreign specimens with ease. Similar things apply to silk; good colours and other inputs are there, as well as skill – what one needs is the final kick-off towards emulation, planting the will, industrial spirit and practical or useful knowledge among the population (XXVI). What needs to be curbed is the foreigners' practice of taking semi-finished products, such as Silesian yarn, out of Austria and implementing the final touch, the finishing process to the products elsewhere. Rather, domestic quality must be enhanced by establishing 'halls, magazines, *Beschauen*' – something which was common in France and which was to become important in the Scottish linen economy after 1727, with the establishment of the *Board of Trustees for the Fisheries and Linen Manufactures*.[41]

40　Rössner, ed. *Martin Luther on Commerce and Usury.*

41　The most comprehensive account on the history of this board is to be found in the works by A. J. Durie, 'The Markets for Scottish Linen, 1730–1775', *Scottish Historical Review*, LII, 1

There is good evidence to suggest that quality control by state officials contributed to a significant rise in terms of overall quality and price in the Scottish linen industry between the 1730s and 1770s. All linen that was put up for sale in Scotland would have to pass an examination by officially appointed stamp masters, usually former weavers themselves.[42] We find similar institutions in the German lands near Osnabrück (famous for its linen industry) where they were called *Leggen*. They were not uncommon in eighteenth-century Europe and represented an important part of the tool-kit of applied Mercantilism. Quality inspection by independent surveyors appointed by the state was crucial in the process of emulation. Bad and sloppy work, adulteration and fraud was to be avoided and punished at all cost. In addition, public contests for best-quality samples should be introduced. This would not only motivate increased domestic efforts for good work and *oecomomy*, but would also attract skilled foreign workers and encourage processes of technology transfer (XXVII).

But there was also a place for the 'free market' and some laissez-faire in the Hörnigk model. Competition should be increased by breaking up guild monopolies and lessening restrictions that prove harmful to industrial development, such as barriers to entry posed by the limitation of journeymen and masters in the cloth industry, or the prescription of a minimum number of years of training before admission and so on. Guilds should not be introduced in those new branches of industry that were yet to be established (high value woollen and silk textiles), so as to induce foreigners from Holland and Italy ('who are unaccustomed', Hörnigk maintains, to guilds and this type of market regulation) to come to Austria. The habitual binge drinking (*das dabey fuergehende Zechen und Sauffen*) would thus be avoided as well, especially as the Italians and Dutch were, apparently, quite unused to this detrimental aspect of German and Austrian guild culture (the German *Saufteufel* was a discursive figuration since the Luther age; the Germans' and Austrians' inclination to intoxication was proverbial). And worst would come to worst if the foreign craftsmen and masters would be forced to incorporate according to German/Austrian custom and thus acquire these traits that proved so detrimental to good habit and productivity, and which were, apparently, unknown to them in the first place. This would also reduce the incidence of riots and Blue Mondays – two of the key pillars of the moral economy of the common people, and main hindrances to Weber's Protestant Work ethic, or Jan de Vries's Industrious Revolution. Skilled immigrants should be supported by all means, with privileges as well as generous credit advancements for the inputs needed for up to a year. This would be made possible by the guaranteed sales of their goods on the protected domestic market. The

(1973), 30–49; ibid., 'The Scottish Linen Industry in the Eighteenth Century: Some Aspects of Expansion', in L. M. Cullen and T. C. Smout, eds *Comparative Aspects of Scottish and Irish Economic and Social History 1600–1900* (Edinburgh: John Donald, 1977), 88–99; id., *The Scottish Linen Industry in the Eighteenth Century* (Edinburgh: John Donald, 1979); ibid., 'Textile Finishing in the North East of Scotland 1727–1860', in J. Butt and K. Ponting, eds *Scottish Textile History* (Aberdeen: Aberdeen University Press, 1987), 1–18; but should be consulted in combination with the first three chapters in C. A. Whatley, *Scottish Society. Beyond Jacobitism, Towards Industrialization* (Manchester and New York: Manchester University Press, 2000).
42   See works referred to in the previous note.

public estimation of a trade in industry and manufacture should be enhanced. Artisans and craftsmen are artists in the very sense of the word, after all, if they deliver upon their task of reconfiguring Austria's productive landscape. No one should be ashamed to be either artisan or entrepreneur; the ubiquitous desire to marry into the nobility and good society were one of the prime reasons why many a manufacturing branch was starved of necessary investment capital these days, says Hörnigk (XXVIII). This was a wrong spirit and wrong pretension that should at all costs be given up. Obviously, Hörnigk had in mind the process of Austrian deindustrialization and the return to agriculture that had set in during the seventeenth century (see Chapter Five). After the 1620s, the number and size of many Austrian cities declined, as well as the share of town and city population in the total Austrian populace. This would have gone hand in hand with an emergent and re-strengthening of the Aristocrat and his values and place in Austrian society. To Hörnigk, it is somewhat clear, if implicitly, that such a sociological trend would have detrimental effects on Austria's chance of effecting positive economic development.

Hörnigk then deals with those Frenchmen who are resident in the Austrian lands and obviously pose a risk to this development strategy due to their high propensity to import French goods for consumption. They should stay but become fully native; their offspring, Hörnigk says, will be as 'German' as anybody else in Austria. They must unfurl their know-how and entrepreneurial instinct within the country (XXIX).

Hörnigk then goes on to discuss the regional or spatial economics of his proposal. The linen industry should stay where it already is, he says, in Crain, Upper Austria, Moravia, Bohemia and Silesia (we must bear in mind that Frederick II of Prussia, when he annexed Silesia in 1740, is said to have consolidated Prussia's economy and finances by incorporating one of the economically strongest manufacturing regions of his time into the Prussian state). Silesia was comparatively rich in terms of manufacturing skill and know-how around 1700. The woollen manufacture should be found in Bohemia. The silk manufacture should be limited by royal privilege to the Austrian Hereditary Lands, due to the proximity of Italy (as a supply of raw silk) and Hungary with its good soils that would be most fit for the cultivation of mulberry trees (*Seiden=Plantagien* as Hörnigk calls them). 'French' manufactures, that is, high-quality cloth production should be limited to Vienna. In this way, Hörnigk formulates something that sounds similar to Thünen's economic geography. It is clear that the high-value manufactures must be located in cities, either established ones or new foundations erected for exactly this purpose (XXX).

If these four main manufactories have been introduced, all the other desired outcomes earmarked in Hörnigk's Nine Rules will be obtained almost spontaneously, that is, the curiosity to try out new things, the willingness to take a risk (entrepreneurial spirit), or an increase in demand for investment (reduction of idle capital). Hörnigk argues for the production of encyclopaedias and other projects in economic taxonomy and lexigraphy – the period of the great economic encyclopaedias and dictionaries such as Krünitz,[43]

---

43 Johann Georg Krünitz, *Oeconomische Encyclopädie, oder allgemeines System der Land- Haus- und Staats-Wirthschaft in alphabetischer Ordnung*, 242 vols. (1773–1858), online: http://www.kruenitz1.uni-trier.de (last accessed 22 January 2015). The encyclopedia was renamed several times after 1785.

Zedler,[44] or Zincke[45] had not yet come, but was imminent. Again Hörnigk names specific branches of improvement and emulation, namely Saxon-Meissen lace making (XXXI). The state should create offices and institutions dealing specifically with the development of the economy; these should be no mere appendices to the princely *Camerae* (XXXII). He then defines how Austria could be above everything and everyone else, not in political (independence, sovereignty) but in economic terms: independence in terms of subsistence requirements, which can be fully provided by and out of the Austrian economy itself. The main aspect that sets Austria (and some German lands) apart is that it has silver mines, which most of the other European powers except for Spain with her American mines (France, Norway, Sweden, England…) have not. Those countries are all dependent upon the trading opportunities and goodwill of other countries to exchange silver and money for manufactures. How powerful could Austria be, if she created, on top of the natural endowment with the monetary input of the time (silver), a flourishing and competitive manufacturing export sector! (XXXIII)

We must not conflate the seemingly primitive-bullionist stance that comes across passim in this text with the Midas Fallacy (see Chapter Four), advanced by Adam Smith (among others) who was among the first and most famous critics of what later became known as 'Mercantilism'. Nor did Becher, in his *Politischer Discurs*, conflate money and real wealth.[46] None of the mid-seventeenth century Cameralists and Mercantilists did so in fact.[47] Hörnigk was well aware that silver (and gold) as precious metals only represented claims to wealth, but no real wealth in itself. But they represented, especially when transformed into money as a means of exchange and storing value, quite powerful economic instruments. Even those countries with a strong export sector but no native gold and silver mines were, in one way or another, 'dependent' upon someone else, as a source of wealth. At a time when everybody agreed that money's intrinsic wealth should equal its physical or material worth (commodity money standard) that was how things went; no one would have accepted paper money in its stead for the payment of export bills. Austria had, on top of this, all the main raw materials a flourishing economy needs. But as Austria had got enough silver, as well as the basic subsistence goods, and many of the 'unnecessary' goods on top of all – in quantities well surpassing domestic demand – she could be, if development were to be promoted wisely, 'over all and everything'.

44 Johann Heinrich Zedler, *Grosse(s) vollständige Universal-Lexicon Aller Wissenschafften und Künste* (Halle and Leipzig: J. H. Zedler, 1732–1754) http://www.zedler-lexikon.de/index.html?c= standardsuche (last accessed 22 January 2015).

45 Georg Heinrich Zincke, *Allgemeines oeconomisches Lexicon: darinnen nicht allein die Kunst-Wörter und Erklärungen dererjenigen Sachen, welche theils in der Oeconomie überhaupt, theils insonderheit in einer vollständigen Landwirtschaft und Haushaltung von Acker-, Feld-, Holtz-, Hopffen-, Obst-, Wein- und Garten-Bau … insgemein zu wissen nöthig…; nebst einem Anhange eines Land- und Hauswirtschafts-Calenders 4th ed.* (Leipzig: Gleditsch, 1764) (original dating from 1731).

46 Roscher, *Geschichte der Nationaloekonomik*, 275–76; on Hörnigk, see ibid., 289–293.

47 Günter Schmölders, *Geschichte der Volkswirtschaftslehre* (Wiesbaden: Betriebswirtschaftlicher Verlag T. Gabler, 1961), 19–20.

Another aim of this work, which Hörnigk noted almost in passing, was that others may be inspired to learn from it as well. This was by no means a strategy for Austria. It was a general strategy towards economic development. It was, we may say with the benefit of hindsight, the strategy nearly all the wealthy European nations had used since the Middle Ages to grow rich. On this strategy was founded the process of industrialization; on the Hörnigk strategy rested the phenomenon we have come to know as the 'Great Divergence'.

Chapter Five

HOW EUROPE GOT RICH – THE AUSTRIAN EXAMPLE

State Intervention and Economic Growth in Pre-industrial Europe

Only for reasons of analytical completeness, a brief sketch of Austrian economic policy and development is given here,[1] mainly because Hörnigk reiterated, *passim* and almost *ad nauseam*, that with '*Oesterreich über alles' wann es nur will*, he had formulated a blueprint economic development model for the Austrian parts of the Holy Roman Empire, extending mainly, but not exclusively, to the 'Hereditary Lands' (*Österreichische Erblande*), that is lands held in hereditary possession by the Holy Roman Emperors, which at that time comprised most parts of Austria proper, Bohemia and Hungary. We have seen, however, that – contrary to the book's title, which is in many ways misleading, especially to the modern reader –, the work represents by no means a peculiar 'Austrian' strategy of development. Other states would – and should, in Hörnigk's opinion – apply the 'Hörnigk' strategy as well.[2] As we have seen in the list of editions (Table 1), the first edition ever to be published within Austrian borders was the last known for the pre-industrial age: the much-amended and commented upon 1784 Vienna edition by Benedikt Franz Hermann. That means literally all known editions prior to the twentieth century were printed within the 'German' parts of the Holy Roman Empire. The 'Hörnigk Strategy' therefore, was more akin to a general 'German', if not continental European model. It picked up on theories and practices that had been long established by the 'Mercantilist' states of early modern Europe and which have been masterfully surveyed in the old, but in this regard by no means out-dated, comparative study by Heckscher.[3]

---

1 The following passages and figure are, if not otherwise indicated, based on and derived from Roman Sandgruber, *Ökonomie und Politik. Österreichische Wirtschaftsgeschichte vom Mittelalter bis zur Gegenwart* (Vienna: Ueberreuter, 1995), esp. 103–42; and ibid., 'Österreich 1650–1850', in Wolfram Fischer et al., eds *Handbuch der europäischen Wirtschafts- und Sozialgeschichte, Vol. 4: Europäische Wirtschafts- und Sozialgeschichte von der Mitte des 17. Jahrhunderts bis zur Mitte des 19. Jahrhunderts* (Stuttgart: Klett-Cotta, 1993), 619–87.

2 There is now an excellent comparative overview contrasting Western Europe with China in the early modern period: Peer Vries, *State, Economy and the Great Divergence: Great Britain and China, 1680s–1850s* (London: Bloomsbury, 2015).

3 Heckscher, *Merkantilismus*. It is chiefly in his interpretation of Mercantilist economics in the history and evolution of modern European political economy that we may we call Heckscher 'outdated' now; as research on the theoretical frontier has advanced considerably since his work. For this, see, e.g., the introduction by the editors in Stern and Wennerlind, eds *Mercantilism Reimagined;* or Magnusson, 'Is Mercantilism a Useful Concept Still?'. But in terms of a practical

It is generally difficult to reconstruct meaningful transmission mechanisms between theory (here: Cameralism, Mercantilism) and practice or economic policy as 'Mercantilism in practice'. First of all, modern research has agreed that prior to 1800 there was no such thing as the 'modern state'. Accordingly, no such thing as 'economic policy' could exist in the modern sense. What we would call economic policy chiefly extended to market regulation and stabilization of the 'common good', or what the German language has as *Ordnungspolitik*, ranging from coin valuations (directed at the stabilization of spot exchange rates of the hundreds and thousands of different coins circulating in medieval and early modern Germany), the regulation of weights and measures, the building of roads and other transport infrastructure, the unification of the territorial economies by an (attempted) standardization of customs and toll duties, the building up and redistribution of grain reserves to the public in times of scarcity, to prohibitions of rent-seeking and usurious behaviour in the market place such as forestalling, charging unduly high prices, the granting of monopolies on certain economic activities (which may obviously clash with the previously mentioned activities); as well as price level stabilization for essentials, such as foodstuffs, in times of scarcity, or 'getting the property rights right', in order to attract foreign capital and make the inhabitants richer and safer – mainly, perhaps, for fiscal needs (but is it always either possible or meaningful to analytically separate the 'fiscal' from 'economic' in the 'policy' of the early modern state?).[4] If we define

survey of Mercantilist policy in pre-modern Europe, Heckscher's work is probably still the best, and in many ways a singular work; what would be desirable would be a comparative new study for pre-industrial Europe along the lines pursued in the aptly written Magnusson, *Nation, State and the Industrial Revolution*.

4   On Germany in the early modern period, see, e.g., Blaich, *Die Wirtschaftspolitik des Reichstags*; id., 'Die Bedeutung der Reichstage auf dem Gebiet der öffentlichen Finanzen im Spannungsfeld zwischen Kaiser, Territorialstaaten und Reichsstädten (1495–1679), in De Maddalena and Kellenbenz, eds *Finanzen und Staatsräson in Italien und Deutschland*, 79–112, (111–12), and Fritz Blaich, *Die Epoche des Merkantilismus* (Wiesbaden: Steiner, 1973). An interesting case study for Württemberg around 1500 is Karl Weidner, *Die Anfänge einer staatlichen Wirtschaftspolitik in Württemberg* (Stuttgart: Kohlhammer, 1931). For early modern Britain, see Parthasarathi, *Why Europe Grew Rich*; William J. Ashworth, *Customs and Excise: Trade, Production, and Consumption in England, 1640–1845* (Oxford and New York: Oxford University Press, 2003); Julian Hoppit, 'Bounties, the Economy and the State in Britain, 1689–1800,' in Perry Gauci, ed. *Regulating the British Economy, 1660–1850* (Farnham, Surrey; Burlington, VT: Ashgate, 2011); Julian Hoppit, 'The Nation, the State, and the First Industrial Revolution', *The Journal of British Studies*, 50, no. 2 (2011), 307–31; Raymond L. Sickinger, 'Regulation or Ruination: Parliament's Consistent Pattern of Mercantilist Regulation of the English Textile Trade, 1660–1800,' *Parliamentary History*, 19, no. 2 (2000), 211–32; Anna Gambles, 'Free Trade and State Formation: The Political Economy of Fisheries Policy in Britain and the United Kingdom, circa 1780–1850,' *Journal of British Studies* 39, no. 3 (2000), 288–316, and C. Dudley, 'Party Politics, Political Economy, and Economic Development in Early Eighteenth-Century Britain', *Economic History Review*, Second Series, 66, no. 4 (2013), 1084–100. In a wider context, see Reinert, *How Rich Countries Got Rich*, or Peer Vries, 'Governing Growth: A Comparative Analysis of the Role of the State in the Rise of the West', *Journal of World History*, 13 (2002), 67–193. On states and property rights in terms of general models, see, e.g., Douglass C. North and Robert Paul Thomas, *The Rise of the Western World. A New Economic History* (Cambridge: Cambridge University Press, 1973); Acemoglu and

'economic policy' in this way, we find good examples of it since the Middle Ages. What we don't find, however, are states that directly interfered with the economic process in the modern sense. This is mainly because they couldn't. This type of modern 'dirigiste' or interventionist state and state behaviour only emerged much later, long after 1800, when the configuration of the economic landscape, as well as 'the state' had changed, both attaining an increasingly 'modern' outlook and shape.[5]

Then there is, of course, the basic fact that good ideas do not necessarily or always or automatically turn into good practice. That is, a theory may be good while totally inapplicable in practice; or else a theory or strategy may not be so axiomatically closed or complex or abstract and still be exceedingly proper and common sense and work 'well' in practice. With regard to the present problem, it is a basic fact, as Freudenberger has noted, that we are often dealing with a state or 'government as an autonomous institution with its own objectives, which do not necessarily coincide with the desires of the populations living within the territory under its control.'[6] Mercantilism and eighteenth-century Europe represent good examples of this problem. Some scholars would, just to take one example, today conclude that literally all measures aimed at creating a unified and uniform Prussian market under Frederick the Great (1712/reign 1740–1786) using a Mercantilist strategy ultimately failed, as did attempts at effectively promoting domestic industry in the dispersed lands that made up the composite Prussian state. Both were cornerstones of the Cameralist-Mercantilist creed. But does this mean that Mercantilist ideas were 'bad'? Or did they simply not unfold as intended, in the repeated attempts to implement them, in 'bad' contexts? Prussia managed, after the 1830s, one of the fastest transitions towards industrialization, as Magnusson has argued – but only after basic restrictions on individual economic activity, which had little to do with the Mercantilist creed, were lifted by the abolition of feudalism and serfdom (*villainage*, manorial system) in 1806–11. The latter had little if anything to do with Mercantilist political economy as such (in fact the Cameralist authors were viciously opposed to and tried to abolish feudalism), but represented regional variations upon a rather restrictive legal-institutional system *in situ* (see Chapter Three), which in fact many contemporary Mercantilist and Cameralist pamphlets sought to redress and abolish. So perhaps we need to turn the problem back on its feet. It was not Mercantilism and Cameralist economic theory that didn't work. It was the context that apparently didn't do the trick.[7]

The problem of translating ideas into different contexts comes across from various other countries. Grafe for instance has argued that, in seventeenth- and eighteenth-century Habsburg Spain, Mercantilist ideas of domestic industry promotion and protection circulated widely. But it was the institutional structure of multi-ethnical and

Robinson, *Why Nations Fail*; Oscar C. Gelderblom, *Cities of Commerce. The Institutional Foundations of International Trade in the Low Countries, 1250–1650* (Princeton, NJ: Princeton University Press, 2013), or David Stasavage, *States of Credit. Size, Power, and the Development of European Polities* (Princeton, NJ: Princeton University Press, 2011).

5 Magnusson, *Nation, State and Industrialization*, chs. 1 and 2.

6 Freudenberger, *Lost Momentum*, 61.

7 This paragraph is based on Rössner, 'Heckscher Reloaded?'.

regionalized Spanish society that prevented the effective application of a national economic policy promoting Spain's common wealth.[8] Grafe argues that a strong tradition of institutional fragmentation in Spain created a bias towards promoting municipal policies at the expenses of the royal or national interest, thus failing to either create an integrated national economy, or to promote industrial policy on the national level. Once the basic restrictions had been lifted, however, many European states after 1800, during the process of industrialization, applied the old, pre-modern Cameralist and Mercantilist ideas and strategies increasingly effectively.[9] And this also happened, to an extent, in Austria.

Austrian Economic Development, 1650–1850

Austria belonged, according to a characteristic and very recent modernization hypothesis, to the losers in Europe's rise to greatness, 1500–1800, but that conclusion depends, of course, on how modernization processes are framed analytically and conceptually.[10] According to Bairoch's estimates, Austria's imputed level of per capita industrialization during 1750 to 1860 was only a little more than a third of the British levels, and lower than France, Italy, Germany and Flanders/Belgium; it was even below the European average.[11] Austria was one of the industrial late-comers during the nineteenth century. Industrialization set in thirty or forty years after England. But there has been much debate about the timing and speed of industrialization in either country; and whether the term 'industrial revolution' can and should be used at all, or whether or not we can pinpoint this transformation in terms of specific chronological dates or rather as a process that was dispersed, drawn-out and unfolded differently across different geographical regions and economic sectors. Moreover it is, of course, difficult to arrive at any meaningful quantitative statements regarding the development of industrial performance and output in the centuries between 1650 and 1850, as no comprehensive output statistics are available for the pre-industrial period. Some have named the process of re-Catholization during the later seventeenth century as a cause for Austria's economic backwardness; something that has much to commend to it in principle, but which is hard to test empirically. 'Intolerant' economies and nations do not have to be performing badly economically *a priori*. There is no reason to suggest, furthermore, a positive correlation between the adoption of a particular faith, say Protestantism, and subsequent rates

---

8 Grafe, 'Mercantilism and Representation in a Polycentric State'.

9 Magnusson, *Nation, State and Industrialization*, 75–121.

10 Acemoglu, Johnson and Robinson, 'The Rise of Europe'; Acemoglu and Robinson, *Why Nations Fail*. Earlier accounts include Fernand Braudel, *Civilisation matérielle, économie et capitalisme (XVe–XVIIIe siècles)*, English trans. S. Reynolds, *Civilization and Capitalism, 15th–18th century* (New York: Harper & Row, 1982–84), and Immanuel Maurice Wallerstein, *The Modern World System*, 4 vols. (London, New York, and San Diego: Academic Press/University of Califormia Press, 1974–2011).

11 Stephen N. Broadberry, Rainer Fremdling and Peter Solar, 'Industry', in Stephen N. Broadberry and Kevin H. O'Rourke, eds *The Cambridge Economic History of Modern Europe, Vol. I: 1700–1870* (Cambridge and New York: Cambridge University Press, 2010), 164–86, (172), Table 7.3.

of economic growth.[12] Lack of capital, social conservatism, the stronghold of the guilds[13] and a high appreciation of aristocratic values and lifestyles may have played a role as well in Austria's somewhat delayed economic development. Others have named the lack of native industrial technology as one of the chief reasons. Most equipment in the textile industries had, since the industrialization, to be imported from England. Industry only surpassed the agrarian sector as the biggest contributor to output and employment in Austria after 1945. As late as 1910, agriculture contributed 60 per cent and industry 20 per cent to total employment, if measured for the entire monarchy. For Austria the figure amounted to 39 per cent for agriculture and 32 for industry.[14] The share of agriculture's contribution to GDP was lower; it had stood at 21 per cent in 1850 (down from 28 per cent in 1830).

Such calculative results are based on aggregate figures for a somewhat artificial polit-ical-territorial unit that covered a wide stretch of geographically, politically, economically and culturally different regions that were also very different from each other in terms of economic potential. As a composite monarchy, Austria-Hungary comprised, during the early modern age, some of the most backward, as well as some of the most developed, regions of her age. Some areas in Lower Austria belonged, by the eighteenth century, to the stronger economic regions of the day, measured in terms of industrial output and its contribution to gross domestic product, and compared well with the more developed English economic regions of the time. Silesia was a quite strong manufacturing region when it was lost to Prussia in 1740. In Bohemia, there were about 400,000 people (or about 18 per cent of the population) active in some form in the manufacturing of wool, cotton and linen cloth around 1790; there were fifty-nine ironworks and a larger number of forges, as well as a flourishing glass-making industry. Access to international markets and the Atlantic Economy was provided through the River Elbe.[15] According to Matis, only 30 per cent of the Austrian landmass was touched by an industrial transformation. Therefore, Austria's backwardness was 'relative'.[16] This is illustrated by the simple fact that, by 1911, the per capita income of the Austrian Alpine lands and Bohemia were three times as high as those of Galicia or Slovenia.[17]

---

12 Davide Cantoni, 'Adopting a New Religion: The Case of Protestantism in 16th Century Germany', *Economic Journal*, vol. 122, no. 560 (May), 502–31.

13 Öserreichische Industriegeschichte GmbH, eds, *Österreichische Industriegeschichte, Vol 1, 1700 bis 1848 – die vorhandene Chance* (Vienna: Ueberreuter, 2003), 45f. (including contributions by well renown Austrian economic historians).

14 Karl Bachinger and Vlastislav Lacina, 'Wirtschaftliche Ausgangsbedingungen', in Alice Teichova and Herbert Matis, eds *Österreich und die Tschechoslowakei 1918–1938: Die wirtschaftliche Neuordnung in Zentraleuropa in der Zwischenkriegszeit* (Vienna: Böhlau, 1996), 51–90, (53), Table 2.

15 John A. Davis, 'The Eighteenth Century', in Antonio di Vittorio et al., eds *An Economic History of Europe. From Expansion to Development* (London and New York: Routledge, 2006), 118–19 (Davis wrongly gives 1764 as the date for Silesia becoming part of the Prussian empire).

16 Herbert Matis, 'Österreichs Wirtschaft im Zeitalter Franz Josephs I', in Harry Kühne et al., eds *Das Zeitalter Kaiser Franz Josephs. Pt. 1: Von der Revolution zur Gründerzeit, 1848–1880: Schloss Grafenegg, 19. Mai–28. Oktober 1984: Niederösterreichische Landesausstellung* (Horn and Vienna: Amt der NÖ Landesregierung, 1984), 113–20, (113).

17 Magnusson, *Nation, State and the Industrial Revolution*, 108.

Some natural geographical barriers to trade (the Alps and Carpathians) made economic integration fairly difficult. There was a lack of effective east-west transport routes. No dense water transport system existed. Austria's only overseas port of note (apart from the Austrian Netherlands and Fiume/Rijeka) was Trieste – a remote port in the Adriatic, far away from Atlantic economy. Industry clustered in select areas in Bohemia, Moravia, Styria, Vorarlberg and around Vienna and Lower Austria. By the 1790s, about 50 per cent of all Austrian manufactories were located in Lower Austria, along a broad spectrum of decentralized industrial production in town and countryside. About a third of total industrial output originated within the area. Around 1800, it was said that the Austrian district of *Unter-Wienerwald* had a higher concentration of factories and manufactories than any other European region of comparable size and dimension. Iron works, tool manufactories, glassworks, paper mills and much more would have created the effects of agglomeration and contributed to industrial know-how in the area.[18] Many of these ventures had been created in the later seventeenth century on government initiative. Around 1700, for instance, there was a colony of cloth makers who were settled at Horn, the silk ribbons and stockings manufactory at Walpersdorf near Herzogenburg, the Vienna *Armaturenmeisterschaft* in Wiener Neustadt, and the mirror or tobacco manufactory in Neuhaus and Heinburg. Most prominent perhaps was the cotton manufactory at Schwechat shortly after 1700. The local nobility was also quite important as a source of entrepreneurship. Think of people such as Fürst Auersperg who established the silk manufactory in Wienersdorf or members of the old aristocratic Esterhazy family who ran the cloth manufactory in Wiener Neustadt. Often, noble entrepreneurs were engaged in brickworks, breweries and distilleries. These products depended on inputs that were yielded as by-products on their big agrarian estates, or rent payments when delivered in kind, such as grain; or labour services provided by the dependent peasants and serfs. Due to statutory rights and grants, the big noblemen usually also ran mills and ironworks. Demesnes usually included wide swathes of forestlands that provided their owners with timber as fuel, effectively free of charge. This aspect often acted as an important stimulus in iron and smelting processes, and often made 'old' and obsolete production processes survive within a more modern industrial environment, where hearths were increasingly fired using mineral fuels such as coke rather than charcoal (there is always a trade-off between technical efficiency and gross profitability, which also depends on cultural and institutional factors such as path dependency).[19] But in many other areas, Lower Austria was still lacking a productive and competitive edge, especially in linen and woollen cloth making (which, however, seemed to have improved after the 1720s, and especially towards second half of the eighteenth century).

18 Roman Sandgruber, 'Historische Entwicklung der Industrie Niederösterreichs von den Anfängen bis zur Gegenwart', in Vereinigung Österreichischer Industrieller, Landesgruppe Niederösterreich, eds *Industrieatlas Niederösterreich* (Vienna: Handelskammer Niederösterreich, 1984), 7–23, (7).

19 Nikolaus Olaf Siemaszko, *Das oberschlesische Eisenhüttenwesen 1741–1860. Ein regionaler Wachstumssektor* (Stuttgart: Franz Steiner, 2011).

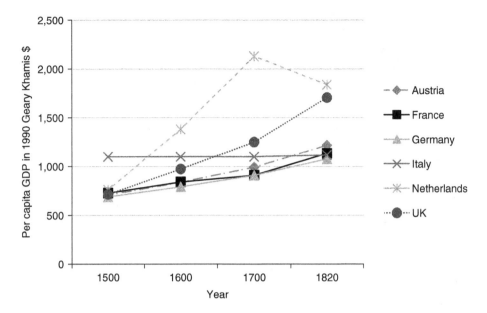

Figure 3 Maddison and the Small Divergence
Source: 'Original' Maddison Database, http://www.ggdc.net/maddison/oriindex.htm (last accessed 26 January 2015.). Note that there are continuous updates on certain countries, mainly England and the Netherlands, which can be obtained from http://www.ggdc.net/maddison/maddison-project/home.htm but which are incompatible with the set of data used for the graph below, especially the Austrian figures.

Maddison's acclaimed figures are in many ways in need of revision. Conceptually, we may be in doubt whether or not the quantification of a country or nation's GDP any time before 1900 in modern values really is a meaningful exercise. But Figure 3 gives the commonly accepted standard of the relative economic position of the countries compared, over time as well as across space; it may help us place Austria in the economic framework of her age, where she started out in the age of Hörnigk and where she eventually was at the eve of and during the early phases of industrialization. New research on the Maddison database by van Zanden and others has suggested that between 1500 and 1800, outside the hotchpotch areas of the northwest/North Sea shore, 'the rest of Europe [was] characterized by no growth' (data for Sweden, Spain, Portugal, Belgium, Germany); but this partly means that incomes in and around 1500 may have been underestimated.[20] By 1700, Austria may well have overtaken France and the German territories in terms of (imputed) per capita wealth. The Holy Roman Empire actually had, according to new revised calculations, suffered a net loss of 14 per cent in terms of GDP in the period 1500–1800, but that loss was nearly completely due to the disruptions of the Thirty

20 Jutta Bolt and Jan Luiten van Zanden, 'The First Update of the Maddison Project: Re-estimating Growth Before 1820', *Maddison-Project Working Paper*, WP-4 (2013), http://www.ggdc.net/maddison/maddison-project/publications/wp4.pdf (last accessed 22 January 2015.) 2013, 6, 14 and tables.

Years War (1618–48) (see Chapter Three). Austria had been the 'biggest loser' of the early modern period. At the same time, The Netherlands had gained, according to the revised estimates, 79 per cent in terms of GDP, and England's economy had grown by an even more impressive 93 per cent.[21] These were the best performers: the 'first modern economy' (Netherlands) and 'first industrial nation' (England). Austria performed, in all likelihood, slightly above the expectable, represented by the continental European average if you removed the two 'odd men out' – the first modern economies. So she had done quite respectably.

The crisis of the seventeenth century, marked out by the consequences of the Thirty Years War, the wars against the Turks, the War of the Spanish Succession, the plague (which struck as late as 1709) and so forth, was over by the early 1700s. The average height of the population began to rise again until mid-eighteenth century, after which it declined again, due presumably to a reduced calorific intake during the early process of industrialization.[22] Population levels began to increase in Austria (in its modern boundaries) from 1.8 million around 1600 to circa 3 million in 1800 and 4 million in 1850. Towards the later 1700s, there was some extensive economic growth, albeit, due to the nature of the available evidence, which is more than sketchy, statements must remain speculative. Measured in terms of the composite monarchy, Austria-Hungary about doubled her population from 13 to 24 million, while the total European population, excluding Russia, only grew by 69 per cent between these dates. In terms of the growth rate of the density of population per square kilometre, Austria-Hungary was at average (regardless whether or not the European parts of Russia are included), between 1500 and 1800. However, the increase was quite strong during the eighteenth century, with a 56 per cent increase from about 24.8 to 38.8 inhabitants per sq km. In the seventeenth century, this increase had been much more modest (22 per cent). But it had been an increase at least. For the Holy Roman Empire, the most recent estimates suggest a decline from 29.8 to 26 inhabitants per square km, and a corresponding increase from 26 to 45.1 (73 per cent growth) during the eighteenth century. The Thirty Years War had wrought considerable havoc to the German lands.[23] There has been controversy about how to interpret the fact that average heights were *decreasing* on the eve of the industrial revolution, with Komlos sketching out an 'Austrian model' featuring an initial increase followed by a subsequent decrease in average heights. Austrian diets, measured in terms of meat intake, may have been above the European average in the 1750s.[24]

---

21 Maddison Project Database, retrieved 18.10.2014.

22 John Komlos, *Ernährung und wirtschaftliche Entwicklung unter Maria Theresia und Joseph II: eine anthropometrische Geschichte der Industriellen Revolution in der Habsburgermonarchie* (St. Katharinen: Scripta-Mercaturae-Verlag, 1994), 49–107.

23 Figures taken from Paolo Malanima, *Europäische Wirtschaftsgeschichte 10.–19. Jahrhundert* (Vienna, Cologne and Weimar: Böhlau, 2010), 22, 29; Tables 6, 10.

24 Others have argued for a changed metabolic schedule of the human body during the process of industrialization, see Hans-Joachim Voth, 'Height, Nutrition, and Labor: Recasting the "Austrian Model"', *Journal of Interdisciplinary History*, 25, no. 4 (Spring, 1995), 627–36, (629).

In terms of population increase – a goal of many Mercantilists (with diverging sub-goals as to the relative wealth level of each in individual member) – Austria did quite well during the early modern age, in spite of the 'brain drain' manifested in the considerable, and at times forced, out-migration of nonconformists, mainly protestant members of the community. In Upper Germany, about 20,000 Protestants left after the Thirty Years War, and in 1732, a similar number, perhaps up to 30,000 of Salzburg Protestants fled the country (one seventh of the regional population).[25] Protestant emigration reached a highpoint in Salzburg around 1730. From 1771, we find repeated prohibitions of emigration. Infant mortality declined by 15 per cent between 1752–54 and 1855–64 (from 56.6 to 48.2 for the age group zero to four years).[26]

The later seventeenth century was also a period of de-urbanization. Only from the beginning of the eighteenth century did Vienna's rise to greatness make itself felt. The number of households, according to careful estimates, increased from 286,000 (1600) to 431,000 (1754). There was considerable immigration from Croatia during the sixteenth and seventeenth centuries. In many parts of Austria, partible inheritance prevailed, and agrarian economies remained relatively poor. Seasonal by-employment and proto-industrialization could be found, especially in Vorarlberg and Western Tyrol. But in many other towns, cities and regions we can observe a process of de-urbanization (1600–1754). The old industrial and mining towns of Schwaz, Villach and others that had experienced a boom in the later fourteenth and first half of the fifteenth century were among those that were hit the hardest by the process of de-urbanization in the seventeenth century. Schwaz had been Austria's second-largest city in the sixteenth century (15,000 inhabitants in 1500), but declined to 6,300 inhabitants in 1754. In the 1600–1754 time period, Vienna, Innsbruck (increased from 5,500 to 8,500 inhabitants,) and Graz (increased from 8,000 to 20,000) grew. Vienna's population tripled between the 1690s and the early 1800s, from between 40,000 and 50,000 inhabitants (1683) to about 130,000 (1741), then 230,000 (1800), making it, by then, the largest city within the Holy Roman Empire.[27] Steyr, the second-biggest city in the early seventeenth century and one of the more important manufacturing centres of Austria, declined by about a quarter between 1600 and 1754, due to the industrial crisis and the forced outmigration of Protestants.[28] Vienna was important as Austria's capital and significant residential city; the nobility, churchmen, clergy and public servants dominated it, but there was not much bourgeois enterprise. The feudal nobility owned up to 50 per cent of the town houses[29]; they were usually freed from tax payments. The process of de-urbanization was accompanied by Austria's cultural and economic 'ruralization'; represented by an increase in fortunes and powers of the nobility and aristocracy; a rise of non-privileged rural market centres, and a gradual deterioration of peasant rights and increase of feudal dues and

25 Sandgruber, 'Österreich 1650–1850', 631.

26 Ibid., *Ökonomie und Politik*, 209, Table 16.

27 Dieter Schott, *Europäische Urbanisierung (1000–2000). Eine umwelthistorische Einführung* (Cologne etc.: UTB, 2014), 158, Tab. 3.

28 Sandgruber, 'Österreich 1650–1850', 637–38.

29 Sandgruber, *Ökonomie und Politik*, 108.

levies in many regions. Counterreformation and the process of re-Catholicization not only caused significant out-emigration; they were also responsible for new waves of social disciplining and the supervision of public and private life through pastors, sexual moral standards, and so forth. The growth of churches and cloisters, also as feudal 'business enterprises', as well as the revitalization of religious shrines and pilgrimages were part of this development.[30] There were also the never-ending struggles between urban and rural industry. Urban guild monopolies were gradually eroded between 1600 and 1800 by country artisans and non-incorporated traders and craftsmen (*Gäuhandwerker, Pfuscher, Störer*), a process that was actively promoted by the government after the 1740s (see later in this chapter).

Agriculture obviously represented Austria's most important sector well into the twentieth century. But there were structural problems. We can observe a decline of viniculture and wine exports via the Danube during the seventeenth century, marked by a slash of about 50 per cent compared to sixteenth-century export levels, which may have been as high as 50,000 hectolitres.[31] Wine cultivation increasingly turned into a by-economy within the peasant economy. The available evidence suggests that there was no extension of cultivated land until the end of the seventeenth century, when the amount of cleared forest and newly cultivated arable fields began to increase. Rye (25 per cent) and oats (20 per cent) dominated arable agriculture and agrarian production, followed by wheat (nine per cent) and barley (4 per cent of the cultivated land). According to Sandgruber, seed productivity (amount of grain harvested divided by the amount of grain put in the earth as seed) would have declined between the mid-seventeenth and the mid-eighteenth century.[32] The three-course rotation system, a fairly traditional method and schedule, prevailed; most peasants were not free but serfdom and *villainage* were rather unknown in the Austrian lands. A form of 'modest feudalism' as in most areas in Germany west of the river Elbe would have been the norm.[33] Towards the end of the eighteenth century, we find a considerable increase in agrarian productivity levels, both in terms of seed corn productivity and productivity per worker; productivity per hours worked, however, may have declined.[34] If that were true, agrarian growth towards the end of the pre-industrial period would have been extensive.

Austria's most important industries were textiles (frequently organized as putting-out or *Verlag*) and, given the geographical conditions, mining.[35] Mining, metallurgy and mineral industry faced a severe decline over the early modern period. At the dawn of the modern period, silver output levels, with the predominant mines at the Falkenstein in Tyrol, had peaked at 25 tons per year; but average yields declined thereafter, especially

---

30 Ibid., 130–32.
31 Ibid., 110.
32 Sandgruber, 'Österreich 1650–1850', 654.
33 Critical: Cerman, *Villagers and Lords*.
34 Sandgruber, 'Österreich 1650–1850', 655.
35 Markus Cerman, 'Proto-industrielle Entwicklung in Österreich', in ibid. and Sheilagh Ogilvie, eds *Protoindustrialisierung in Europa. Industrielle Produktion vor dem Fabrikzeitalter* (Vienna: Verlag für Gesellschaftskritik, 1994), 161–76.

in the age of the South American silver influx since the mid-sixteenth century, which turned the American mines into the world's largest silver supplier. Between 1650 and 1800, silver output further contracted from about four to little more than one ton per year. Copper output declined from 1.7 tons to 0.4 tons in the period 1500–1650, but somewhat recovered to about 0.53 tons by the early 1800s.[36] Iron production in Styria (Erzberg) contracted from 9,000 to 3,000 tons per year from the 1560s to the 1650s. The production peaks of the 1560s were not reached again until the 1830s and 1840s.[37] Total Styrian production may have declined from 13,000 or 14,000 tons in 1550 to 8,000 tons a century later.[38] Total Austrian iron production declined from 20,000 tons (representing up to 30 per cent of total European production) circa 1550 to 15,000 tons by 1650 (minus 25 per cent). The 1550s output levels were reached again in 1750, after which date they doubled from 20,000 to 41,000 until 1810.[39] Therefore, observed over the whole early modern period, Austria's iron production doubled. But the lion's share of the increase fell in the Theresian period after 1740.[40] Silver, gold and lead mining declined; copper and brass industry kept up. The regional armaments industries would have received some boost during the Thirty Years War.[41]

After 1600, the traffic volume contracted on most routes between the 1560s and the late seventeenth and sometimes the early eighteenth century (Brenner, Tauern; Danube). The traffic on the Tauern road collapsed, by 1655, to one third of the mid-sixteenth century figures. The Brenner toll yields – this was the important passage towards Italy – were, by circa 1694, still a third below their 1601 high point. The amount of recorded through-traffic had reached around 20,000 tons before 1620. The West-East traffic on the Danube declined from 1652 into the 1680s. In 1700, the toll values still were below those recorded around 1600.[42] The native merchant capital was, in Sandgruber's words, 'weak'.[43] Contemporary cameralists such as Wilhelm von Schröder mocked an apparent tendency among the merchants to strive to become cavaliers as soon as they could afford a noble lifestyle and habits. Foreigners frequently dominated the native commercial landscape. Only during the eighteenth century did the volume of Adriatic trade (Trieste) increase significantly. Vienna's rapid population increase would have stimulated commercial activity and the accumulation of mercantile capital. In 1667, the Oriental Trading Company ('Orientalische Kompanie') was founded and endowed with a monopoly on Turkish trade; also engaging in cattle imports from Hungary. In 1719, a second oriental trading company was founded which operated from Vienna, Trieste and Fiume/ Rijeka; lasting for only thirty years. In 1722, the Ostend Company (East India Trade) was established in the Austrian Netherlands (but liquidated again in 1731 after a series of

---

36 Sandgruber, 'Österreich 1650–1850', 662.
37 Sandgruber, *Ökonomie und Politik*, 114, graph.
38 Ibid., 113.
39 Ibid., 115, Table 8.
40 Sandgruber, 'Österreich 1650–1850', 664, Table 20.
41 Ibid., *Ökonomie und Politik*, 112, 115–17.
42 Ibid., 117–19.
43 Ibid., 119.

political conflicts about the nature and legitimacy of the Company). Towards the 1780s, the on-going processes of liberalization of foreign trade were intensified, manifested by a gradual decline of *Niederleger* (merchants and companies enjoying staple rights), as well as the abolition of internal tolls and privileges, staple rights and price regulation.[44] Foreign merchants, Turkish, Serbian and Christian Armenians were important as middle men, as were Greeks and Sephardic Jews later on. After the 1630s, there is a rise of the privileged Bolzano Fairs as focal points for south-north trade between Italy and the German lands. Bolzano developed, between the mid-seventeenth and mid-eighteenth century, into a 'regional trade and exchange fair with partial international relevance', as for the first time trading places and exchange partners outside the traditional range of exchange rate notations, covering the Italian Cities, the Habsburg lands and Upper Germany, appeared, namely Hamburg, Amsterdam and London. This suggests the development of more or less regular business links between Bolzano merchants and the northern European fringe.[45] The elevation of Trieste into a Free Port in 1719 and the somewhat forced development of Austria's overseas trade would have further stimulated traffic and commerce in the region. Bolzano represented the connection point between Northern Italy and the Southwest German/Austrian economic areas, with goods such as woollen cloth and linens imported from the north and silk, oil, raw cotton sent back in return.[46]

After the 1740s, an age of economic growth and development set in, ending the 'long seventeenth century crisis'. The quantitative evidence points towards an increase of raw materials and foodstuff imports, perhaps even the movement towards a more 'industrialized trade balance'. Labour input increased, but growth remained extensive. We may doubt whether there really was the same 'industrious revolution' that some have found at work in seventeenth- and eighteenth-century England and the Netherlands.[47] The apparent decline in popular piety, the number of masses sung and church stipends, as well as the prohibition of pilgrimages in the 1770s may support the view that some sort of cultural change towards a more market-oriented outlook and economy had occurred, but a priori, these things should not be assumed to have affected economic activity directly, either positively or negatively (pious people can be as productive as atheists; likewise, Protestants in the same way as Catholics).[48] Cloisters and monasteries were secularized. Workhouses and orphanages were increasingly put to 'productive' use. Under Maria Theresia and Joseph II the number of holidays was reduced by a total of 24; many were declared to be 'half holy-days': after mass people had to return to work. The length of

44 Sandgruber, 'Österreich 1650–1850', 677.
45 Markus A. Denzel, 'Ex merce et cambio pulchrior. Bargeldloser Zahlungsverkehr auf den Bozner Messen (17. bis Mitte 19. Jahrhundert', in Andrea Bonoldi and Markus A. Denzel, eds *Bozen im Messenetz Europas (17.-19. Jahrhundert) / Bolzano nel sistema fieristico europeo (secc. XVII–XIX)* (Bolzano: Athesia, 2007), 149–86, and the larger study by Markus A. Denzel, *Die Bozner Messen und ihr Zahlungsverkehr, 1633–1850* (Bolzano: Athesia, 2005).
46 Franz Mathis, 'Handelsgüter und Handelsströme durch Tirol', in Bonoldi and Denzel, eds *Bozen im Messenetz*, 123–34.
47 Sandgruber, *Ökonomie und Politik*, 144, after de Vries, *Industrious Revolution*.
48 Ibid., 145.

the working day was also increased among industrial workers as well as civil servants (the latter from six to eight or nine hours per day after 1800). The 'Hirtenbrief' (Pastoral Care Letter) by Emperor Joseph II in 1783 attempted to introduce the 'ungemessene' working day for civil servants, which meant that civil servants could retire from their daily tasks only when they were actually done with them.[49] After 1807, the Austrian working day was extended to up to 16 hours. Spinning schools were erected following an edict of 1765. In the 1780s, 50 per cent of Tyrolean children visited a school. Schools, training and knowledge were increasingly perceived as a main developmental goal; Austrian's literacy rates increased.

Woollen remained Austria's main textile manufacturing branch until late. As late as 1841, the total value of woollen output came to 9.4 million Gulden, while cotton weaving came to less than one half of this (3.96 million Gulden). Linen was only comparatively negligible (with a production value of 1.5 million in 1841). But linen had clearly been more important during the early modern period, especially in Upper Austria and those regions in Silesia, Bohemia and Moravia where it had dominated the industrious landscape.[50] The production of cottons only took off in the later eighteenth century (and it had not featured so much on Hörnigk's agenda, either). In 1723, the *Schwechater Zitz- und Kottonfabrik* was founded on account of the Oriental Company. This manufactory enjoyed a monopoly on the lower and upper Austrian market. But between 1740 and the end of the 1760s, the cotton cloth sales in Austria rose six-fold, furthered by the subsequent liberalization of this manufacturing branch and the foundation of new manufactory enterprises in Himberg, Kettenhof, Fridau, Ebreichsdorf, St Pölten and so forth. The number of spinsters and weavers of cotton in Lower Austria is said to have surpassed 100,000 towards the 1770s. Output grew considerably (but took off even faster after the 1800s). Up to 900 tons of raw cotton were imported annually into the Austrian lands.

The silk industry likewise experienced a benevolent phase after the early 1700s, but remained – as predicted by the model von Thünen, as well as Hörnigk's remarks – centred on Vienna. The number of people employed in the manufacture of silk rose from about 2,000 around 1760 to about 15,000 around 1813, making it the most important Viennese industry of the time.[51] The linen industry fared less favourably, due to the loss of Silesia in 1740 (which in accounting terms boosted the shares of the other linen producing regions within the composite monarchy), and the slump in sales due to the general crisis of the later seventeenth century (with linen being the chief item of domestic consumption other than foodstuffs, as well as a source of by-employment for a significant share of the population, sales levels were highly sensitive to the general trend in population). Also, there was much competition from Bavarian and Bohemian producers. The liberalization of the industry in 1755–73 would have boosted sales and led to a boom in linen production towards the later eighteenth century. But subsequently, the industry faced stiff competition from the rapidly growing cotton textiles sector. The

---

49 Ibid., 155.
50 Sandgruber, 'Österreich 1650–1850', 668–69.
51 Ibid., 670.

number of independent artisans and craftsmen in Vienna increased considerably; from about 1,700 in 1679 to about 11,000 or 12,000 in 1736. This number would have remained about the same into the 1780s.[52] In the 1840s, Vienna contributed about one-seventh of total industrial units, but between one fourth and a third of Austrian industrial output,[53] which suggests not only that average productivity of industry in Vienna was significantly above average, but also that the share of value added in the total sales price was higher than elsewhere, again corresponding to the Thünen model of regional industrial distribution. Viennese industry would have been dominated by high-value and luxury manufacture more than anywhere else, including paper, leather and hat making and the like (to be expected in any residential and capital city of the size and reputation). For other parts of the monarchy it is much more difficult to quantify trends in industrial output.

Often, the state acted as an entrepreneur, but usually after initial private initiatives had run into troubles. The production of cotton cloth only began to pick up towards the end of the eighteenth century.[54] The flagship project of the industry was the *k.k. priv. Wollenzeugfabrik* in Linz (literally: royal and imperial private woollen stuff manufactory at Linz), founded in 1672 under privilege, including a monopoly for thirty years on specific types of cloth, and their marketing and sale. This was meant to be part of a Listian 'learning period' and schedule, also intended to break guild monopoly and create a more powerful industrial productive landscape.[55] Upon experiencing economic problems, the manufactory was sold to the Empress for 926,000 Thalers in 1764. It is said to have experienced mixed success for the best part of hundred years, a fate shared with many manufactories across the Empire. Manufactories often lacked sufficient capital (which could be generated inter alia through lotteries).[56] At the time of sale, the manufactory would have been the biggest state-run enterprise in the Austrian lands. In 1771, its workforce numbered more than 26,000. Usually a considerable share of the workers were out-workers, that is, working from home or in decentralized production sequences, as was the case in Prussia's state-run manufactories such as the *Zeughaus*; but, these figures were still huge (three or four times the size of a medium-sized town). In various years between the 1760s and 1790s, total employment reached levels near

---

52 Ibid., 666.

53 Ibid., 666; 674, Table 22.

54 Ibid., 669.

55 *Österreichische Industriegeschichte* II, 171–72.

56 With a focus on Prussia, see Rolf Straubel, *Kaufleute und Manufakturunternehmer. Eine empirische Untersuchung über die sozialen Träger von Handel und Grossgewerbe in den mittleren preussischen Provinzen (1763 bis 1815)* (Stuttgart: Franz Steiner, 1995); see also Karl Heinrich Kaufhold, 'Schwerpunkte des preußischen Exportgewerbes um 1800', in Franz Mathis and Josef Riedmann, eds *Festschrift für Georg Zwanowetz anläßlich der Vollendung des 65. Lebensjahres* (Innsbruck: Universität Innsbruck, 1984), 243–60, (243), as well as Karl Heinrich Kaufhold, 'Manufakturen im Alten Reich. Aspekte einer vorindustriellen gewerblichen Betriebsform', in Torsten Meyer and Marcus Popplow, eds *Technik, Arbeit und Umwelt in der Geschichte. Günter Bayerl zum 60. Geburtstag* (Münster and New York: Waxmann, 2006), 41–52.

50,000 staff, many of whom were spinsters working out-house for the much smaller number of weavers.[57] The Schwechater cotton manufactory had more than 20,000 employees in the 1750s.[58]

Between 1764 and 1811, the return on the investment, based on the evidence available, would have averaged about 12 per cent per year. Under Ancien Règime conditions, this was considerable, given that interest rates (usury legislations were at work also) stood at around five to six per cent per annum.[59] But we must consider the wider goals and circumstances that surrounded the establishment of such manufactories. Whether they were state-run or private enterprises, even if they did not always or constantly work under profit-yielding circumstances, manufactures served several goals, which all need to be considered in order to reach a balanced assessment:

- Profit (business administration);
- Reduce unemployment (social; promotion of general welfare);
- Mother of subsequent manufactory foundations – emulation and spreading of industrial know-how;
- Technology transfer and generation of useful knowledge;
- Production of state-relevant goods such as uniforms, rifles and munitions which the market may not supply either at all or at quantities necessary (for the survival of the state; symbiotic with development goal, see earlier).

That, based on modern efficiency criteria, many of the state-run manufactories were unprofitable or inefficient at times should neither come as a surprise, nor should it be valued detrimental to their assessment. As a specific type of business organization, manufactories were quite advanced, after all. Smith's magnum opus on the *Inquiry into the Nature and Causes of the Wealth of Nations* (1776) commences with the example of a pin manufactory in (Book I, chapter one) as a prime example of the positive nexus between division of labour, the streamlining of manufactorial processes and economic and productivity growth.

It needs to be remembered (see earlier) that while, in average terms, Austria or Cisleithania, most of the time probably remained below the European average figures for per capita industrialization, there were areas, such as Lower Austria and Vorarlberg that had a higher density of industrial production per capita and per square mile and that enjoyed output growth rates and possibly also productivity levels that would have been above the European average and closer to the better-performing areas such as England or Belgium. The period under Charles VI and Maria Theresia, especially the 1720s and 1730s, is also held to have been comparatively beneficial for the development of Hungary, even though Hungary – which usually contributed about a quarter of the taxes raised in the Habsburg Empire – bore a not inconsiderable share of the costs of

57 *Österreichische Industriegeschichte*, II, 176, 181.
58 *Österreichische Industriegeschichte*, I, 62.
59 *Österreichische Industriegeschichte* II, 180

Austria's military campaigns, especially the wars against Prussia in 1741.[60] It is quite a moot point to try to estimate the contribution Hörnigk's text made to this development. But the cornerstones of Austrian industrial policy after 1740 resemble Hörnigk's programme closely – as closely as the programme of any other eighteenth-century mainstream economist.

Policy Development, 1650–1850

It has often been argued that pre-modern states were 'soft states' with the simultaneously strong desire and lack of practical leverage to implement anything that would resemble a 'national' economic policy of development (see earlier in this chapter).[61] Historians have de-constructed the concept of 'Absolutism', that is, the mainstream political theory of princes and rulership in the later seventeenth and eighteenth century (what we may call the *Westphalian* State System); something which earlier scholars such as Gustav von Schmoller had seen as the crucial ingredient of their symbiosis between national economic policy ('Mercantilism') and the making of modern nation states (*Mercantilism-as-state-building-hypothesis*). Nevertheless, Martin Luther's Reformation (1517) had opened up a whole array of new fields of state action and intervention, ranging from confession and confessional (religious) politics as a means of strengthening the emerging (proto)-state, to the establishment of public primary and elementary schools and the stripping of the monasteries and altars (secularization) which led – in the reformed/Lutheran areas – to an increase of the rulers' political strength. In the reformed areas, the rulers were by definition the first bishops or *Kirchenherren*, attaining key functions previously held by Curia and Pope under the old confession pre-1517. The stripping of the altars and dissolution of the monasteries frequently also led to an increase of the state's assets and wealth, especially from the treasure accumulated by churches and monasteries for endowment and ritual ornament since the Middle Ages.[62] And even those rulers who chose or elected for their territories to remain Catholic after 1555, when the politics of Reformation became consolidated in the state's hands, were forced to opt into this new system of power politics and state craft, even if in a slightly antagonistic way. Even though recent historical research has urged us not to overstretch the importance of the sixteenth-century Reformation, we should be aware that it decisively changed the political landscape of

---

60 István Kállay, 'Wirtschaft und Gesellschaft der königlichen Freistädte Ungarns zur Zeit Maria Theresias', in Anna Maria Drabek, Richard Georg Plaschka and Adam Wandruszka, eds *Ungarn und Österreich unter Maria Theresia und Joseph II: neue Aspekte im Verhältnis der beiden Länder: Texte des 2. Österreichisch-Ungarischen Historikertreffens, Wien, 1980* (Vienna: Verlag der Österreichischen Akademie der Wissenschaft, 1982), 121–30. More recently, Antal Szántay, ' "Vitam et sanguinem, sed avenam non" – Habsburg State Finances and Hungary in the 18th Century', in the *Proceedings of the Fondazione Istituto Internazionale di Storia Economica "F. Datini" / THE FINANCIAL CRISES: Their Management, Their Social Implications and Their Consequences in Pre-industrial Times, 10–13 May 2015* (forthcoming).
61 Magnusson, *Nation, State and the Industrial Revolution*.
62 Rössner, *Martin Luther on Commerce and Usury*, ch. 4.

Europe, not only within the Holy Roman Empire (Germany). It paved the way for fundamentally restructured patterns of governance (but also agency for the subjects under consideration) and would thus also have major economic consequences.

One of these consequences was in economic policy. The late medieval boom, but especially the collapse and problems experienced in the central European mining regions, focused around Hall in Tyrol, the Saxon and Bohemian Erzgebirge and the Harz Mountains (mostly ruled by the Dukes of Brunswick/Braunschweig), but also certain processes in the Thuringian Saiger industry, where argentiferous copper deposits were separated into silver and pure copper, using imported lead, had led to an increasing degree of state intervention in the mining economies. In the words of Wakefield, many a German state was based upon a silver rock, with the mining industries (iron, silver, tin) representing, due to the facture that minerals were usually subject to regalian rights, a domestic interest par excellence.[63] Many of the mines were either run by the states themselves – that is the princely administrators (*Direktionsprinzip*); or else tightly supervised, as every entrepreneur had to pay tithe and taxes on mining yields to the rulers. Mining regions were areas where rulers tried to directly and actively interfere with the regional economies and their very peculiar cultural and social configuration. *Bergordnungen* (literally: mining ordinances) were frequently issued. They marked these regions out as peculiar fields of economic and social interaction, with peculiar privileges and conditions that wouldn't prevail to the same or comparable extent elsewhere. Mining society and economy were structured using quite particular schedules. Frequently – as was the case with the sixteenth century Dukes of Brunswick-Wolfenbüttel – the rulers directly interfered in the running of the mines, including the supervision of production processes, with repeated aims at streamlining and thus raising overall productivity. Detailed statistical records were kept denoting output and productivity levels. Inefficient administrators were sacked.[64] For many German states within whose territories mines and mining works were located, the industrial landscape provided a testing field for the core field of action of the emerging 'modern' states in later centuries: administration and rationalization of productive processes. It is no coincidence or wonder that mining featured prominently in German economics and Cameralist textbooks during the sixteenth to eighteenth centuries, and that Hörnigk included observations of mining in his general schedule of development and economic policy (see earlier in this chapter).

Mountains were also important for a stable supply of silver, money and coins, which in turn were crucial for maintaining economic as well as social stability and equilibrium.[65]

---

63 Andre Wakefield, in an unpublished paper given at an international workshop held at the Universität Leipzig, July 2014.

64 Hans-Joachim Kraschewski, 'Wirtschaftspolitische Grundsätze des Herzogs Julius von Braunschweig-Wolfenbüttel und seiner leitenden Montan- und Finanzbeamten, in Angelika Westermann and Ekkehard Westermann, eds *Wirtschaftslenkende Montanverwaltung – fürstlicher Unternehmer – Merkantilismus Zusammenhänge zwischen der Ausbildung einer fachkompetenten Beamtenschaft und der staatlichen Geld- und Wirtschaftspolitik in der Frühen Neuzeit* (Husum: Mathiesen, 2009), 195–226, as well as the other contributions to the volume.

65 Rössner, *Deflation – Devaluation – Rebellion*, esp. ch. IV.

Mountains provided, in the words of Georg Agricola, one of the leading authors in scientific mineralogy of his age, alongside agriculture the most important branch of domestic production. After the Thirty Years War, a policy of promoting growth and development was implemented on the level of the Holy Roman Empire (*Reichsmerkantilismus*). The abolition of internal tolls and customs duties, some price regulation on markets, the promotion of infrastructural improvement and currency standardization (monetary integration), industrial legislation, as well as the protectionist measures after 1675–76 – with the imperial edict towards prohibiting French imports in 1676 (here Hörnigk was involved) – was said to have constituted an imperial programme or strategy towards growth and development (Blaich).[66] Indigo – the Devil's plant, as it was labelled in early modern German usage (as it was bound to destroy the economic basis of the woad-producing regional economies, especially in the Central German/Saxon territories) – was finally admitted by imperial decree into the productive landscape of the German economies in 1671. This was after a bitter struggle fought about the matter since mid-sixteenth century, especially as this directly harmed the economic interests of the woad-producing economies such as Saxony (for which Indigo was a direct substitute, but it was more effective and cheaper for colouring than woad).[67] Luxury debates were resumed in 1666, after sumptuary legislation had been part of the 1548 and 1577 Imperial Policy Edicts (with no practical effect in terms of limiting the import of luxury manufactures). They are a major feature in Hörnigk's text. Luxury imports put a drain on the balance of payment, which would have a direct impact on monetary policy, as the majority of circulating monies were made of/based upon silver those days. Moreover, it was said that being overburdened with payments for luxury was a main reason for the many bankruptcies among contemporary businessmen, tradesmen and entrepreneurs (which is, of course, difficult to verify). Finally, too much money and thus productive capital left the German-speaking economies for imports of chiefly French manufactures, thus also jeopardizing the competitive position of German manufacturing industry – one of the main points of departure in Hörnigk's *Oesterreich über alles*.[68]

That these measures may not have been as effective as intended or may have failed to unfold the productive potential of the German Economies is less a fault of these legislations than the political, cultural, legal and geographical structure of the Empire. Formally organized as a sort of confederation of about three hundred independent territorial states and an ever-changing number of semi-independent political subjects and entities enjoying state-like status (for example, imperial knights) which are sometimes said to have reached into the hundreds if not thousands, it is obvious that 'Imperial Mercantilism' and its success was dependent upon the extent and degree of translation into practice at the individual territorial or state level. However, recent research has begun to rehabilitate the Holy Roman Empire as something that may have worked better than usually thought. The 'Empire' was a level of policy reasoning manifest before the

---

66 Blaich, *Wirtschaftspolitik des Reichstags*, 183–213; Bog, *Reichsmerkantilismus*, passim.

67 Blaich, *Wirtschaftspolitik des Reichstags*, 214–16; most recently Timmermann, *Indigo*.

68 Blaich, *Wirtschaftspolitik des Reichstags*, 208–14.

eyes of contemporary politicians and regents; and while not every protective measure may have been completely enforceable, it is important to realize that people genuinely *believed* in the virtues and necessity of negotiating these legislative measures and policies. These measures were part of the politico-cultural mind map or 'discourse', to use a more modern term, towards the end of the seventeenth century. And there is every reason to believe that they laid the foundations for later theories and trajectories of state-supported industrial development, as witnessed in England post-1688, in Prussia, France, Sweden, Austria and many other countries after the early 1800s.[69]

Most of the practical or applied political economy, however, took place on the level of the individual or territorial state. It has been said that Austria's growing wealth after 1700 would have been a direct consequence of the 'Hörnigk strategy' turned into practice; the protective economic legislation under Leopold I (1640–1705), Charles VI (r. 1711–1740) but especially Maria Theresia (1717–1780) seem to resemble closely the wording to be found in Hörnigk's work.[70] According to Otruba, the 'foundations of Austrian economic policy were based on a crude or improvised Mercantilism found in the old works by Becher Hörnigk and Schröder, updated in the light of the more recent developments in Cameralist economics and theory a la Justi and Sonnenfels.'[71] Especially the 1740–90 period seems to have been a period of prosperity and economic success and the transformation from an economy in crisis – the early 1740s saw a pan-European harvest crisis; furthermore Frederick the Great annexed Silesia, one of the more powerful industrial economies of the time, from Austria – into an early industrial economy that was performing relatively well, according to the sparse quantitative evidence that we have. The main goals of economic policy at the time were, in a nutshell, (a) to raise industrial productivity and output; to (b) increase competitiveness (exports), as well as (c) abolish local privileges and monopolies, especially of the guilds (labour market, output restrictions on industrial production), thus attempting to (d) create an integrated national economy – and, most importantly, a market that classified as comparatively free and as competitive as possible given the circumstances of the time. Measures included the encouragement of technological transfer and cultural emulation, not only from neighbouring Germanic states such as Prussia, Bavaria and Saxony; the regulation of industrial production, especially by the establishment of quality controls and the curbing of guild powers; promoting domestic key and high value-added industries such as iron smelting and cloth manufacture (especially silk and cotton); a pro-active commercial and fiscal policy directed at the generation of a positive balance of payments and so on – that

---

69 Magnusson, *Nation, State and Industrial Revolution*.

70 H. J. Bidermann, *Die technische bildung im Kaiserthume Oesterreich. Ein Beitrag zur Geschichte der Industrie und des Handels* … (Vienna: C. Gerold und Sohn, 1854), 26 cited after Otruba, ed. *Österreich über alles*, 33.

71 Gustav Otruba, *Die Wirtschaftspolitik Maria Theresias* (Vienna: Bergland Verlag, 1963), 29: 'Die Grundsätze der Maria-theresianischen Wirtschaftspolitik bestanden in einer mehr oder minder improvisierten Anwendung der merkantilistischen Theorien eines Becher, Hörnigk und Schröder, allerdings in stark modifizierter Form des modernen Kameralismus eines Justi und Sonnenfels.'

is, nothing less than the standard Cameralist toolkit designed for creating a competitive domestic free market economy.[72] The main problems of the domestic productive landscape were a lack of capital (investment) as well as demand, as the market was too limited to allow high-powered, large-scale industry. Obviously, the problem was one of synergy – only a larger, integrated national economy would provide the demand and thus sources for investment necessary to build up a more capital-intensive and larger-scale domestic industry; and only a high-powered capital-intensive industry would produce goods that would fetch a large market. So the creation of a national economy – a *Volkswirtschaft* – stood at the heart of Austria's economic problems.

Sometimes it has been said that post-1780 policy under Emperor Joseph II would have been informed by a Physiocratic model, with an emphasis on the abolition of guild monopolies and other prerogatives, tax privileges, feudalism and other barriers to market entry.[73] But if we study the Cameralist texts carefully, especially Justi's *Staatswirthschaft*, but also Becher's *Politischer Discurs* (1668) and Hörnigk's *Oesterreich über alles*, we can see immediately that these points also represented the cornerstone of High Mercantilism and Cameralist economics. There was nothing peculiarly 'Physiocrat' nor 'Mercantilist' about them. This was just common sense – good economics so to speak. The promotion of industry, chiefly the protection and granting of privileges to manufactories, set in during the second half of the seventeenth century. But Sandgruber's dictum that the Mercantilists' eyes were focused on the luxury industries[74] is somewhat misleading and at variance with the modern evidence, not least the strategy laid out by Philipp Wilhelm von Hörnigk. We find a *Commerzcollegium*, a government agency or board concerned with monitoring and raising industrial prowess, as early as 1666 (it existed until 1678). Presumably it had been initiated by Johann Joachim Becher, modelled upon the French example of the *Conseil de Commerce* established by Jean Baptiste Colbert in 1664.[75] Lack of staff, financial resources (both problems were connected), the character of such offices as sinecures, as well as the lack of executive powers of such board members usually acted against these initiatives which, on paper – and from the viewpoint of economic reason and theory – looked rather promising. The war campaigns against the Turks brought an end to them, somewhat disrupting a pattern of 'good' industrial policy. Under Charles VI, *Kommerzräte*

---

72 Basic works on Austrian economic and industrial policy include Otruba, *Wirtschaftspolitik Maria Theresias*; Karl Pribram, *Geschichte der österreichischen Gewerbepolitik von 1740 bis 1860: auf Grund der Akten*, Vol. 1, *1740–1798* (Leipzig: Duncker & Humblot, 1907); Freudenberger, *Lost Momentum*, esp. 61–130; Bernhard Hackl, 'Die staatliche Wirtschaftspolitik zwischen 1740 und 1792: Reform versus Stagnation', in Helmut Reinalter, ed. *Josephinismus als Augeklärter Absolutismus* (Vienna, Cologne and Weimar: Böhlau, 2008), 191–272; and Komlos, *Ernährung und wirtschaftliche Entwicklung*, ch. III. Hackl's dictum that Mercantilist economic policy would have resembled a 'planwirtschaftliches Modell' for which the economic freedom of the individual was 'sacrificed' is entirely at variance with the historical facts and the more recent literature, empirical as well as theoretical.

73 As stated by Hackl, 'Die Staatliche Wirtschaftspolitik', 194.

74 Sandgruber, 'Österreich 1650–1850', 668.

75 Hackl, 'Die Staatliche Wirtschaftspolitik', 198.

were founded for several countries; a *Hauptkommerzkollegium* was established in Vienna in 1717–18, after a similar institution had been in place for the Bohemian lands since 1710–14. The *Hauptkommerzkollegium* was the superordinate agency for the subsidiary boards and institutions (*Länderbehörden*) of the component parts of the Austrian monarchy, such as Bohemia and Silesia.[76] The impetus of these policies seems to have lost its drive in the 1730s.

In the 1740s, renewed efforts at promoting domestic industry were put in place.[77] The main problem was, in the perception of the contemporaries, the territorial and institutional (and thus economic) fragmentation of the Austrian possessions. Economic and industrial policy had been seen as the affairs of the *Länder*; but what prevented the high-end manufacturing branches, especially in the textile sector, from taking off was the lack of an integrated market and a unified national economy. In 1746, the *Universal-Commerzdirektorium* was created, made up from members of the Vienna Hofkammer, the Hungarian, Bohemian and Austrian Court Chamber. But as this institution lacked much staff and infrastructure, it is said to have remained a mere 'think tank' (*Planungsbehörde*). This board was especially concerned with textiles, silk and iron manufacture, as well as commerce and transport infrastructure. The board was re-constituted in 1749 as the *Commercien-Ober-Direktorium*. It remained in place as a centralized agency into the 1750s, with regular correspondence and coordination with its counterparts in the Austrian Netherlands, the Italian and Hungarian branches of administration. The administrative separation between *Kommerzialgewerbe* (producing for distant markets, especially textiles, metal works) and *Polizeygewerbe* (producing for local markets; mostly foodstuffs, tailors, carpenters etc.) was important – the former were to be left much more deregulated and free of guild power and other restrictions to output and entrepreneurship than the latter.[78] In 1768, the *Staatswirthschafts*-Deputation was founded, with similar responsibilities especially relating to the monitoring of industrial and agrarian production, as well as demographic management. According to some scholars, this did not lead to a modernization of Austrian economic policy since a 'Mercantilist' outlook was retained. But that, of course, hinges upon the definition of both what we mean when we speak about 'modernization' and 'Mercantilism', and whether the introduction of Physiocracy in economic policy really represented a process of modernization or rather a change in economic outlook. The two should be strictly separated; in many ways Physiocracy was more a fashion thing than anything else. Justi would have called it a 'Chimera', a new discourse, while most of the underlying ideas, especially relating to 'free' markets, good economics and market governance that had been existent for ages, did not change much. In many other European states, more 'Physiocratic' policies were adopted in the wake of the Seven Years War; policies that were focused, mostly, upon a gradual liberalization of agriculture and food markets.[79]

76 Ibid., 199.
77 Ibid., esp. 200ff.
78 Sandgruber, 'Österreich 1650–1850', 666.
79 Most recently the contributions in S. Reinert and Røge, eds *The Political Economy of Empire*.

Since the mid-1740s, the so-called *Kommerzkonsesse* were founded (1749 in Styria and Lower Austria; 1752, in Bohemia, Moravia and Upper Austria; 1757, in Inner Austria and Vorarlberg; 1763 in Tyrol). Their function was to coordinate government activities addressed at raising industrial productivity and promoting local and regional entrepreneurship. This included production licenses for new masters and entrepreneurs; the organization and procurement of raw materials, quality supervision, as well as the monitoring of industrial production by compiling and using output statistics. Infrastructural processes such as hydraulic engineering directed at improving Austria's traffic and transport system were also actively encouraged.[80] The *Konsesse* usually consisted of several princely administrators (*Landesfürstliche Räte*) as well as at least two native, private entrepreneurs.[81] We may perhaps compare them with the *Board of Trustees* in Scotland, or practices in France under Colbert, and again find that such processes were, at the time, quite common, especially in the more backward or 'catching-up economies' of Europe.[82]

We find an increasing trend towards liberalization, a gradual curbing of guild monopolies and powers since the 1760s and 1770s in Austria, especially for those production branches that catered to foreign markets. If shoemakers produced for export mainly, they were allowed to have more than the prescribed maximum number of journeymen and apprentices, as an edict of 1771 under Maria Theresia addressed at Vienna shoemakers said.[83] From the 1720s, we find an increasing level of support by the state for artisans and craftsmen intending to set up and pursue business outside the guilds' umbrellas via protective decrees (*Schutzdekrete*). Industrial statistics (*Manufakturtabellen*) were compiled from 1749. In 1762, inspectors for the manufactories were created in Bohemia.[84] In 1753, Maria Theresia prescribed that the *Ungarische Hofkanzlei* and the Vienna *Hofkammer* were to meet weekly so as to monitor the performance of the Hungarian economy, especially as a source of taxation (with the aim to reduce the debt by the Royal Free Cities). From 1762 we find first national-level statistics for the composite monarchy in the Hörnigkian spirit, first of livestock. From 1789 onwards, detailed statistics are available on grain output, with up to 24 types recorded, including legumes, fruits, forage crops and vegetables used in industrial processes, mainly sugar beet, hops and tobacco. Statistics from that date were also produced for the fisheries, silviculture and forestry, including game hunting.[85] Industrial output statistics were produced from 1841, but they are incomplete. The first and only complete industrial census was taken in 1902.[86]

---

80 See, e.g., Nikola Petrović, *Die Schiffahrt und Wirtschaft im mittleren Donauraum in der Zeit des Merkantilismus: der Bau des Donau-Theiss-, des Franzens-Kanals und die Bestrebungen gegen Ende des XVIII. Jahrhunderts, den mittleren Donauraum mit dem Adriatischen Meer zu verbinden* (Belgrade: Institute für Geschichte; Novi Sad: Akademie der Wissenschaften und Künste der Wojwodina, 1982).

81 Hackl, 'Die Staatliche Wirtschaftspolitik', 205.

82 See no. 83.

83 *Österreichische Industriegeschichte* I, 56–57.

84 Herbert Knittler, 'Die Donaumonarchie 1648–1848', in Fischer et al., eds *Handbuch*, 880–915, (907).

85 Roman Sandgruber, 'Wirtschafts- und Sozialstatistik Österreichs 1750–1918', *Vierteljahrschrift für Sozial- und Wirtschaftsgeschichte*, 64, no. 1 (1977), 74–83, (77–78, 81).

86 Ibid., 81.

Under Maria Theresia, there also occurred a lessening of restrictions on the agrarian economy, which, according to Voth

> improved the legal position of tenants and reduced their labor obligations (Robot). [...] The second, which fostered the growth of the bureaucracy, allowed the data necessary for effective policy measures to be collected for the first time and censuses to be conducted at regular intervals [...]. The third element promoted direct state intervention in the economy to subsidize new enterprises, limit the power of the guilds, and import skilled laborers.[87]

Voth has speculated that the reduction of holy days (by about 24) between 1750 and 1770 and the concomitant increase in labour input may have amounted to about 18 per cent.[88] This would, according to Voth, have increased claims on energy intakes and thus may have reduced heights, without leading to a decrease in well-being as an earlier hypothesis advanced by Komlos had it.[89] People worked longer because they desired to do so, in order to interact more closely with the market economy and increase their consumption of goods.[90]

After 1765–68, domestic trade and sales in victuals were liberalized,[91] followed by similar edicts in 1783 for timber, and 1790–91 (for grain). The focus of government policy since the 1750s had increasingly switched towards productivity-enhancing strategies, ranging from agricultural melioration (introduction of clover, potatoes, reduction of fallow, fertilizers); the curbing of *rinderpest* as well as the number of sparrows haunting farmers (quota of killed sparrows for every household); a rise of private property and reduction of large noble units of production; drainage of swamps; up to the clearing of woodlands. In Bohemia, the *Kommerzienkonsess* debated whether or not journeymen should be allowed to continue the traditional pattern of peregrination, the common requirement on the way to become a fully accredited master incorporated in a guild. It concluded that peregrination should be retained in all industrial manufacturing branches bar glass making, as it was only in the latter that Bohemian producers had built up a comparative advantage that would allow for the product to be exported. All other branches, especially linen weaving and leather

---

87 Voth, 'Height, Nutrition, and Labor', 629–30.

88 Ibid., 630; Ibid., 'Physical Exertion and Stature in the Habsburg Monarchy, 1730–1800', *The Journal of Interdisciplinary History*, vol. 27, no. 2 (Autumn, 1996), 263–75, (273). Critical response to this in John Komlos, Markus Heintel, 'The Threat of a Malthusian Crisis in the Habsburg Monarchy', *The Journal of Interdisciplinary History*, vol. 30, no. 1 (Summer, 1999), 91–98.

89 John Komlos, *Nutrition and Economic Development in Eighteenth-Century Habsburg Monarchy. An Anthropometric History* (Princeton, NJ: Princeton University Press, 1989).

90 Voth, 'Height, Nutrition, and Labor', 636.

91 Roman Sandgruber, 'Marktökonomie und Agrarrevolution. Anfänge und Gegenkräfte der Kommerzialisierung der österreichischen Landwirtschaft', in Anna Maria Drabek, Richard Georg Plaschka and Adam Wandruszka, eds *Ungarn und Österreich unter Maria Theresia und Joseph II: neue Aspekte im Verhältnis der beiden Länder. Texte des 2. Österreichisch-Ungarischen Historikertreffens* (Vienna: Verlag der Österreichischen Akademie der Wissenschaft, 1982), 131–45, (131–32).

making were, as yet, too far below the international standard marked, for instance, by the Dutch.[92] So Austrians had to continue wandering about, learning and emulating, studying foreign practices.

The processes of economic liberalization after the 1750s were, indeed, a European phenomenon. They can be found at work literally anywhere, be that England, Scotland, Saxony or France. Especially, the losers of the Seven Years War perceived the need for economic reform and the benefit of lessening the tight grip of the feudal economy. In Austria, such measures extended, for instance, to the *Vorkaufsrecht* (preemptory purchase or drawing rights) of the manorial lords for the products of their subjects or the *Mühlenzwang*. The hunger crisis of 1770 further promoted liberal ideas in the economic discourse of the day, as elsewhere across Europe.[93] Scholars have stated that the level of market integration increased in Austria towards the last decades of the eighteenth century.[94] The idea was to increase competition and market participation, thus increasing efficiency in agriculture. This expansion and increasing integration of markets may have made itself felt in the decline in living standards (as societies where a major share of output is marked locally, when markets are weakly integrated, apparently have a higher level of nutritional intake per person in the countryside, where the agrarian products originate),[95] as measured in terms of reduced height on the eve of the factory age. But, if contemporary reports are credible, increasing prices for agrarian products in the last quarter of the eighteenth century made peasants rich and sloth and overindulgent in the consumption of eggs and meat, which in earlier times they would have brought to the market.[96]

Did the 'Hörnigk Strategy' Make Austria Rich?

How successful was Austrian economic policy in the Baroque period and the era of Maria Theresa? Answers remain difficult, not least because no reliable statistical material exists – excluding the (in)famous Maddison database, which is constantly being updated by new findings on select European countries, often for benchmark years different from the original Maddison file, compounding any reliable comparisons of economic development and national income figures for European states before 1800 (after which the data becomes much better). Assessments of Austria's economic performance, therefore, need to remain mixed, to say the least. Eminent economic historian Wilhelm Treue called Austrian Mercantilism 'undecided', 'shapeless' and 'amorphous', without *telos* or goal.

---

92 Reinhold Reith, 'Arbeitsmigration und Technologietransfer in der Habsburgermonarchie in der zweiten Hälfte des 18. Jahrhunderts', in Ulrich Troitzsch, ed. *"Nützliche Künste". Kultur- und Sozialgeschichte der Technik im 18. Jahrhundert* (Münster etc.: Waxmann, 1999), 51–65; (61); reprint of an article that also appeared in the *Blätter für Technikgeschichte* 56 (1994), 9–33.

93 Rothschild, *Economic Sentiments*.

94 Sandgruber, 'Marktökonomie und Agrarrevolution', 140.

95 See, e.g., John Komlos, 'Modernes ökonomisches Wachstum und biologischer Lebensstandard', in *Anthropologischer Anzeiger*, 58, no. 4 (Dezember 2000), 357–66.

96 Sandgruber, 'Marktökonomie und Agrarrevolution', 132–34.

But that assessment would have to include other Mercantilist economic policies of the day, as well; perhaps even England and Scotland.

Other accounts have painted a more favourable picture. Butschek, for instance, saw moderate growth in the Austrian economy until the 1770s and some more visible development thereafter. He called the measures of industrial policy and protectionism since the later seventeenth century, but especially under Maria Theresia, highly successful, especially by the institutional reforms designed for 'unifying' the Austrian economy (or rather economies). The introduction of a comprehensive school system promoted education, cultural techniques and economically useful skills (or 'useful knowledge', to borrow a famous term from Joel Mokyr).[97] Some select – or shall we say, stray – output and other economic index figures suggest a rapid catch-up in key branches, such as the eightfold increase in manufacturing employment in Lower Austria from about 20,000 (1760) to 182,000 (1790), the rise of iron production figures, for the same period and for the entire monarchy by 50 per cent – at a time when population figures were almost stagnant. Agricultural yields literally exploded in Upper Austria between 1770 and 1790 (by 77 per cent) and rose, in the other provinces, between 12 and 25 per cent (except Vorarlberg and Tyrol, where they declined); agrarian output continued to rise at regionally different rates between 30 and 100 per cent, between 1789 and the 1830s. An increasing share of raw cotton imports, as well as iron and cloth manufactures on Austria's export balance sheet, led to a gradual transformation or 'industrialization' of Austria's trade balance towards the later decades of the eighteenth century.[98]

We must be careful not to conflate an increase in economic activity with decisive changes in per capita income. Here, Sandgruber has painted a rather gloomy picture. According to his calculations, nominal wages remained stagnant and real wages, expressed as the purchasing power of wages in terms of grain and meat products, even declined in Austria proper throughout the entire eighteenth century (1700–1790). Only after 1790 was there a very modest increase in nominal (day) wages. Since day wages don't tell us about the actual wage bill in terms of size and composition, with labour only reflecting one among several inputs in gross domestic product (alongside capital and knowledge), it is impossible to derive from this evidence statements as to the development of Austria's gross domestic product per capita.[99] In fact, Sandgruber's data tie in with Komlos' findings on nutritional intake (see earlier in the chapter), but are by no

97 Felix Butschek, *Österreichische Wirtschaftsgeschichte. Von der Antike bis zur Gegenwart*, 2nd ed. (Vienna, Cologne and Weimar: Böhlau, 2012), 90–94.

98 Ibid., 87–88, Tables 11, 13.

99 Roman Sandgruber, 'Einkommensentwicklung und Einkommensverteilung in der zweiten Hälfte des 18. Jahrhunderts – einige Quellen und Anhaltspunkte', in Richard Georg Plaschka / Österreichisches Bundesministerium für Wissenschaft und Forschung, eds *Österreich im Europa der Aufklärung. Kontinuität und Zäsur in Europa zur Zeit Maria Theresias und Josephs II. Internationales Symposion in Wien 20.-23. Oktober 1980* (Vienna: Österreichische Akademie der Wissenschaften, 1985), 251–63, (263). That rising total rewards to labour (i.e., wage bill and total consumption expenditure) may well be reconcilable with declining real or day wages, if total labour input increases more than real wage decline, setting off 'early capitalistic' transformation processes, has been masterfully demonstrated in De Vries, *Industrious Revolution*.

means unusual for the European economy on the eve of industrialization. In fact, Austria seems, on balance, to have performed at least as well as the European average, except England and the Netherlands – possibly even slightly better. As Matis and Sandgruber, two distinguished economic historians of Austria in the early modern period, conclude in a preface to a study entitled 'Lost Momentum':

> At the watershed of the late 18th century, under the reign of Maria Theresa and her son Joseph II, Austria's economic development accelerated at a remarkable rate of growth. The speeding-up process was driven by structural and organizational reforms since the end of the Prussian war. They should partly compensate the loss of the richest province Silesia. For a European Great power it seemed quite inevitable to introduce an institutional modernization process as a pre-requisite for a modern market economy. Contemporaries felt that Hörnigks's famous patriotic tract of 1684 now had a more realistic chance to become true than ever before. Freudenberger (i.e. the basic study referred to in this introduction, PRR) identifies entrepreneurship as the single most important element of this momentum: Industrialization was promoted by foreign wholesalers, bankers and investors, by noble landlords and by capable managers.[100]

But during the 1810s and 1820s, this economic upswing was nipped in the bud and growth was stalled. Nevertheless, it seems as though, based on the original Maddison figures (which reflected the state-of-the-art until 2008), as well as most of the available corroborative evidence, Austria as Hörnigk would see it – that is, the Hereditary Lands – would have caught up and possibly even slightly surpassed the average national income of western Europe by the 1740s or 1770s at the very latest. Obviously, there was still a large income gap between Austria and the high-fliers, represented by the Netherlands as the richest (until the 1820s), and England as the second-richest (and after 1820, the richest) and most developed or 'modern' economies of their age.[101] Whether or to what extent this development was due to a successful application of the Hörnigk strategy is a different question – and likewise nearly impossible to solve or 'prove' in exact quantitative terms. But all the evidence presented in the preceding sections suggests that the 'Hörnigk Strategy' did make a great contribution to Austrian economic development in the long run.

The question is furthermore whether there has always been a unified economic policy paradigm in European history. Economic policy usually is, as with other branches of policy-making, the result of constant negotiating, re-negotiating and balancing interests among actors competing for political and economic resources and private benefits. Very often, 'national' economic interests coincide more or less fully with private interests of rent-seeking (the positive scenario); sometimes private interests of powerful economic actors are camouflaged as representing those of the 'Common Weal'. When balancing individual interests and national development, maximizing the latter without either suffocating private entrepreneurship, or subscribing to the interest of the individual's 'free

---

100 Freudenberger, *Lost Momentum*, 8.
101 Ibid.

enterprise' as the prime goal of economic development (a modern invention that easily creates rent seeking at the expense of the community, if the state completely withdraws from the economy) is the main challenge for successful economic policy and development. Those mechanisms and dynamics were tested in the pre-industrial landscape of early modern Europe.

Basic challenges included aspects that were to be found in other countries of the time as well and that were based on the different economic structures of the Austrian provinces, regions and countries that made up a very mixed economy that was never as 'Austrian' as Maria Theresia and other rulers would have intended. Creating a 'national' economy proved, under these circumstances, nearly impossible. Promoting domestic industry under the Mercantilist paradigm included measures such as prohibiting the importation of Italian wines – which ran counter to the interests of Carinthia (through which a considerable share of Austrian iron exports went), leading to an import boycott (in Italian cities) of Austrian iron products via Senigallia in retaliation. A general ban on imported silk in 1756 led to mirroring retaliation on imported Austrian manufactures in neighbouring states, such as Prussia, Bavaria or Saxony. It did not necessarily help that most of her neighbours to the north were member states in the Holy Roman Empire, as the Austrian Hereditary Lands were, which allowed formal litigation before the Imperial Chamber Court (as in the case of Austria against Bavaria in the tariff dispute of 1771). Sometimes the standardization of the tariff for all Austrian lands and provinces led to complaints between individual provinces, reflecting once again that concepts and discourses on competitiveness unfolded, not on the national, but, regional level. When it was decreed that Hungarian imports must be routed through the Austrian lands – rather than, as previously common, the large international trading fairs of Leipzig and Breslau – there were Prussian retaliatory tariffs on Hungarian wines, paper and iron manufactures, which were damaging to the Hungarian economy. And so on.[102] As in the case of France in the age of Colbert – where the agrarian, wine-exporting provinces favoured 'free' trade and moderate or no import duties and the manufacturing provinces advocated domestic industrial protection and a high tariff on imported manufactures (mostly cloth from England) – it was difficult to integrate the economic interests of provinces and lands that were, in terms of economic structure and stage of development, very different.[103]

The evidence assembled so far confirms that a gradual economic transition had taken place, visible in Austria's improved economic position as early as 1700. To what extent this was due to 'good policy' must, for the reasons given above, remain ambiguous. But what is clear and unambiguous is the sheer scale of acts, documents, reports and other written sources, documenting, since the later seventeenth century, an increasing awareness of government and its role in the economic process. Whether or not those economic and industrial policies were successful is hard to determine. How are we to define 'success'? How are we to measure and establish the productivity record of industry in the pre-modern world that was dispersed, often across the countryside, intermingling with other

---

102 Otruba, *Die Wirtschaftspolitik Maria Theresias*, 142–46.
103 On France under Colbert, see Isenmann, 'From Privilege to Economic Law'.

types of activity throughout the agrarian working year, with a lack of even remotely reliable industrial statistics and similar census material? Then, of course, government papers and acts usually originated in the circumstances when things went wrong, when problems arose. 'Normal' conditions (or business as usual) do not normally find much resonance in government documents. What is obvious, especially from the post-1740 record, but also much earlier, and not only in the Austrian lands, but also in Prussia, Saxony, Scotland, and England, at least since the 1720s, is an increased attention paid by governments to problems of industrial performance and raising industrial productivity. That is, governments developed and sharpened their conceptual understanding of what would become known as 'economic policy', especially why it was important to support domestic manufacturing and industry. Whether these measures were immediately successful *in situ*, or with time lags of a few years or decades, does not matter. What matters is that European governments built up, from the seventeenth century, an increasingly sophisticated apparatus of monitoring and steering techniques directed at industrial improvement. And it is also clear that these strategies greatly facilitated Europe's transition towards industrialization and the emerging Great Divergence or global inequality between Europe and the rest of the world after 1800. Hörnigk's text represents a foundational stone of this development in modern political economy.

Appendix

THE KNOWN PUBLICATION RECORD OF HÖRNIGK'S BOOK

Kenneth Carpenter, formerly Kress Librarian at
Harvard University

HÖRNIGK, PHILIPP WILHELM VON, 1638–1712

This book is unusual in that there were so many editions in German, but no translation. One need look no further than the title to ascertain the reason.

Gustava Otruba's list, in his [1964] edition of the text, derives from K. Th. von Inama-Sternegg, 'Über Philipp Wilhelm v. Hornick', in *Jahrbücher für Nationalökonomie und Statistik* NF II (1881), 194–200; and H. Gerstenberg, 'Philipp Wilhelm v. Hörnigk', in *Jahrbücher für Nationalökonomie und Statistik*, III. Folge, Vol. 78 (1930), 813–71. Otruba and other writers on this work have not provided locations for some 'editions' and, indeed, some are exceedingly rare.

It is worthy of note that there were two 1784 piracies of the Berlin, 1784, edition. No. 17 is clearly Viennese, and it is possible that no. 18 is also Viennese, perhaps published by Trattner.

1. German edition, 1684.

Oesterreich uber alles wann es nur will. Das ist: wohlmeinender Fürschlag wie mittelst einer wolbestellten Lands-Oeconomie, die Kayserl. Erbland in kurzem über alle andere Staat von Europa zu erheben / und mehr als einiger derselben / von denen andern Independent zu machen. Durch einen Liebhaber der Kayserl. Erbland Wolfahrt.

[Nürnberg?] Gedruckt im Jahr Christi 1684.

π⁴ A-M¹² N⁸ ($7; – G6); [viii], 303 p.

i title; ii blank; iii-viii *Verzeichniss der Abtheilungen*; 1–303 text

L7 missigned L5; p. 206 mispaged 106, and p. 270 mispaged 370.

According to the preface to the 1708 edition, the printer was Johann Hoffmann, who brought it out in the summer of 1684.

Oesterreich

Uber alles
wann es nur will.

Das ist:
wohlmeinender

Fürschlag

Wie mittelst einer wol-
bestellten Lands - Oeconomie, die Kayserl. Erbland in kurzem über alle andere Staat von Europa zu erheben / und mehr als einiger
derselben/ von denen andern Independent zu ma-
chen.

Durch einen Liebhaber
der Kayserl. Erbland
Wolfahrt.

Gedruckt im Jahr Christi
1 6 8 4.

VD17 23:307898G, with fingerprint: 18ss k:I. usie nokai 3 1684A (BSB, Wolfenbüttel, Gotha); VD17 gives his name as Hörnigk.

MH-BA* KBD (two copies, one with early underlining and marginalia) Columbia* Stanford* This title page is reproduced on Wikimedia Commons. UB Salzburg

2.   German edition, [n.d., 1684?]

Otruba notes an edition without place of publication (1684?) with the title-page statement: "zum andern mal auffgelegt."

This may be the edition referred to in the preface to the 1708 edition as having been brought out in the fall by Johann Hoffmann of Nürnberg.

Not located. Not recorded in VD17.

3.   Oesterreich über alles wann es nur will. Das ist: wohlmeinender Fürschlag Wie mittelst einer wolbestellten Lands-Oeconomie, die Kayserliche Erbland in kurzen über alle andere Staat von Europa zu erheben … Durch einen Liebhaber der Kayserlichen Erbländ Wolfahrt.

[n.p.], 1685.

[8], 303 p.; 12°.

[i] title; [ii] Pro captu Lectoris habent sua fata Libelli; [iii-viii] Verzeichnus der Abtheilungen; 1–303 text

Published in Passau according to Otruba.

VD17 3:604208K, with fingerprint: 18ss k:I. usie noka 3 1684B (BSB, Göttingen, Halle, Dresden) A copy is also recorded in in BL(1388.a.30)* Title page downloaded from BSB, with my agreement that the copy is not for commercial use.

4.   German edition, 1705.

Oesterreich über alles, wann es nur will. Das ist: Wohlmeinender fürschlag, wie mittelst einer wohlbestellten lands-oeconomie, die kayserlichen erb-land in kurtzem über alle andere staat von Europa zu erheben, und mehr als einiger derselben, von denen andern independent zu machen.

[n.p.] 1705.

[12], 342 p.

Humpert records a Leipzig, 1705, edition, but without providing a location.

Minnesota* (written on 2/20/15) UB Graz (12° I 26019)

5.   German edition, 1707.

'Oesterreich über alles/ wann es nur will'. Das ist: Wohlmeynender Fürschlag/ wie mittelst einer wolbestellten Lands-Oeconomie, die Käyserlichen Erblande in kurtzem über alle andere Staate von Europa zu erheben/ und mehr als einiger derselben/ von denen andern independent zu machen. Durch W. F. V. S.

Oesterreich

Uber alles
wann es nur will.
Das ist:
wohlmeinender

Vurschlag

Wie mittelst einer wol-
bestellten Lands - Oeconomie,
die Kayserliche Erbland in kurzem
über alle andere Staat von Europa
zu erheben / und mehr als einiger
derselben / von denen andern Independent zu machen.

Durch einen Liebhaber der
Kayserlichen Erbland
Wolfahrt.

Gedruckt im Jahr Christi
1685.

Oesterreich
über alles/
wann es nur will.

Das ist:

Wohlmeynender

Fürschlag/

Wie mittelst einer wohlbestellten
Lands-Oeconomie, die Käyserlichen Erb-
Lande in kurtzem über alle andere Staate von
Europa zu erheben/ und mehr als einiger dersel-
ben/ von denen andern independent
zu machen.

durch

W. F. V. S.

Leipzig/
bey Thomas Fritschen. 1707.

Leipzig / bey Thomas Fritschen. 1707.

)(⁴ A-O⁸ P-Q⁴; [8], 244 p.

i title; ii blank; iii-viii Verzeichniss der Abtheilungen; 1–235 text; 235–244 Anhang oder Unvorgreiffliches project, zu stellung einer armee von hundert tausend mann aus den Käyserl. erb-ländern

Pp. 112–115 are omitted in pagination.

The Anhang appeared in this edition for the first time; it was included in subsequent editions.

Otruba, referring to the preface to the 1708 ed., says that this one was soon withdrawn.

Houghton (from the Stolberg Library, with many underlinings by an early reader) KBD

6.   German edition, 1708.

'Oesterreich über alles/ wann es nur will'. Das ist: Wohlmeinender Fürschlag/ wie mittelst einer wolbestellten Lands-Oeconomie, die Kayserlichen Erblande in kurtzem über alle andere Staate von Europa zu erheben/ und mehr als einiger derselben/ von denen andern independent zu machen. P. W. v. H.

Regensburg/ Verlegts Joh. Zacharias Seidel/ 1708.

):(⁶ A-N⁸ (-N8) ($5); [xii], 206 p. The first gathering consists of 2 inserted leaves, the second signed):(2; leaves 3–6 are conjugate, with 3 unsigned, 4 and 5 appropriately signed)

i title; ii blank; iii-vi Gönstiger Leser; vii-xii Verzeichniss der Abtheilungen; 1–198 text; 198–206 Anhang/ oder Unvorgreiffliches Project, zu Stellung einer Armee von hundert tausend Mañ auss den Käyserl. Erbländern

p. 64 mispaged 46.

Gönstiger Leser reads:

Dieses Wercklein hat Anno 1684. im Sommer zum ersten/ und im nechsten Herbst darauff zum andern mahl zu Nürnberg durch Herrn Johann Hoffmann/ Buchführen/ das Tage-Licht gesehen. Seine erste Erziehlung war zu Dressden/ von einer selbigen Orts ausheimischen Feder. Ein hoher/ allda gleichfals nicht einheimischer Minister, liesse ihm/ um seiner Auffrichtigkeit und Wohlmeinung willen/ die Gnad seiner Protection wiederfahren. Es hatte damahls den Nahmen seines Erzeugers nicht auffgedruckt. Dannenhero als Herr Thomas Fritsch zu Leipzig es verwichenen Frühling abermahl auffzulegen Sinnes worden/ bewarbe er sich guter Intention, denselben in Erfahrung zu bringen. Als ihm aber der Zufall darinnen nicht fügen wolte/ indem so gar auch des ersten Verlegers Erben keinen Bescheid mehr davon geben konten: wurde er durch einige Vermuthung auf einen unrechten geleitet/ unter dessen ersten Nahmens-Buchstaben auch/ ein gute Parthey Exemplarien gleich Anfangs fortgangen. Gleichwie aber dem Irrthum nach der Hand/ auff bessern Bericht/ von ihm gantz willig/ so viel annoch seyn könten remedirt worden: also wird solchem in dieser vierdten Edition nachgegangen/ indeme doch sowohl der hohe Protector, als der Autor an einem in der Welt sehr bekandten Ort/ noch führhanden seynd. Was den zu Leipzig neu-beygedruckten Anhang belangt/ will sich der Autor des Büchleins nichts davon zuschreiben; so auf allen Fall ebener massen allhie angemerckt werden sollen.

Oesterreich
über alles/
wann es nur will.
Das ist:
Wohlmeinender

Fürschlag/

Wie mittelst einer wohlbestellten
Lands-Oeconomie, die Kayserlichen Erb-
Lande in kurtzem über alle andere Staate von Europa zu erheben/ und mehr als einiger derselben/ von
denen andern independent zu
machen

P. W. v. H.

Regenspurg/
Verlegts Joh. Zacharias Seidel/ 1708.

MH-BA BSB(digitized) UB Salzburg*

7.   German edition, Regensburg, 1712.

'Oesterreich über alles/ wann es nur will'. Das ist: Wohlmeynender Fürschlag/ wie mittelst einer wolbestellten Lands-Oeconomie, die Kayserlichen Erb-Lande in kurtzem über alle andere Staate von Europa zu erheben/ und mehr als einiger derselben/ von denen andern independent zu machen. P. W. v. H.

Regensburg/ Verlegts Joh. Zacharias Seidel/ 1712.

π^4):(^{4} A-N^8 ($-); [xii], [208] p. The preliminaries consist of two gatherings of four leaves. The fourth of the first signature is signed):(2; the first leaf of the second signature is unsigned; the second is signed):(2; the second is signed):(4; and the third is signed):(5.

i-iv blank; I title-page; II blank; III VI Vönstiger Leser; VII-XII Verzeichniss der Abtheilungen; 1–198 text; 198–206 Anhang/ oder Unvorgreiffliches Project, zu Stellung einer Armee von hundert tausend Mann aus den Kayserl. Erbländern; 207–208 blank

p. 195 mispaged 185.

Gönstiger Leser reads:

Dieses Wercklein hat Anno 1684 im Sommer zum ersten/ und im nechsten Herbst darauff zum ndern mahl zu Nürnberg durch Herrn Johann Hoffmann/ Buchführen/ das Tage-Licht gesehen. Seine erste Erzielung war zu Dressden/ von einer selbigen Orts ausheimischen Feder. Ein hoher/ allda gleichfals nicht einheimischer Minister, liesse ihm/ um seiner Auffrichtigkeit und Wohlmeinung willen/ die Gnad seiner Protection wiederfahren. Es hatte damahls den Nahmen seines Erzeugers nicht auffgedruckt. Dannenhero als Herr Thomas Fritsch zu Leipzig es verwichenen Frühling abermahl auffzulegen Sinnes worden/ bewarbe er sich guter Intention, denselben in Erfahrung zu bringen Als ihm aber der Zufall darinnen nicht fügen wolte/ indem so gar auch des ersten Verlegers Erben keinen Bescheid mehr davon geben konten: wurde er durch einige Vermuthung auf einen unrerchten geleitet/ unter dessen ersten Nahmens-Buchstaben auch/ eine gute Parthey Exemplarien gleich Anfangs fortgangen. Gleichwie aber dem Irrthum nach der Hand/ auff bessern Bericht/ von ihm ganz willig/ so viel annoch seyn können/ remedirt worden: also wird solchem in dieser vierdten Edition nachgegangen/ indeme doch so wohl der hohe Protector, als der Autor an einem/ in der Welt sehr bekandten Ort/ noch fürhanden seynd. Was den zu Leipzig neu-beygedruckten Anhang belangt/ will sich der Autor des Büchleins nichts davon zuschreiben; so auf allen Fall ebener massen allhie angemerckt werden sollen.

MH (library label on spine, reading in two lines: T2h. / 88.) BSB (digitized) Steimärkische Landesbibliothek

8.   German edition.

Oesterreich über alles/ wann es nur will. Das ist: Wohlmeinender Fürschlag/ wie mittelst einer wohlbestellten Lands-Oeconomie, die Käyserlichen Erb-Lande in kurtzem über alle andere Staate von Europa zu erheben/ und mehr als einiger derselben/ von denen andern impendent zu machen. P. W. v. H.

Regenspurg/ Verlegts Joh. Zacharias Seidel/ 1717.
Sächsische Landesbibliothek-Staats- und Universitätsbibliothek Dresden (digital)

8.   German edition.

Oesterreich über alles, wann es nur will. Das ist: Wohlmeinender fürschlag, wie mittelst einer wohlbestellten lands-oeconomie, die kayserlichen erb-land in kurtzem über alle andere staat von Europa zu erheben, und mehr als einiger derselben, von denen andern independent zu machen. P. W. v. H.
[n.p.] 1719.
[vii], 229 p.
Humpert.
UC Santa Barbara (HC264.H7)*

10.   German edition.

Oesterreich über alles/ wann es nur will. Das ist: Wohlmeynender Fürschlag, wie mittelst einer wohlbestellten Landes-Oeconomie, die kayserl. Erb-Lande in kurtzem über alle andere Staaten von Europa zu erheben/ und mehr als einiger derselben/ von denen andern independent zu machen. P. W. v. H.
Regensburg/ Verlegts Johann Conrad Peetz/ 1723.
The title is in red and black.
π2)(⁶ (with leaf 1 signed)(2 and leaf 2 signed)(3) A-N (N8 blank); [16], 208 p.
i blank; ii frontispiece; iii title-page; iv blank; v-x Vorrede. An den geneigten Leser; xi-xvi Verzeichnuss der Abtheilungen; 1–206 text; 207–208 blank
p. 176 mispaged 117.
Vorrede reads:
Wann unter die Kennzeichen eines guten Buchs besonders dessen wiederholte Auflagen gerechnet werden/ so darff wohl niemand zweifeln/ dass gegenärtige Schrifft/ **Oesterreich über alles** genannt/ einen allgemeinen Beyfall und Lob verdiene: dann es ist bekannt/ dass sie seit 1684. da sie das erstemahl durch öffentlichen Druck zum Vorschein kommen/ wegen ihrer Güte in Leipzig/ Nürnberg und Regenspurg zu verschieden mahlen wieder ediret und aufgekauffet worden.
Der gelehrte Autor derselben war ein Herr v. Horneck, nicht zwar der berkannte Ottocarus von Horneck aus Steyermarck/ welcher ein MS. einer Oesterreichischen Historie in Teutschen Reimen hinterlassen; sondern/ wie die Literæ initiales auf dem Titul-Blat bezeugen/ der berühmte Phil. Wilh. von Horneck, weyl. Sr. Durchl. Eminenz des Hrn. Card. von Lamberg/ Bischoffens zu Passau und Käyserl. Principal-Commissarii zu dem fürwährenden Reichs-Convent in Regensp. geheimden Rath u. Hochansehnl. Gesandter/welcher diesen Aufsatz zu Dressden verfertiget/ daselbst er auch von einem hohen Minister, seiner guten Intention und Absicht wegen/ billig patrociniret/ und gleich im ersten Jahr zweymal zum Druck befördert worden.

Z

Oesterreich
über alles/
Wann es nur will.
Das ist:
Wohlmeynender
Fürschlag,
Wie
Mittelst einer wohlbestellten
Landes-Oeconomie,
Die Käyserl. Erb-Lande in kurtzem
über alle andere Staaten von Europa zu
erheben/ und mehr als einiger derselben/ von denen
andern independent zu machen.

P. W. v. H.

Regenspurg/
Verlegts Johann Conrad Peez/ 1723.

Der eigentliche Inhalt dieser Schrifft bestehet in allerdings practicablen Vorschlägen zu nützlicher Verbesserung der Lands-Oeconomie in Oesterreich/ oder dass ich die rechte Wahrheit sage/ in einem mehr als Sonnen-klaren Beweiss/ dass das Ertz-Hauss Oesterreich mit seinen zugehörigen Erb-Landen/ als Ungarn/ Böhmen/ Schlesien und Mähren/ in Betrachtung deren natürlichen Gaben und Uberflusses aller erdencklichen Nothwendigkeiten eines beglückten Staats/ über alle andre Staaten von Europa seyn könnte/ wann es nur solche Gaben geniessen/ und sich dieselben durch Errichtung

nöthiger Manufacturen und Commercien zu nutze machen wolte. Ich achte für
überflüssig/ ein mehrers hievon zugencken/ weilen der Herr Verfasser dieses Werckleins
gedachtgen Titul selbsten gleich in der ersten Abtheilung seiner Schrifft weitläufftig
erkläret hat; zugeschweigen/ dass das vorgedruckte Kupffer-Blat quasi in frontispicio
den Haupt-Zweck und Inhalt des gantzen Buches also deutlich præsentiret/ dass ich mit
demselben [e with tilde] viele Worte ersparhen kan.

Wolte aber jemand den glorieus-anscheinenden titul dieses Werckleins wider die
Intention des Autoris auf eine andere Art attaquiren/ und von dem Oeconomischen
Ingeresse auf politische Prærogativen verfallen/ so würde er auch hierinnen bald
totum Argumentum concediren müssen. Dann consuliret er die Geographos, so zeiget
ihm Mart. Zeilerus in einer Topographie von Oesterreich/ wie die gütige Mutter der
Natur dieses Ertz-Hauss und dessen Erb-Königreiche mit allen Beneficiis, die nur zu
Vollkommenheit eines glücklichen Landes desideriret werden können/ ga reichlich
versehen habe.

Wer sich die Mühe geben will/ in die Historie zu lauffen/ um darinnen das
Oesterreichische Alterthum und dessen heutigern Ehren-Ruhm aufzusuchen/
der wird aus Joan. Cuspiniani Descriptione Austriæ, und Ger. de Roo Annalibus
Rerum ab Austriacis Principibus gestarum, besonders aber aus Sigmunds von Birken
Oesterreichischer Ehren-Spiegel/ ingleichen aus Joh. Jacobs von Weingarten Fürsten-
Spiegel oder Monarchie des Ertz-Hauses Oesterreich davon völlig überzeuget
werden. Der über 300. Jahr lang geführten Käyser-Würde, und aller mit solcher
verbundenen Reservaten anjetzo nicht zu gedencken/ weil es wider unser Institutum
lauffet; wir haben durch diese Schrifft mehr nicht gesuchet/ als den Geneigten [e
with umlaut] Leser zu animire/ [e with umlaut] nicht nur Oesterreich sein Glück
zu gönnen/ sondern auch zu der hernach intendirten Staats-Verbesserung unsers
Teutschen Vagterlandes/ soviel an ihm ist/ beyzutragen. In Hoffnung dessen/
wünsche dem Geneigten Leser/ nebst allem Seelen-und Leibs-Vergnügen/ ein
gelassenes Gemüth/ die Wahrheit zuhören/ und einen also kräfftigen Vorsatz/
derselben zu folgen. Adieu.

MH MH-BA (ONE OF THESE IS THE STOLBERG COPY) Princeton KBD
(Staysv. 17285/80) KU* BSB (digitized)

11. German edition, 1727

Oesterreich über alles/ wann es nur will. Das ist: Wohlmeynender Fürschlag, wie
mittelst einer wohlbestellten Landes-Oeconomie, die kayserl. Erb-Lande in kurtzem über
alle andere Staaten von Europa zu erheben/ und mehr als einiger derselben/ von denen
andern independent zu machen. P. W. v. H.

Regensburg/ Verlegts Johann Conrad Peetz/ 1727.

$\pi^2)(^6$ A-N (N8 blank); [16], 208 p.

i blank; ii frontispiece; iii title-page; iv blank; v-x Vorrede. An den geneigten Leser;
xi-xvi Verzeichnuss der Abtheilungen; 1–206 text; 207–208 blank

p. 176 mispaged 117.

Oesterreich

über alles/
Wann es nur will.

Das ist:

Wohlmeynender

Fürschlag,

Wie
Mittelst einer wohlbestellten

Landes = Oeconomie,

Die Kayserl. Erb=Lande in kurtzem
über alle andere Staaten von Europa zu
erheben/ und mehr als einiger derselben/ von denen
andern independent zu machen.

P. W. v. H.

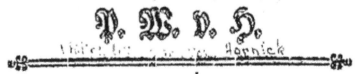

Regenspurg/
Verlegts Johann Conrad Peetz/ 1727.

Although the entries for the 1723 and 1727 editions are bibliographically identical, even to the extent of having p. 176 mispaged in both, these are printed from different settings of type, the 1727 being to a considerable extent a line-for-line reprint of the 1723.

MH-BA NN KBD BSB (digitized) Steiermärkische Landesbibliothek* UB Graz* UB Salzburg*

12. German edition, 1729.

Oesterreich über alles/ wann es nur will. Das ist: Wohlmeinender Fürschlag/ wie mittelst einer wohlbestellten Lands-Oeconomie, die Keyserliche Erb-Lande in kurtzem über alle andere Staaten von Europa zu erheben/ und mehr als einiger derselben/ von denen andern independent zu machen. Samme Anhang oder Project, zu Stellung einer Armée von 100000. Mann/ aus den Käyserl. Erb-Ländern. Von P. W. v. H.

Franckfurt / M DCC XXIX. [1729]

π^6 (1 & 6 + 2–5, i.e., fspc. & title are 1 and 6) A-M^{12} N^6; [12],299 p.

i̲ blank; i̲i̲ frontispiece; i̲i̲i̲ title; i̲v̲ blank; v̲-x̲i̲i̲ Verzeichniss der Abtheilungen; 1̲–299 text

Errors in signing: A7, B7, C6–7, D7, and H7 are unsigned; H5 is missigned H4.

MH (MOMW erroneously states that pp. 216–217 are missing from the Widener/ Houghton copy; MOMW also erroneously gives the date as [1729]) ÖNB (digital)

13. 1750, Franckfurt u. Leipzig

Oesterreich über alles/ wann es nur will; Das ist: Wohlmeynender Fürschlag, wie, mittelst einer wohlbestellten Landes=Oeconomie, die Kayserl. Königl. Erb=Lande in kurtzem über alle andere Staaten von Europa zu erheben/ und mehr als einige derselben von denen andern independent zu machen. Zu welchem noch ein Anhang, von unpartheyischen Gedancken über die Oesterreichische Landes=Oeconomie, und leichteste Vermehrung der Cammer=Gefälle, beygefügt worden. Neueste Auflage von P.W.v.H.

Franckfurt und Leipzig, 1750.

i̲ blank; i̲i̲ frontispiece; i̲i̲i̲ title; i̲v̲ blank; v̲-i̲x̲ Vorrede an den geneigten Leser, signed at end: Geschrieben in der Michaelis-Messe 1750; x̲-x̲i̲i̲ Verzeichniß der Abtheilungen; 1̲–420 text

π2 2π4 A-2C8 2D2; [xii], 420 p. illus. 17 cm.

Anhang: p. 3̲1̲7̲–420 has special title-page: Unpartheyische Gedancken über die Oesterreichische Landes=Oeconomie und leichteste Vermehrung der Ertz=Hertzoglichen Cammer=Gefälle, wie auch bequemer Aufstellung eines Militis Perpetui. Aus dem Manuscript eines erfahrnen Cameralistens gezogen, und als eine Zugabe zu Hornecks Tractat: Oestereich über alles, wenn es nur will, mitgetheilet. 1750.

KBD Chicago (HC263.H69)* Minnesota* Berkeley* BSB (digitized) The title page reproduction is from BSB, with my agreement that it's not for commercial use. Steiermärkische Landesbibliothek (with imprint of Frankfurt u. Leipzig) UB Graz* UB Salzburg*

Oesterreich

über alles/
Wann es nur will.

Das ist:

Wohlmeinender

Fürschlag/

Wie

Mittelst einer wohlbe-
stellten Lands-Oeconomie, die
Keyserliche Erb-Lande in kurtzem über
alle andere Staaten von Europa zu erheben/
und mehr als einiger derselben / von
denen andern independent
zu machen.

Sammt Anhang oder Project, zur
Stellung einer Armée von 100000,
Mann/ aus den Käyserl. Erb-
Ländern.

Von

P. W. v. H.

Franckfurt/
M DCC XXIX.

Oesterreich
über
Alles, wann es nur will;
Das ist:
Wohlmeynender
Fürschlag,
Wie, mittelst einer wohlbestellten
Landes-Oeconomie,
die Kayserl. Königl. Erb-Lande in
kurtzem über alle andere Staaten von Eu-
ropa zu erheben, und mehr als einige dersel-
ben von denen andern independent zu
machen.
Zu welchem noch ein Anhang, von unpartheyi-
schen Gedancken über die Oesterreichische Landes-
Oeconomie, und leichteste Vermehrung der
Cammer-Gefälle, beygefügt worden.
Neueste Auflage.
Von
P. W. v. H.
Franckfurt und Leipzig, 1750.

14.   1753, Frankfurt u. Leipzig

Oesterreich über alles, wann es nur will; Das ist: Wohlmeynender Fürschlag, wie mittelst einer wohlbestellten Landes-Oeconomie, die Keyserl. Königl. Erb-Lande in kurtzem über alle andere Staaten von Europa zu erheben, und mehr als einige derselben von denen andern independent zu machen. Zu welchem noch ein Anhang, von unpartheyischen Gedancken über die Oesterreichische Landes-Oeconomie, und leichteste Vermehrung der Cammer-Gefälle beygefügt worden. Neueste Auflage. Von P. W. v. H.

Oesterreich

über

Alles, wann es nur will;

Das ist:

Wohlmeynender

Fürschlag,

Wie, mittelst einer wohlbestellten

Landes-Oeconomie,

die Kayserl. Königl. Erb-Lande in kurtzem über alle andere Staaten von Europa zu erheben, und mehr als einige derselben von denen andern independent zu machen.

Zu welchem noch ein Anhang, von unpartheyischen Gedancken über die Oesterreichische Landes-Oeconomie, und leichteste Vermehrung der Cammer-Gefälle beygefügt worden.

Neueste Auflage.

Von

P. W. v. H.

Franckfurt und Leipzig, 1753.

Franckfurt und Leipig, 1753.

i title; ii blank; iii-vii Vorrede an den geneigten Leser, dated at end: Michaelis-Messe, 1750; viii-ix Verzeichniss der Abtheilungen; 1–206 text; 207–316 Historische Anzeige von denen Privilegiis des Durchlauchtigsten Ertz-Hauses Oesterreich, nebst Chur-Manntzischen Vidimus gedachter Privilegien; 317 divisional title; 318 blank; 319–420 Unpartheyische Gedancken über die Oesterreichische Landes-Oeconomie, und Leichteste Vermehrung der Ertz-Hertzoglichen Cammer-Gefälle, wie auch Bequemer Aufstellung eines Militis Perpetui. Aus dem Manuscript eines erfahrnen Cammeralistens gezogen, und als eine Zugabe zu Horneck's Tractat: Oesterreich über alles, wenn es nur will, mitgetheilet. 1753.

Pagination errors: P. 191 mispaged 181; p. 225 mispaged 222.

π^2 $2\pi^4$ A-2C^8 2D^2; [12], 420 p.

MH-BA GL (MOMW) KBD Syracuse* U. of Cincinnati* Washington U.* Bayerische Staatsbibliothek (Austr. 3410)* Steiermärkische Landesbibliothek (with imprint of Frankfurt u. Leipzig)* UB Salzburg*

15. German edition, 1764

Franckfurt und Leipzig, 1764.

[xii], 420 p. front.

Comparison of the BSB copy on Google with the 1753 edition shows that this is a reprint, basically page for page, of the 1753 edition, with the "Vorrede an den geneigten Leser," also dated at end: "Michaelis-Messe, 1750."

Bayerische Staatsbibliothek (Austr. 3412; digitized)* ÖNB (digital) UB Salzburg* BnF*

16. German edition.

Herrn Johann von Horneks Bemerkungen über die österreichische Staatsökonomie. Ganz umgearbeitet und mit Anmerkungen versehen von Benedikt Franz Hermann, Professor der Technologie, der röm. kais. königl. patriotischen Societäten in Oesterreich und Steyermark, der naturforschenden Gesellschaft in Berlin, der freyen ökonomischen Gesellschaft in St. Petersburg und der litterarischen Gesellschaft in Laibach Mitglied, dann der rusisch-kaiserlichen Akademie der Wissenschaften Korrespondent.

Berlin und Stettin. Bey Friedrich Nikolai, 1784.

*^{5} A-M^8 N^3; [10], 198p.

i title; ii blank; iii-vi Vorbericht, signed at end: Geschrieben in St. Petersburg den Iten May 1783. B. F. Hermann; vii-x Inhalt; 1–198 text

Reviewed in *Allgemeine literatur Zeitung*, Bd. 4 (Dec. 1785): 370–71:

Hr. Prof. H. hat das bekannte Buch des von Hornek, *Oesterreich über alles, wenn es nur will*, in Absicht der Schreibart umgearbeitet, und es zur Grundlage einer grossen Menge von Bemerkungen gemacht, worinn er die Producte des östreichischen Länder ungleich vollständiger angiebt, die seit der Erscheinung jenes Buchs gemachten Verbesserungen in der Staatshaushaltung nachträgt, und so den grossen Unterschied zwischen dem itzigen Zustande, da sie reich, mächtig, und voll Fabriken und Manufacturen sind, und dem

Herrn Johann von Horneks
Bemerkungen

über die

österreichische
Staatsökonomie.

Ganz umgearbeitet und mit Anmerkungen
versehen

von

Benedikt Franz Hermann,

Professor der Technologie, der röm. kaif. königl. patriotischen Societäten in Oesterreich und Steyermark, der naturforschenden Gesellschaft
in Berlin, der freyen ökonomischen Gesellschaft in St. Petersburg und
der litterarischen Gesellschaft in Laibach Mitglied, dann der
russisch-kaiserlichen Akademie der Wissenschaften
Korrespondent.

Berlin und Stettin.
Bey Friedrich Nikolai, 1784.

fast ganz entgegengesetzten vor hundert Jahren anschaulich macht. Er zeigt dabey eine gute Kenntniss dieser Länder, und eine reife Beurtheilungskraft, wovon wir unter vielen nur ein Beyspiel anführen wollen. "Dass die Macht eines Staates nach der grössern oder kleinern Menge seiner *natürlichen Produkte* abgemessen werden müsse, (sagt er S. 23 in der ersten Anmerk. zum 9ten Absehn.) ist ein Satz, der mit eben so viel Einschränkung anzunehmen ist, als der, dass die Menge des Volkes den eigentlichen wahren Reichtum der Staates ausmache, und dass daher das Augenmerk des Regenten vorzüglich dahin gerichtet seyn müsse seinen Ländern die grösstmöglichste Menge von Einwohnern zu verschaffen. Beyder Meinungen haben ihre Berühmten Verfechter. Aber ein Ueberfluss an natürlichen Produkten, ohne eine hinlängliche Menge Menschen, um sie zu erzielen, zu verarbeiten, zu verzehren, und auszuführen, wozu sollen sie? Und umgekehrt: eine übergrosse Menge Einwohner, die bey dem grösstmöglichsten Fleisse nicht Nahrungswege genug finden, welch Glück würden sie geniessen? Wir glauben also in der Vereinigung dieser beyden Sätze einen andern zu finden, die Macht eines Staates in der *grösstmöglichsten* Menge *wohlhabender* Bürger bestehe[.]" Diesen Satz, darinnen Hrn H. schon andre gründliche Staatskundige, auch Philosophen, z. B. Sulzer, vorgegangen, erläutert er noch durch einige Zusätze, indem er bewerden könne, dass, wenn ein Staat bey der besten Cultur nur für eine Million Einwohner Nahrungsmittel hervorbringen kann, und deren doch zwo besitzt, wenn er nach politischen Verhältnissen mit seinen Nachbarn, bey den vortrefflichsten Manufacturen, und bey dem lebhaftesten Handel doch nicht so viel gewinnen kann um sich dafür die abgängigen Bedürfnisse einzutauschen, oder für baares Geld zu erhalten, ein solcher Staat nach und nach verarmen, und durch seinbe Uebervölkerung unglücklich werden müsse.

MH-BA ÖNB (digital)

17. German-language pirated edition, [n.p.], but Vienna, 1784

Herrn Johann von Horneks Bemerkungen über die österreichische Staatsökonomie. Ganz umgearbeitet und mit Anmerkungen versehen von Benedikt Franz Hermann, Professor der Technologie, der röm. kais. königl. patriotischen Societäten in Oesterreich und Steyermark, der naturforschenden Gesellschaft in Berlin, der freyen ökonomischen Gesellschaft in St. Petersburg und der litterarischen Gesellschaft in Laibach Mitglied, dann der Russisch-kaiserlichen Akademie der Wissenschaften Korrespondent.

[Vienna: Georg Philipp Wucherer] 1784.

π^4 ($\pi2$ + inserted leaf) A-P^8 Q-R^4 (-R1= leaf inserted after $\pi2$?) chi^4; [10], 253, [1], [8] p.

i title; ii blank; iii-vi Vorbericht, signed at end: Geschrieben in St. Petersburg den Iten May 1783. B. F. Hermann; vii-x Inhalt; 1–253 text; 254 blank; I divisional title: Nachricht von dem Verkäufer dieses Buchs an das Publikum; II blank; III-VIII text of Nachricht, signed at end: Wien, im November 1784. Georg Philipp Wucherer, k. k privilegirter Grosshändler

The "Nachricht von dem Verkäufer," a defense against the charge of piracy, is available as part of two digitized versions of this book. One is MOMO; the other is on

Herrn Johann von Horneks

Bemerkungen

über die

österreichische

Staatsökonomie.

Ganz umgearbeitet und mit Anmerkungen versehen

von

Benedikt Franz Hermann,

Professor der Technologie, der röm. kaif. königl. patriotiſchen Societäten in Oesterreich und Steyermark, der naturforſchenden Geſellſchaft in Berlin, der freyen ökonomiſchen Geſellſchaft in St. Petersburg und der litterariſchen Geſellſchaft in Laibach Mitglied, dann der Ruſſiſch-kaiſerlichen Akademie der Wiſſenſchaften Korreſpondent.

1 7 8 4.

Google Books: http://books.google.com/books?vid=HARVARDHW7VWX&printsec
=titlepage

There are extensive additions, some marked by asterisks, which are added remarks, others marked by letters, which contain information on current economic conditions and are drawn, as the Vorbericht points out, from B. F. Hermann's <u>Abriss der physikalischen Geschaffenheit der österreichischen Staaten, und des gegenwärtigen Zustandes der Landwirthschaft, Gewerbe, Manufakturen, Fabriken und der Handlung in denselben</u> (1782).

In some copies the Nachricht is at front, preceding the Vorbericht; thus in BL copy, which is digitized on MOMW.

MH KU* BL*

18. German-language pirated edition, n.p., probably Vienna, 1784

Herrn Johann von Horneks Bemerkungen über die österreichische Staatsökonomie. Ganz umgearbeitet und mit Anmerkungen versehen von Benedikt Franz Hermann, Professor der Technologie, der röm. kais. königl. patriotischen Societäten in Oesterreich und Steyermark, der naturforschenden Gesellschaft in Berlin, der freyen ökonomischen Gesellschaft in St. Petersburg und der litterarischen Gesellschaft in Laibach Mitglied, dann der Russisch-kaiserlichen Akademie der Wissenschaften Korrespondent.

[n.p.] 1784.

*[6] (- *??) A-; [10], 198 p.

[i] title; [ii] blank; [iii-vi] Vorbericht, dated: Geschrieben zu St. Petersburg den 11ten May 1783; [vii-x] Inhalt; [1]-198 text

Wirtschafts Universität, Wien, Universitätsbibliothek has 3 preliminary leaves only, with *4–5, the Inhalt, bound at end. Because a catchword for the first page of text is on *5v, the printer intended the Inhalt to be bound at front. The catalog for their copy gives the imprint as St. Petersburg, no doubt because the editor's Vorbericht is signed from St. Petersburg. In fact, that place of publication does not appear on the title page, and it is like the other copies recorded, that is, with no place of publication but with a small circular ornament on the title page, between the end of text and the double rule above the date. It is much more likely that this pirated edition was printed in Vienna by Johann Thomas Edler von Trattner.

Kansas* Bayerische Staatsbibliothek* Wirtschafts Universität, Wien, Universitäts-bibliothek* UB Salzburg

AUSTRIA SUPREME (IF IT SO WISHES)

That is: a well-intentioned proposal for
quickly raising the hereditary Imperial domain, through well-ordered oeconomy,
above all other European states and rendering it more independent of the others
than some of them are.

By one who is devoted to the welfare of the hereditary Imperial domain
[Philipp Wilhelm von Hörnigk]

[no place of publication] 1684

Translated by Keith Tribe

Footnote annotations by Philipp Robinson Rössner

Index of Sections

I. Intention of the author and justification of the title

I have taken it upon myself to prove that *Austria could be supreme if it only wished*. I consider myself justified in giving this small work an unusual title by the same right that parents have of calling their children whatever they will. And, according to another right of all men, I want these words to contain a promise, hence a harbinger. By "Austria" I do not merely mean the world-renowned duchy of that name on both banks of the Danube; but also every part of the hereditary kingdom and lands of the German-Austrian house, whether located within or without the Roman Empire, thereby including Hungary. When I write that Austria can be supreme over *all*, I place only Christian Europe in the balance, with which we have incomparably more to do than with all other parts of the world. The *supremacy* on which the whole question turns *I define as a surplus of human requisites and comforts* (in real goods, gold and silver), *a surplus independent of other nations, whether actual or even a possibility;* a hitherto little remarked, hence unsuspected, advantage that I credit to our Austria and at the same time place at its disposal. I pray my reader does not come to the premature and inward conclusion that I present here senseless paradoxes and empty talk, or impracticable suggestions. He should allow himself to have a little patience and be so good as to consider the success of this small work, which will I hope show seriousness, faith and expediency. And God willing, if Austria allows its natural gifts and advantages to be infused with the will to be used to their proper benefit, it will be manifestly proved that its salvation and elevation alone, after God, rests in its own hands.

II. Occasion for this work: Germany can have no better example in the improvement of domestic manufactures and commerce than your Imperial Majesty

I admit that what has prompted me was the appearance at the beginning of this year of the well-known pamphlet *Teutschland über Frankreich, Wenn es klug seyn will*, in which, among other things, it was shown that, if Germany were to trouble itself to do without French goods, it could meet its requisite needs at home and also keep its good but rapidly dwindling money in its purse. Not only would it see its poverty and many other wants ameliorated, but also could exceed in wealth and powers the French nation, which, hitherto has been pumped up by German money – causing Germany's ruin. France would now be humbled by Germany. However, the author recognises that such a fortunate course for our fatherland is not likely to be adopted by general imperial decree at Regensburg. In my own opinion that fact is not necessarily a bad thing, unfortunately! It is as clear as daylight how little succour and salvation we can expect, even in our present extreme need brought about in the east and west by our two sworn foes. And furthermore, even if all the German Electors (Archbishops) of Mainz were like Johann Philippsen,[1] understanding as he did how to best promote commerce in the Empire, and with the will and enthusiasm to do something about it, while having the courage to talk about it and find support among others, then something might be hoped for along these lines. But since these great hopes are now reduced to ashes along with this great Duke, the author points out that each of the most noble rulers, in their own houses, should allow themselves to be advised on how to improve the true oeconomy of their country through better arrangement of industry and manufacture – for there is a great difference between this and the Cameral [domainal] oeconomy. These rulers will then, in a spirit of praiseworthy emulation and attracted by expediency and profit, be joined by all the others since the remnants of meaner spirit would be quickly overcome. Whatever praise might be due for this proposal, I consider a good example is needed in order for this kind of movement to find its initial momentum. If I review the whole of Germany, there is no one of greater renown, of more reassuring expediency and success than your Imperial Majesty, and not only in regard to your supreme imperial dignity and office. In particular, you possess an extent of kingdom and lands blessed by God and nature, in which all are equally subject to the same head. All are mixed together, forming one body, each satisfying another's want and need with his own surplus, so that practically every wish is met with an abundance of raw goods and their great inland consumption. This advantage is something of which they can be justifiably proud. Few states in Europe could join them and become a small world in themselves, without any external action, in respect not only of essentials, but also of comforts, if only the proper institution would come to their aid. This hope is what prompted me to take up my present endeavor.

III. Given the current wartime unrest, is it timely to address the oeconomy of the country?

I am perfectly aware of the kind of judgements and complaints that may be heaped upon me following this work. I can hear them say: *how absurd it must seem, at a time when everything shakes from the crack of musket and boom of cannon, to fill people's ears with talk of the elevation of commerce*

---

1   Johann Philipp von Schönborn (1605–1673), archbishop (and by this means imperial elector) of Mainz, an important politician of the empire, renowned for his Mercantilist policies of developing the territories of the Mainz Archbishopric.

and manufactures and the improvement of the nation's oeconomy (Landes=Oekonomie) as the fruit and work
of the most tranquil peace. The thunder of war breaks out on all sides and over our heads; how ridiculous it is
to flatter one and all about imaginary states of happiness that neither our fathers nor our grandparents enjoyed,
even in their most pleasant and secure times. However, what might be seen as most inopportune
could be seized upon as the most convenient opportunity by people who are better able to
take care of themselves than we are. None can deny that, if a few months before the present
Turkish invasion, a few more million taler had been in hand than was actually the case, and
had been spent in a timely manner, with ducal rather than merchant oeconomy; if the callup
was more promptly arranged, regiments enlarged earlier, the army placed at the right time in
a completely different state than it was afterwards found to be; if magazines and other contingencies had been made ready and generously and substantially supplemented, it would
have been possible to field a considerably greater quantity of men and regiments. If these
had been placed in the field earlier, had conceived and undertaken proper action against the
approaching enemy power, it would have robbed the same of all appetite for advancing on
Vienna and have blocked their path to it. A few million taler more, I say, would in all likelihood have effected this. However, what say one million? Just a few hundred thousand taler
well-placed would initially have willingly brought us, in good time and order, the greater part
of the assistance that later was indeed gained, but that rushed in panic to save the imperial
residence. If, therefore, the shortage of money is the source of our so great and enduring
unhappiness, when would it not be more timely to do something about this than when need
is the greatest? When will the spirit of those who live in these lands, whether great or small,
be receptive to innovations that in another time might appear somewhat unusual and difficult to entertain? When, other than in the time of danger that now confronts us, when its is
clearly and completely realised that matters can be assisted primarily through a change of
direction in agriculture? When will neighbours be less trouble than in a crisis, since extreme
necessity forces a decision upon us? And what is several hundred or a million taler against
that which the hereditary imperial lands could save in one year through better institutions?
Finally, if the wartime conditions we presently have did not permit the establishment of
new commercial undertakings and manufactures, they do at least deserve protection from
foreign, useless goods for which our most noble blood, the most inward mark of our powers,
and millions of our good gold and silver flow to our arch foes and sworn enemies. One
would spare oneself for only a few years from foreign-made goods – silk, wool and cloth
fabrics and so-called French goods – and enjoy the most extreme hardship and danger of
the entire undertaking with that which God and nature has so freely and comfortably placed
within our borders. Have not other nations in straightened times considered themselves fortunate while mortifying themselves in sackcloth and ashes. How much easier it should be for
us, given our present travails (for we must either give Christianity up or believe such a thing),
to atone for our pride awhile by using our good Silesian, Moravian and Bohemian cloth,
and our Silesian, Upper Austrian and other domestically-produced canvas; hence leaving
in their own country the silken and woven goods, Dutch lacquers, Indian bombazine, the
pestilential French fashions – sparing us them, if they are really so important, for just as long
as it takes until we have learned how to imitate them in sufficient quantities? To bring this
about we need neither armies, nor deep and far-ranging counsel and advice, nor unaffordable capitals. It can be done with paper, pen and ink without any expense, so long as the plan

is stuck to. And then the Emperor would, in a few years, have gained a powerful kingdom within his lands without injustice, blood, flight and bad conscience, the land giving as much as a Peruvian mine[2] now does to the Spanish monarchy. Whoever may contradict this, *sit nobis velut ethnicus et publicanus ac Patiae hostis.*[3] The truth is plain to see, and can be grasped with the hands, if one only wants to.

IV. What has stood in the way of previous advocates regarding matters of the country's oeconomy, with respect to merchants as well as themselves?

Many will say, *God protect us from such hawkers and preachers of commerce, those who made the Emperor and his lands rich! As is said at the tollgate at the Red Tower in Vienna, so many of them have emerged in the last twenty years, but all they brought into the world was an empty beaker* [Becher[4]]. My answer: that may be so, but it is not at all clear whether this is their fault, or that of others. No one can deny that their proposals were in fact reasonable, their reasoning was sound, and that is shown by those parts of the Empire where manufactures are now blossoming. Why do we not follow on? They have discovered sedem et radicem morbi.[5] Why should one not use it as a cure? Their propositions were founded upon clear reason, irrefutable rules for the common economy, and the example of other nations. Why were they not taken up? They bore themselves badly, did not know how to behave at Court, could not make themselves liked by a few people, more often fell out with someone, drew their Imperial payments and wiped their mouths. Is this any reason to have dismissed the good that they offered? If they were unreliable, inconstant and better at starting things than finishing them, why did others not do what was lacking? If their presence was an obstacle, why did nothing happen with their absence? If they bridled the horse back to front, they soon overloaded the poor horse and brought it to a halt. If they were not masters of manufacture, but rather mastered by manufacture; took matters up in places where there was neither resolution nor sufficient capital, why were they not dismissed so that one might do it oneself? The difference between them and others was that they undertook more for the public than they were able, while others did less than they should. Moreover, if I were to speak the real truth, if one demanded inland commerce, ten others opposed, both merchants and lords, the former not being prepared to put up the money for it. I say that the merchants were opposed either because they were foreigners, little

---

2   Hörnigk is referring here to the mines of Potosí, once – mainly during the second half of the sixteenth century – the world's largest silver mining complex.

3   Translates as 'may be to us like a pagan, tax collector and fatherland traitor'. The first bit taken from Matthew 18:17, where Jesus said (King James Version) 'And if he shall neglect to hear them, tell it unto the church: but if he neglect to hear the church, let him be unto thee as an heathen man and a publican'.

4   This is a pun on the German word for "cup" or "beaker" (Ger. Becher), which was also the last name of Hörnigk's brother-in-law Johann Joachim Becher (1635–1682), one of Germany's most famous alchemists, project-makers and economists, who married Hörnigk's sister Maria Veronika von Hörnigk in 1642.

5   Meaning 'the seed and root of the disease'.

concerned about the welfare of our dear Fatherland, concerned more about their purse, and in time of need they could run away like an absconding tenant. Or if they were in fact of our country, they dealt with foreign capital and with credit, or they were only factors for foreign businesses, not understanding manufactures and other useful things, but had only learned how to buy up finished goods somewhere else and then give them to us for much more. Or if they do have an understanding of manufactures, they pretend they do not, only out of hatred of domestic fabrications of which they either have a superfluity, or for which they are indebted, so that one can suspect that their profit is dishonestly come by. Never do they trouble themselves to consider whether they benefit or harm the common weal, are not capable of making such a distinction, not to speak of being enlightened enough to improve it. Much less are they commanded to recognize and do their best by the authorities.

V. Concerning the kind of merchants from this place who will be discussed here

While I might have a quarrel with several domestic merchants, I must say clearly that what I say and undertake does not involve any passion or animosity against merchants in general, with none of whom, thank God, I am involved for good or evil. I would in truth be ill-advised to despise trade in itself and its works, or invite disparagement. Rather, my intention is almost entirely devoted to their honour and advancement and for the improvement of the nation's oeconomy (Landes=Oekonomie), for which, I propose, merchants are the best of all instruments. What I do is motivated by an undeviating fervour for the welfare of the land, whose bread I eat, a land that I cannot work against. For this reason, I divide traders into two sorts: those who benefit the common weal, and those who do it harm. The former are those, first of all, who export surplus domestic goods, not in their raw state (apart from those that cannot be used in any other way), but as manufactures, and so bring foreign money into the land. Also, there are those who buy at one place abroad so as to sell at another foreign place, the kind of trade that the Dutch practice to a great extent in Europe as much as India, without setting as much as a foot in their own country. No less, when, within their own country, raw material is taken and worked up into manufactures and then brought to somewhere else in this country. In this way, foreign goods remain outside, while one's own money is kept at home. Likewise to be praised is when raw goods that are lacking are purchased from other countries, but worked up at home and either retained or sold back abroad. However, the second sort of merchant simply buys manufactures abroad in order to sell them again, just as they are, at home. In so doing, they are carrying good money out of the land or merely running foreign concessions – which is unworthy, corrupt and insupportable huckstering that every Jew can do, and which can only be excused by an extreme and unavoidable shortage of foreign goods of this kind. I have nothing against the first kind of traders, of whom, I may hope, there are many in the hereditary lands. Rather, I honour them and consider that they deserve to be borne on hands aloft. I also wish that someone would be as concerned as I am to increase their number, for the hereditary lands would be better for it. But with the second kind, I admit that I know so little to compare, that I could not forgive myself if I forgot the welfare of my second Fatherland, making me an accessory in the deterioration wished upon it by the most harmful foes to its development and well-being. And these are part of the trading community who raise objections to those who seek a reformation of the previously-existing disorder of industry, because they foresee that their disguise will be stripped off and their works opened up to the light of day. For which they will, if God wills, not remain unpunished.

VI. The kind of obstacles advocates have encountered from the Court

What, however, should I say about those who are officially responsible for the promotion of the nation's oeconomy, and who are either coldly indifferent to it, or even secretly or openly show themselves to be against it? Some time ago, I hear it said that some of them were involved with merchants. I don't know in what way. Some had their capitals invested in trade, some were in business with them, some received regular sums of money from them, some had particular arrangements or could be persuaded by mere words. Others were said to be unconcerned with matters of commerce and manufacture, or had little ability, or were otherwise prevented or too taken up by excess work or by Court affairs, or would not admit it nor allow others to take it in hand, since no one other than they should have control of the most important powers. Others were unsuited to the work because it was not the kind of thing they were familiar with, and they did not wish it to seem as though they had to learn from others. They either did not know what to do or had not done before what their profession required. There was also no lack of those, it was said, who did engage with the work, but only for their own private ends, so they began manufactures, but directed water only to their own mill wheels, and similar things about which it is not for me to judge or to write. But I rather believe and claim that most of them do occur too often. While I cannot persuade great ministers otherwise, knowing myself one or two, a better organisation of activity is to be wished from the bottom of one's heart. If this does not come about, then most unfortunate times will follow. But all the same, one evil-intentioned minister can at a stroke destroy or prevent more good work than nine well-meaning true servants of their lord and their Fatherland can do, work which would be invaluable for them. Moreover, it must be hard for a master to plough with unwilling oxen. If all else failed, there would only be means for putting them back to pasture, to put an end to it. I do not know what kind of president advised the Castilian King Philip IV that if he should first take Madrid, then Lisbon would soon follow. Nonetheless there is no call for that with us, nor is there any intention; but the faint-heartedness that has followed on from earlier events, or the mistrust arising from other circumstances, is no reason for a minister to deny what is in itself a good cause. Thus the state expects that the ruler will take in hand such faint spirit, pour in courage and resolve and then stand fast by, rock-like. King Henri IV of France developed the manufacture of silk cloth against the advice of his minister the Duke of Sully (whom no-one could accuse of being disloyal or lacking in understanding), directly overseeing and managing the undertaking in his own kingdom, as is shown again and again in the memoirs of noted rulers. Similarly, it is known how the great Duke Maximilian in Bavaria established against all advice the state regulation of beer-brewing, and the great success of his doing so. And so even the most famous heroes and most prudent rulers have not been ashamed of becoming involved in such matters, laying eye and hand on the economy of their lands and sustaining its manufactures with real goods. But in certain cases and circumstances, one needs just as many heroic souls – almost none fewer – than have to stand at the head of an army.

VII. Whether descendants ought to do more than their forefathers in matters of industry

Our ears have to suffer yet more stupidities, having to listen to people say: our forefathers were people themselves and knew nothing of such novelties, but it did them no harm; and so we could carry on just like our elders. Of course our predecessors were different people than us, and certainly were so in matters of economy. They did not chase three or four million Gulden[6] out of the Imperial lands just for disgraceful French goods, but mostly made use of what their own house provided. Their expensive ornaments were solid gold and silver, gems, sable and the like which, while they were in part foreign, could be passed down to children and then on to their children. They did not acquire French rags that tear so easily, but which are made useless every six months by the change in fashion. They dressed in good woollen cloth and fustian, knew nothing of French goods, and so little about foreign silks that, even one hundred and thirty years ago, a great King feared it might be a sin to wear pure silken tights. Their cloth was made locally. Cloth-making then flourished within our borders and, with it, everything else. Now everyone wants foreign cloth and foreign silks. The domestic woollen industry lies vanquished. Thus, together with that industry, all welfare and benediction seems to have died and disappeared. And again, where our forefathers made do with one item of domestic clothing, four foreign ones are barely good enough for us. Then, what left the country went mostly to our friends. Now, nearly all flows to our foes, as if it were quite absurd. Besides poverty, this also brings about the declining state of our oeconomy as punishment. If we were still living in former times, our purse, and everything upon which its welfare depends, would fair better, and it would be finally possible, with more certainty and greater honour, to

---

6   In the seventeenth century, several currencies circulated in the Holy Roman Empire and the Austrian hereditary lands. The Rix dollar (*Reichsthaler*) was set, by imperial decree in 1623, at 90 kreuzer or one Gulden (florin) and 30 Kreuzer (that means the silver florin or 'Thaler' was equal to 60 kreuzer or two-thirds of a Reichsthaler or Rix dollar. In Saxony and most other southern and central German lands, the Gulden or florin circulated, in nominal terms, at 24 groschen (groats) which was a different relation from the gulden-kreuzer accounting ratio. In 1667, the Rix dollar – which was nothing more and nothing less than an accounting ration – was set at 96 kreuzer (or 1 fl./Gulden 36 kreuzer) but exchanged, in day-to-day commerce and business, at higher rates usually. This was due to the fact that most payments were settled in underweight small change coins such as pennies, Groschen and kreuzer. The currency relations in southern Germany and Austria were immensely complex, to say the least, and those coins mentioned by Hörnigk in the text are too unspecific to be translated into discrete currency ratios. Further information in Michael North, *Das Geld und seine Geschichte* (Munich: C. H. Beck, 1994), esp. pp. 107–11; Bernd Sprenger, *Das Geld der Deutschen. Geldgeschichte Deutschlands von den Anfängen bis zur Gegenwart* 3rd ed. (Paderborn etc.: Schönigh, 1991), 124–32.

do something about reforming commerce and raising up manufacture. Everyone shouts about the olden times being better than those of the present. The lands can no longer bear the present poverty and the continuing burdens and expenditures. But no one studies the reason for the difference between the olden times and those of the present. No one takes to heart the cause. No one wants to take the first blow with the axe on the tree and fell the abuses listed above. Moreover, for ages, our neighbours were never so powerful and unruly, so aggressive and dangerous, as they are now. That should be very illuminating for us, and encourage us more that our forefathers. Today, whether a nation is powerful and rich does not depend on the limitation of its own powers and wealth, but primarily on whether its neighbours possess more or less than it does. To be powerful and rich has become a matter relative to those who are weaker and poorer. One hundred years or more ago, France, England, Holland and others were far less rich and powerful than they are today. Against them, Germany could extol itself as strong and well-off, and be easily content with the condition of our forefathers. Since our neighbours have so incomparably exceeded and outgrown us and their older themselves, then, if we are virtuous people who consider our future responsibility, it will be worth our while not to leave things as they were in older times. Instead, we should seek to set ourselves again on an equal footing with our neighbours – that is, at least equal our neighbours in welfare, if not to achieve a higher degree of welfare. For this is what our descendants demand of us, owing them the liberty that we inherited from our own predecessors, together with the means for its maintenance that we have so irresponsibly neglected. In the whole of Europe, commerce is in an incomparably different condition than that of former times. Other nations are no fools in leaving behind the deficient conduct of their forefathers and improving themselves. It will certainly be no absurdity for us to do likewise. Rather, it would be for us the height of foolishness if, in our present condition of want, we neglected to do just that which our insightful forefathers would have done if they were placed in the same straits as we are now. It makes as much sense as a fist in the eye to say that this or that has not happened for one hundred years, so today it can wait. Altri tempi, altre cure.[7] Usually one does not set much store by the works of our predecessors. Why then should antiquity here enjoy eternal protection? If we want to imitate our forefathers, in many things meet and fair, why should we not imitate their virtues more than their faults? I am not talking about a hundred years or more, but only fifty years, when the Imperial Court still knew nothing of French cookery, nothing of French wines, both of which have made inroads into us along with French and Latin sicknesses of mind and body. We should resist and consider antiquity, not the good things that our forefathers might have neglected to do. If posterity had stopped with our predecessors, then we would, like Adam and Eve, still be wearing sheepskin back and front. One hundred years ago, our predecessors could, in their own time of need, faced with Turks and others, still depend upon the Holy Roman Empire and their neighbours. But in our own times, thanks to the cunning of the French, everything has fallen into such a state that one can rely only upon God and oneself, and almost none of the others, if one seeks the least neighbourly assistance without offering to pay for it in cash. Hence, everyone is best advised to look out for themselves. For he who, in

7   Italian for 'other times, other cares'.

straightened times, has a full purse at home, good luck to him! If not, he might as well resolve to become a mean servant, not only to the foe, but to his friends and their helpers. Austria can, if it only so wishes, make provision against such misfortune with one third of the capital that flows out for all kinds of unnecessary things, and nearly always towards France. God is a God of wars, large armies and victories – but no less a God of peace and its benefits of superfluity and tranquillity. No time is set for God to have compassion for whomever he will. He can certainly move the hearts of our princes, so that they put their shoulder to the wheel and create something that our predecessors had never imagined. But he does want to be begged to do it.

VIII. That which is to be considered as belonging to the nation's or country's oeconomy (*Landes=Oekonomie*) in general

An idiot or any other kind of reluctant soul can say what they like, but one thing remains true and constant once and for all: *when a country is blessed with all things belonging to human need and welfare in fullness and independence, or the better part of such things, and whose inhabitants have sufficient natural skills to use them properly; then it will necessarily enjoy wealth, superfluity and power; and if not, then their absence is merely a matter of will.* Now, I will make the first part of this crystal-clear about our Austria. Then, it will be far easier to reach a conclusion about the second. A few sections are needed for this, and some reflection.

In respect of our purpose with regard to the oeconomy of the country, there are two things needed for all human subsistence: the matter in itself and its proper care, or its acquisition and use. The former depends on nature alone, with the suitability of the land contributing; the latter, partly from nature, partly from human will, understanding playing a part. Now these substances are at the most basic level of two kinds. On one side I place gold and silver (copper, in some places taken for money, I will not discuss here, because this is not usual among us) which are in their value and use equal to all other things, and which in their civil use are of a completely different kind. On the other side, I place all other things that are included in human purpose and industry, and which either sustain the body, or clothing, or the home, or to instruments of human subsistence and property. Now, it must be considered here that a country which had only gold and silver, although in a sufficient amount, would of course be rich, but still a long way from true perfection and independence; since one can neither eat gold and silver, nor clothe oneself with it. Such a country would depend on others for its remaining needs, if these countries were so inclined to exchange them for money. By contrast, a country that had everything apart from any gold and silver could exist longer than the former, even against the will of its neighbours. While gold and silver are indispensable for the majority of human circumstances, the second country would still depend on foreign goodwill, whether its neighbour wanted to buy its goods in exchange for gold and silver or not. However, where nature has granted a country neither gold and silver, nor other things in appreciable quantities, such a country would be in the worst of circumstances and would be dependent on the caprice and power of all others. Even if it quickly followed the example of the Genoese and the Dutch, and turned to industry or bustling activity, buying raw goods somewhere, working them up, then selling them again as manufactures, and, through this effort, gaining gold and silver to buy all remaining needs; then other countries would still decide whether to let them have the goods necessary for sustenance or to buy the fabricated goods for money. In the absence of either the one or the other, such a state would necessarily fall apart and decline. Also, if such a state were doing so well that its industry and trading flourished and it thereby gained wealth, it would never be the equal of its neighbour that, besides having moderate success in trade, possessed its own domestic raw goods. England and Holland give us a clear example of this. The first, with its commerce in Europe, the Mediterranean and East India, cannot be compared with the second in any way. It is commonly accepted that England is richer in coin, can contribute more to the public treasury and sustain a war for longer than the second. The cause is that the Dutch not only have to purchase raw materials that their manufactures fabricate for their own use and for export, but must also purchase their foodstuffs from abroad, for which a large part of the coin they have earned is used. Against this, England possesses, apart from silk, wine, oil and spices (and a good proportion of these last come from its own West Indian colonies), almost all other bodily necessities. Also, a great part of the things that it exports are fabricated from its own domestic raw goods. While it does not acquire so much foreign money as Holland does, it retains what it has acquired – the Dutch gold magnet is stronger at attracting, the English more powerful at keeping. Finally, how much a country is blessed by nature, that alongside gold and silver it is also able to meet all human needs and requirements from its own soil, is applauded most completely because it is a small world in itself and is independent of others. I know of nothing to compare with this ideal under the sun apart from China, which reaches from a climate close to that of temperate European skies into much hotter regions. Hence, the natural perfection of our European countries is only to be measured against England, noting whether such a country is endowed with domestic gold and silver, and for the rest, with the most necessary, noble and abundant gifts of nature, or not. For according to a standard of this kind, each is more or less dependent on the other, hence more or less perfect and to be ranked higher or lower accordingly.

As regards the care of goods, this consists first of their domestic production, with regard to that which grows on the surface, in the planting and cultivation; as regards animals and that which moves itself, their breeding and husbandry; and finally, regarding subterranean things, their quarrying and extraction. Secondly, in giving form to raw goods, which is what manufacture and its processes consists of. Third, in properly using all of these, both within the country and without, which is mostly effected through the convenient establishment of domestic and foreign commerce and trade. Here, it can be considered that a country rich in raw goods is generally poorer than another where manufactures flourish. But the difference is that the former should, through the proper advancement of its raw materials, replace its deficiency as quickly as it can; the latter however cannot, if others refuse to supply it with raw commodities. The latter thus depends upon others, the former not. Neither of them has much about which to boast if it does not set about commerce, but instead allows foreigners to control it alone. For they can certainly be assured that foreign merchants will, in short order, suck the best coin from their body. They will never admit that their position is precarious, and that they must endure foreign favours. For the finesse of merchants is infinite, especially of those who graze on foreign grass. Upper Austria experienced this to its great disadvantage when its linen trade was destroyed by some foreign monopolists, and its hard-working inhabitants were subjected to such reduced wages that they could hardly afford to pay for the bench upon which they sat. A similar misfortune also befell Silesia, with its wool and linen spinning. Not only could this yarn be worked with far greater advantage domestically than elsewhere, but also many Dutchmen sit in this duchy, each of whom bought up yarn to the value of some hundred thousand in value. They not only paid the locals poorly, but also, by so doing, prevented others from enjoying the benefit if they themselves had traded it abroad.

IX. Nine leading economic principles

If the power and excellence of a country consists in its superfluity of gold, silver and all other things requisite for its subsistence and comfort, to as great an extent as possible on its own account without depending for them on others, and also being capable of their proper care, use and application without assistance; then it follows that the general management of the nation's oeconomy has to direct itself to the way in which superfluity, care and enjoyment drawn from one's own capacities, without depending upon others (or where this is not totally possible, limited as much as is possible considering external dependence and domestic coin) can be brought about. To which end, the following nine rules must serve.

First: Observe most carefully and become acquainted with the nature of the country, leaving out of account no corner, no piece of land, and whether it is capable of cultivation. Nothing that might be useful from all plantations under the sun should remain untried, whether it might do well in the country, and how well, the closeness or distance of the sun not being everything. For everything that concerns silver and gold, no effort nor cost is to be spared in extracting it.

Second: All the goods contained in the land that might not be consumed in their raw state are to be worked up domestically. Compared with the wage of their fabricator, the value of raw goods is commonly two, three, ten, twenty, even one hundred times more, neglect of which is an abomination for the experienced householder (oeconomist).

Third: To realise that, for both the above rules, people are needed, to both transport and cultivate raw goods, as well as to work them up. Hence, only just as many people as can sustain themselves can form the the population of a well-ordered state, although this is unfortunately a matter often neglected. Such people are to be brought by all possible ways out of a life of idleness into a sustainable profession, taught all and encouraged in all kinds of inventions, skills and craft techniques; and where necessary the teacher for such purposes should be brought from abroad.

Fourth: Gold and silver, once in the country, whether extracted from one's own mines or brought in from outside through one's own industry, must in no respect and for whatever cause, as much as possible, be borne out of the country again, provided that it is not buried in caskets, but always kept in circulation; nor diverted into works in which it is at once destroyed, and no longer able to bring some use. For then it would be impossible for a country to accumulate any appreciable supply of ready coin, even if it possessed its own gold and silver mines, before it declined into poverty.

Fifth: Strive with all effort to make the inhabitants of the country content with domestic goods, seeing that they limit their lasciviousness and finery, disregarding those from foreign countries (apart from that for which extreme want leaves no other recourse, rather than recurring unavoidable abuses, exemplified by Indian spice).

Sixth: It would be essential in recovering from a situation of want or irremediable abuse to engage the assistance of foreigners, so far as possible not with gold or silver, but by exchanging other domestic goods.

Seventh: Foreign goods should be taken in their raw state, and fabricated within the country. Thus, the manufacturing proceeds are thereby earned.

Eighth: The effort must be made night and day to establish how goods that are superfluous to the country can be sold to foreigners in finished form, so far as this is necessary; and also to use gold and silver to find their consumption at the farthest end of the world, seeking to promote the same by all ways and means.

Ninth: Besides very particular cases, it should in no case be permitted to bring into the country goods already present within the country in sufficient amount and quality, showing foreigners neither sympathy nor compassion, whether they be friends, relatives, allies or enemies. For there all friendship ends, where it leads to my weakening and corruption. And that remains true even if the domestic goods are inferior in quality, or even higher in value. For it would be better, however strange it may seem to an ill-informed person, to spend two talers that stay in the country, than only one, but which goes abroad.

There is no need to add to this illumination of the basic principles for the general management of the nation's oeconomy. Their rational nature is obvious to any prudent person. I do not claim to have ruled out all exceptions. The circumstances of each country might lead to one or other of the principles being replaced, but this seldom occurs. To which lands these rules and their stewardship are applied can be shown with little effort, since it will be clear in the general state of their economy. I do not take it upon myself to lecture anybody, but can say without any desire for fame that every husbandman or overseer of a local rural economy, whether he be high or low, who proves and studies these rules, will easily be able to determine whether he is up to the task, or not. They are not the invention of a speculative spirit. They present the way things are, reason confirms them, and at all places where wealth blossoms, they are practised in whole or in part. For this reason, my reader will credit me if I delay him awhile with such a small theory. And if he has understanding, which I do not doubt, he will easily find out what they are about. I believe that, little by little, if it has not already long happened, it should dawn upon him to do what he can and decide whether the well-known shortage of money in the Austrian heritable lands can be attributed to nature; or lack of skill and inattentiveness – hence, pure human will. Some will no doubt say that this is all old material, and much like the merchants' or cameralist's alphabet, with which we have long been familiar. But why is such an alphabet unfortunately so little practised in many places, or learned? But now we want to guide Austria according to this touchstone, studying it primarily with regard to its natural advantages, and examine how they might be cultivated.

X. The natural advantages of the hereditary Imperial lands and the goods cast up for the purpose of human subsistence

It is not my intention here to talk in general terms about the position, climes, rivers, sea harbours, mountains and similar things that either contribute to, or hinder, commerce and manufactures, and which otherwise are counted among the natural advantages of countries. Here I am only interested in the goods that the hereditary Imperial lands cast up.

According to the above section, gold and silver come first. Some places in the hereditary lands are especially renowned for this: Hungary on account of its mining town Chremnitz, Schemnitz, Neusohl[8]; Bohemia because of Guttenberg and others, also previously Ilowa or Eyl; Tyrol because of Schwaz; Silesia because of the 'golden ass' of Zueckmantel and others. In the hereditary lands as a whole, however, there is not one major place. Then Austria also shows the imprint of valuable buried metal; and it has been reported to me that, in the opinion of the Imperial residence, the Vienna Woods are supposed to be pregnant with silver ore. It is all the same whether it is left there because of strictness in sparing the timber, or as some say, that it is not yet proper time. Some time ago, Styria also had in Judenburg a very rich silver mine, which was however ruined by water four or five hundred years ago. It makes one think that these uplands must have still more in them. It is said far and wide that the Carinthian uplands are full of gold ore, and there are published books in circulation concerning the details of the way that the local peasantry process the ore in many hundreds of sites. Carniola perhaps should not be omitted, since other metals have been found there, and I have been assured by Moravians that there is alluvial gold somewhere. The shire of Glatz did have gold and silver mines, and perhaps has them still if one is to believe what one hears. It is known that the major rivers of the hereditary lands are rich in alluvial gold, if there were sufficient interest in working them. How much has been produced by working mines in the hereditary lands is uncertain, nor is any really exact calculation here needed. It is enough that, in sum, what the domains, principalities, works and mines produce, taking away the costs (for these costs also stay within the country), leaves quite a few million guilders to be put into circulation in the hereditary lands.

The next issue, following both noble metals, concerns physical nourishment, and what is proper to it. The principal spice, esteemed salt, is possessed by Austria and Upper Styria in abundance, Silesia also has its share, while Hungary has such a quantity of rock salt and other salt as to be able to supply the hereditary lands two and three times over. Besides that, there is the much-valued bread, for which corn, mostly wheat and barley, is relevant. Following this, there are vegetables and pulses, then fruit from tree and bush, not least all kinds of herbs and garden produce. Then meat, which includes animal husbandry – cow, sheep, goats and kids, pig, with their proper pasture and feeding, and also what they produce for eating – milk, butter, cheese, bacon, fat; also from the wild, pigeon and duck; and not forgetting bees and their honey. Also that from river and pond, in Trieste and Dalmatia fresh sea-fishing. Then for drinking, primarily wine, beer with its hops, also vinegar and brandy. Finally, of all noble spices Austrian saffron, famous throughout the world.

---

8   In modern terms, Kremnica, Banská Štiavnica (Ger. Schemnitz) and Banská Bystrica (Ger., Neusohl), all located in contemporary Slovakia. These used to be the most important mining towns in the historical landscape then known by the name of *Upper Hungary* (Oberungarn).

Anyone still unfamiliar with the common saying, the hereditary Imperial lands were made for eating and drinking, can easily surmise that all of the above things are not only available in quantity, but in superfluity. Practically none of all the hereditary lands is short of what they need (besides saffron) from the items listed. And if one, such as Silesia, is short of wine, then it can be brought from the neighbouring hereditary land, so that the money disbursed upon it stays at home. Tyrol takes bread from some neighbours, more for the sake of ease than necessity; while perhaps other Austrian corn magazines could well be relocated. And for those other things – salt, grain, wine, beef, pig, freshwater fish, vinegar, brandy, fruit and so on – these are to be found in such abundance that the only complaint is what should be done with it all. Inhabitants find themselves almost forced to become crafty in trying to use everything before it should decay. Austria and Bohemia lead all others in such superfluity, most of all Hungary, to be praised for this as much as the European country. Its soil is fertile, so that in many places the most ordinary corn produces from the second sowing the purest wheat, and the grass grows so high that it almost covers the grazing cattle. Its waters are so fruitful, that it is not really even a joke to say that the River Theiß (Tisza) in Upper Hungary runs with two parts water and one part fish. The wine in some places, for instance around Tokaj, stands comparison with the best in the world. The fields are filled with the lowing of cattle, great and small. The farmyards are brimming with ducks and geese; the air teems with their feathered brethren. In sum, Hungary is a real mine for bread, fat and meat; about which I will here cease talking, before I am taken for a hired advocate.

The inner man is followed by the outer, that is, clothing and all its sorts. For its purposes, the hereditary lands yield wool, linen and animal skin. For wool, Bohemia is the best, especially the long wool from around Pilsen[9], which is good for making cloth. Closely following Bohemia comes Silesia in regard to quality and quality. Moravia is a little further behind. Austria and Hungary have sufficient quantity, but it is coarse. Linen was also produced in Silesia, Upper Austria and partly Inner Austria, supplying many neighbouring areas and some quite distant, and not because they did not have enough from the hereditary lands. There is less doubt about the superfluity of skins of all kinds (apart from fine furs), since it is a necessary by-product of the cattle husbandry and hunting described above. Here the tame wren and beaver hair should not be omitted. Following the outer man is the roof, that is, house and home, for which earth and clay, wood and stone are needed. There is no shortage of any of this in the hereditary lands as regards useful quantities, nor much lack elsewhere. There is even no shortage of splendid marble and other notable stone, if one is not spared the effort of quarrying and transporting it. The Caplier's Milnschaw Castle in Bohemia[10] is built on a crag of pure jasper. Finally, there are the great variety of tools need for human needs, for house and also ornaments, many of which are made from stone, ore, gold, silver, wool, linen, leather and the like, as already mentioned. Others are made from the lesser metals, of which the hereditary lands have no shortage at all, something which is not, as far as I know, true

9 The German term for the town of Plzeň in today's Czech Republic.
10 Presumably Hörnigk refers to Milešov Castle in northern Bohemia, owned by the noble Kaplirz family.

of the rest of the known world, apart from China. Copper and iron are found nearly everywhere. Tin has been mined in Bohemia at Schlaggenwald[11] since time immemorial, without which even the English tin could not be profitably mined. And now there is such a surplus at Geyerberg that it attracts attention, as if half the world could be supplied from there, partly ceding not a hair to the English. There is lead at Villach in Carinthia, somewhere in Bohemia, and also so much in Hungary that is sufficient; and in Upper Styria at Admont, near the village of Schlamming, there is an ore that is supposed to give sixty pounds to the hundredweight, but which is not mined. Idrija (aeterni liquori vomica) produces so much quicksilver that, if sufficient effort were made and it was sold far and wide, the whole world could be supplied with it. Hence, it is regarded as one of the treasures of the hereditary lands. Minerals also belong here, the most important like sulphur, iron sulphate, antimony being so plentiful in Hungary alone, to say nothing of the other lands, that again the whole world could be supplied. All the others are present in such quantities and superfluity, one here, another there. Hungary also has a relative monopoly of green earth. In the Tyrol, there is calamite, and everywhere there some brass is made. This place has all the metals and minerals, so it cannot lack mineral dyes, at least if no trouble is spared in getting it. There is sufficient salt, whether as rock salt or saltpetre, in all places, but in abundance in Hungary. Bohemia seems that it will be the home of alum, if compared with the unbelievable mine on the Meissen border[12], if anyone wished to do sufficient for its sale. As for timber, the prime and serviceable material for all kinds of human subsistence, it is in some places in such great, although unfortunate, abundance that anyone who could indicate how it might be used up would be rewarded with no little thanks, lacking nothing for masts and for shipbuilding, let alone other uses. Gemstones also belong here as the most elegant ornament. Of these, Hungary gives us opals and jade, Bohemia the finest garnet, although small, also glaze, then also diamonds, amethyst, sapphire, topaz, carniola, aquamarine, agate, jasper, all kinds of dyes, pearls, although of a rather lower quality, including the pleasant serpentine.

Nothing more is to be said here about wax, tallow, horn, glass, bone, paper, pitch, horse and deer hair, feathers and various other things, which are no less important to human needs than many of those items listed above, since there is a superfluity in the hereditary lands of bees, cattle, linen and other things from which these products are made. There will never be a shortage of them. But we must not forget the horse, a very prominent and living instrument of human subsistence; all of Hungary, then Bohemia, these are both famed for their horses, and the remaining hereditary lands have no shortage, abundance being present everywhere. There is no lack of other European beasts of burden, where they might be needed.

XI. Needed and missing goods in the hereditary Imperial lands

Following our listing of the goods with which nature has endowed the hereditary Imperial lands, we now must look at those we lack, so that we might better determine whether this

---

11 Ger. *Schlackenwald*, literally 'slag' or 'dross wood'.

12 Meaning the border with the Saxon states; Meissen being both an out-dated term for the Saxon lands as well as the name of a once-important town and bishop's seat in Saxony.

derives from nature, or from lack of human effort. Among the edible goods that are lacking are northern dry and salt fish, secondly Indian spices, Southern European and other foreign confectionery and sweets, especially oil, then bitter oranges, lemons, figs, raisins, olives, capers, oysters, sardines, rice, (of which Bohemia is not entirely barren, and of which, given its abundance of ponds and low-lying ground, could have a lot more), tobacco, chocolate, tea, coffee, and more of the same sort. Among fabrics, we lack delicate furs, such as sable, ermine and similar sorts, as well as cordovan, Russian and saffiano leather. Second, the so-called camelhair, or rather Turkish and Persian goat hair. Third, cotton, which is now so much used in Europe. Fourth, and above all else, silks. In building, as well as in household goods and ornaments, we have to do without delicate Chinese porcelain, and proper lead glaze; in timber, no West Indian pernambuco wood, Brazilwood and real bloodwood; also ebony, cypress, cedar and similar foreign wood, like elephant wood. Also delicate fur materials. Stones such as ruby, emerald, turquoise, coral, small oriental stones and pearls. Finally, various sorts of material commodities. Not to mention apothecary's goods, because with respect to the country's oeconomy they will be treated in a quite different way to other means of human subsistence, bearing in mind that no land under the sun is supplied with each and every medication, nor will be, given the different and hostile climates required.

XII. A balance of missing goods in the hereditary Imperial lands

If our surplus and our lack are held against each other, then at once the latter suffers embarrassment once it is, in all its superfluousness and ease of substitution, laid on the balance and compared with our surplus. For really, what is more valuable in regards to human sustenance than simple bread and salt, wine which is never regarded highly enough and despised only from its abuse, and animal husbandry together with all the works of field and garden, the two prime and sole activities of our first parents and the patriarchs? What kind of comestible dishes can be made with the spices that not only serve to foster an unnatural appetite (about which the Swedish Imperial Counsellor Julius Coyet would say not unjustly: the Dutch should ship East Indian stomachs along with East Indian fodder), but also make rotten salted and smoked fish edible; or mead brewed out of honey, syrup or sugar? As far as our clothing, what is silk against our wool? In cold lands, silk is nowhere as usable as in the warmer climes, nor can it be imported in great enough quantities for all the people. Our wool is, by contrast, wearable and useful in all climates, and there is everywhere enough of it; Even in the coldest of all climes, where sheep-keeping is unknown, it is replaced with leather and animal skins. I am not at at all talking here of the outward value which human foolishness attributes to certain curious things just because of their short supply, itself brought about because they are not available in sufficient quantities for human needs. My concern is with an inward value, the use that the human race can make of these goods. Consider, common furs and hides are to be preferred to fine furs, since the former cover nakedness and protect against the cold and other intemperate atmospheres, and the latter are used only by a thousandth part of the human race simply as ornament. The same goes for porcelain, foreign timber, attractive stones and similar things, all of which have no general use, are kept only for ornamentation and have no value other than that which human caprice places upon them. They are, compared to our abundant common timber, metals, minerals and other endowments, of little account. Let us instead make our judgements according to necessity: who can do without bread, wine or beer, the common fruits of the earth, meat, fresh fish, firewood and timber for building, wool and linen, leather and fur, metals and minerals, all of which are articles of human need; even if we were at the same time surrounded by all kinds of tasty dishes and Indian spices, expensive foreign timber and furs, and draped with precious stones and pearls? By contrast, how easily can we go without all these useless things for sustenance and subsistence, while the former are so needed? Anyone who does not believe this should try taking away from a land its salt, bread, wine (or beer where it is drunk), fresh meat and fish, wool – leaving only spices, tasty dishes and silk goods. Insight will quickly follow. It is the same with whether substitutes can be found for goods, or not. Something can be introduced into a country in one of two ways: with the thing itself, if the land is made suitable and real effort is made to introduce it; or by using something else that is close to it in use and so can replace it. Where a country is unsuited through lack of persistence in the cultivation of field and garden, in wine growing, animal husbandry in general, and especially in sheep pasturage, where there is no hunting and so no furs, nor any metals; here there is really nothing that can substitute for the bread, wine, the fruits of the earth, meat, butter, cheese, wool, leather and the essential iron, much less for gold and silver. For one can import these things, but that is not the issue, for this brings with it foreign dependence, which is of no use to good order and oeconomy, gold and silver excepted. Bread in Lapland, in part Norway with its air-dried fish, and the Swiss in Emmertal and elsewhere with dry cheese – for all these people our ordinary bread seems like a very special and tasty confection (as Tavernier also writes in his *Orientalische Reise-Beschreibung* (1681) about fortunate Arabia). For our part, we could easily do without Indian spices when we have our good domestic herbs; or use honey instead of sugar, as the Romans and Greeks once did; and use butter instead of oil (for we would not miss oil, apart from using it for salad). I recall being told by people whose words I trust that the old Swedish General Königsmark once gave a feast for all the Swedish generals and many fine people. Afterwards, the guests, in praising the excellent meal, noted that the East Indians had not thereby become one pfennig (penny) richer, since only German herbs were used – rosemary, sage, marjoram, melissas and the like. And although without any doubt there was no lack of sugar, this is after all more something from the West rather than the East Indies. Which leads me to remark that everything that comes from the West Indies is far more acceptable than from the East, since the latter has to be paid for with coin, while the former can be exchanged for European manufactures. A great Polish nobleman is said to have held a banquet like that of General Königsmark at the Imperial Diet. And I would think a great deal more of our Austrian cooks if they studied such Swedish soups, rather than the French. But to come back to the point: we can cultivate silk here, and as for bombazine, we can replace it with our fine wool and linen. As for cordovan, Russian and saffiano leather, no one has made a serious effort to produce it, since this has already been done elsewhere. We can replace scurvious, indigestible, salted, bone-dry fish with our quite edible freshwater fish from river and pond, and with our good fresh beef, veal and mutton, plus our nice domestic fowl, not forgetting venison. Indeed, we can substitute many things almost directly, so instead of northern fish, we have our abundant Hungarian fish, using our surplus salt and smoking it. Without any doubt, we can grow and cultivate an unbelievable amount of foreign foods in our own soil, even if this will need rather more hard work here than would be the case in their natural soil. I do not wish to say very much about the lack of proportion between our surplus and lack, the latter being little, the former great; nor about unequal consumption, since there is far less application in the world for the goods we lack than the goods which we have in abundance, and which also provide much usable material for manufacture and industry. It is an irrefutable truth that the hereditary Imperial lands are far more fortunate in their abundance than unfortunate in their lack. If otherwise, it should be thought a misfortune to be spared the instruments and attractions of the disorderly desires of opulence and pride.

XIII. Conclusion to be drawn from this balance

How wise, some will say, *to write down with such fuss things with which even our children in the street are not unfamiliar!* Answer: that may be true, if you are lucky. But I wish to conclude from this either: that even those who know most are unaware of all this; or worse, if they do know of it, they do not want to be thought to know it. Least of all, are they concerned to do what they could and should for the good of their fatherland and the common weal, applying their knowledge to good ends. Or there are those who would gladly use such knowledge (I have certainly known some of these among great and the good), but they receive such a bludgeoning that they never put their intention into effect. But what I conclude is the following: *A country that so fully possesses within its own borders, independently of others, all life's essentials, and also the major comforts of human subsistence, and indeed in such abundance that it can supply its genuinely needy neighbours with a large part of the same for money; if that country were short of money, powerless against its neighbours, and weak in opposing its enemies then it would really be poorly advised and have conducted its economy very poorly – its poverty and all the evils and misfortune thence arising being entirely a matter of its own will, and its own fault.* These are only a few words, but they are true words whose certainty requires no philosophy in support, and whose clarity requires for their understanding no cameralistic nor commercial sciences. They are based upon one simple principle that even children can understand: *he who has a large income and spends little will either quickly become rich; or if not, he must have wilfully wasted it.*

XIV. False objections concerning why the Imperial lands have a natural abundance, yet lack money

Perhaps some well-educated person might wonder *why it is that those lands most blessed by nature are those which are poorest in money. If we consider this in detail, we find that hereabouts the peasants living in rough, infertile mountains and unfelled land, who have to feed themselves through spinning, woodcutting and a hundred other chores, usually have more money, deal with the qualities of their land and order themselves better than those who live in the best lands for corn and wine.* The answer is that this is very often true, but hardly praiseworthy. At the same time, it is no less clear that the peasants in the mountains are hard-working people, and the others often lazy good-for-nothings. Both are respectively rich and poor because this is what they want for themselves, which is exactly what I claim. Whosoever is not ashamed of making such a stupid objection, would neither be ashamed for the answer to apply to him. Moreover, if something is to be added to the examples, then one follows the good, rather than the bad, example. There are still some countries in the world whose inhabitants are no less industrious, substantial and rich. Let us emulate these.

Others say: *water, air and all the elements do not favour the chances of the hereditary lands becoming as rich as other countries.* But if the elements are so gracious as to place all kinds of wealth in my lap, which element can be so merciless and tyrannical as to force me, against my will, to tip such wealth into the mud and dung again? Foolishness and malice talk past each other in such useless objections.

What can we do about this? It will perhaps seem laughable enough to some that, *following the natural implantation of commerce and manufactures, no worthwhile genius can be found to speak for them?* Such unhappy genius consists only in ignorance and clumsiness. Now there are two kinds of ignorance and clumsiness: a wilful variety, properly called idleness, inattentiveness, diffidence and often spite; of which everyone, if he only wishes, can easily cure himself. The other kind kind can be ascribed to nature: except that, to be honest, there are few nations under the sun that can complain of this. Nonetheless, we wish shortly to investigate whether someone, from among the Austrians or those living in the hereditary lands in general, might allow himself to suffer abuse to his own and his fatherland's disgrace, so that the genius presently lacking in commerce and manufacture might excuse itself?

XV. Whether the Germans do not actually possess sufficient natural intellect and skill for the commerce and manufactures of the hereditary Imperial lands

I am aware that many people consider that the Germans, in comparison with other nations, must seem rather dense as regards intellect. Among the French in particular, this has become an established saying. Insofar as this relates to an apparently wilful stupidity, I can do no other than for the most part agree. For if I wanted to dispute the proposition, I would simply be struck by the unanswerable irrelevance of its contrary; considering the way in which we Germans serve our own true interest so badly, making such poor provision for our general well-being and our liberty above all with regard to the French, who mock us for it. We also take from them that which we could just as well have at home, and better; giving them our precious gold and silver, leaving them bearing witness to our suffering. So we justly deserve to be laughed at by them for such poor use of our own money. There is however another explanation for natural understanding. In this, I do not disagree over-much with the French, what they rightly call 'esprit' lies perhaps more in the general fluency of their speech and their way of presenting themselves, rather than in any especially significant light of reason. Not that we should have any natural deficiency in this, but we have for the most part been brought up differently, giving us a greater sense of custom and tradition. Besides, as regards what healthy common sense, judgement and ingenuity in the serious sciences can give to a nation, the French should credit me if, in comparison with the Germans, I admit neither their advantage, nor equality. In the four principal [University] faculties, we are at least in balance with them, despite what they might imagine. In matters of state, they will recall what kind of people they use to deceive us, and what kind of nation their foremost envoys and instruments among us think they belong to. For as in the proverb, where the Devil cannot go himself, he sends an old woman. Where for us, French wit is wanting, they invent the kind of German about whom they make light. In the mathematical sciences, they will perhaps have sufficient modesty to share first place. In any case, it is a different story with the two leading inventions of the Germans [printing and artillery] that have practically transformed the world of the sciences and of artillery, together with other inventions (among them clocks) which, while of lesser importance, are also important in themselves, as testified by their present king. A few years ago, the inventive brothers Hautsch of Nuremberg set up a squadron of model horsemen for him on a table, their inner workings able to emulate in an almost unbelievable fashion all kinds of field manoeuvres; and having had them presented to him, the king said: "It has to be said that the Germans are inspired [*ont bien de l'esprit*]". A French noble in attendance sought to claim the same for his nation and dared to add: "Sire, the French however have the advantage". But the king wasted few words in noting the difference, saying "Yes, in inventing new fashions in clothes". Now that mathematical art plays such a role in manufacture, it is easy to tell if the Germans are lacking in this, and one would only have to look at Nuremberg and Augsburg. These two cities deserve praise for being practically the only major trading cities in the entire Empire that benefit the fatherland, by drawing money from abroad with their manufactures, since the others mostly buy from abroad, simply letting German money flow abroad without having learned how to bring it back again. And what is there to learn? If the German nation has been such an example in manufactures and in trade to the French and its neighbours, if still today the Germans remain in the lead, how can their understanding of it be any less that that of others? Now it is known the whole world over that four or five hundred years ago the Hansa cities had almost a monopoly in manufacture and industry throughout the greater part of Europe, and that it introduced such industry into the Netherlands (and into Germany), then England and France. It is no less evident that, when a German worker arrives among French or Dutch workers, he soon shows them up in skill and hard work. And that is true of the Germans as a whole.

Regarding the hereditary Imperial lands, it should not be forgotten how flourishing manufactures were before the great Bohemian and German Wars, and had been continuously so for the two or three hundred years previously. Like Bohemia, Silesia and Moravia (all of which I think had kings from the House of Lützelburg[13]), they teemed with wool and linen mills (which both certainly come first among all manufactures). Anyone who claimed that the understanding that our forefathers had of manufacturing was completely lost by their own children in one generation would be a laughing stock; doubtless he might venture to conclude that, since then, climate and other heavenly influences had altered. That also, in other iron-making pursuits the Austrians have no peer is demonstrated by Upper Austria, Crain and Silesia, not forgetting Styria. And more, Breslau's good order, trade and manufactures could, if necessary, claim the honour of the hereditary lands. The hard work and assiduousness of the inhabitants of Silesia, a land that now in many places lies in the most terrible neglect, would be sufficient to process all the wool and flax grown in the hereditary lands, supplying themselves and their neighbours with their product. These honest people work up their own cloth and linen, as is well-known. Now

13 Here referring to the imperial House of Luxembourg.

in the hereditary lands, everyone is buying up foreign goods, and the Silesians neglect their own resources. So the Dutchmen[14] come along, pick the material up and specially prepare it elsewhere, finishing and dyeing it, then send it back to us through a quite laughable trading arrangement as good Dutch wares; which they are, not only in quality, but at two or three times the price. Whoever gets as far with cloth or linen as combing, carding, teasing, spinning and weaving so that he only lacks proper finishing does not have to be a man of genius to see that he can do this as well. If he only applied the same amount of work and thought (no more than this is needed) to silks, then France and Italy could certainly save themselves the trouble of supplying us. Some areas are more hard-working than others; those in the wine-growing areas being accused of being more fond of drinking than working, and allowing the import of manufactures to turn them within a few years into loafers and idlers. By contrast, those in the beer-producing lands are far more industrious. And if the plains of Bohemia are suited everywhere to grain and animal husbandry, and wine-growing is worthwhile, there is a general lack of industriousness. The mountainous areas of German Bohemia are full of hard-working people. In Vienna itself, where pleasure-seeking and a desire for a merry life have become the custom, there is no lack of skill or industry if there be sufficient will, encouragement and direction. The example can be given of the well-known French hat makers who were so poor, yet in a few years grew very wealthy. They produced neither for themselves, nor for their countrymen, but for Germans – in particular, for Austrians. It is often the same with adornments, wigs, embroidered goods and the like, which can be made by good Austrians, but are bought from the French. And in the best shops the latest fashions can be found that are born, bred and worn out in the city, but which have to be called French so that it can be sold without punishment by unchristian profiteers. There is so much like this. If only the authorities would get to work, the instruments, means and opportunity for cheating and idleness would be swept away. Above all, it requires no great study and investigation regarding spirit and genius to discover how to make the hereditary lands rich. It needs a simple broad approach and quite moderate understanding. If our spirit is not subtle enough to invent or establish new manufactures, then things should be left as they are for a few years, and we should content ourselves with such domestic goods as we have, closing the door on foreign goods. The German spirit will soon enough show itself once it sees that the consumption of its products is certain, that its work is valued, profit guaranteed, and that, since the inadequacy of its goods no longer leads to their being displaced from abroad, no longer does anything stand in the way of their enjoyment and use. With the inducement of profit, and that of the buyer's desire for good curious wares, one artisan will emulate the other and so encourage work and diligence. Every peasant can have the sense that, if he can meet his needs himself, he can do without foreign things. Why then can we not do the same?

XVI. What should be the first rule of a well-ordered oeconomy in the hereditary lands?

If then the hereditary Imperial lands have at home sufficient for their own subsistence, or can have such sufficiency almost completely, then they can be rich if they want to be

---

14 Later editions, for instance the Frankfurt/Leipzig 1753 one (p. 58) changed the original 'Dutch' and 'Dutchmen' into 'foreign'/ 'foreigners' (*Auslaender*).

so. Now we shall, on the basis of the above rules, show how this wish should be exercised by us.

According to the first rule, no patch of land that could possibly benefit us for anything shall remain untilled. However, I am reliably informed that there are some areas belonging to the Bohemian crown where there is so much barren or overgrown land available that many thousand peasant families could exist there. What then of the entire kingdom, and of all the other hereditary lands? How much wooded mountainside is there, how many shallow valleys could be made suitable for wine-growing or arable cultivation or other no less useful employment if there were only an industrious hand behind it? With what incomparable effort do the Dutch look after their inundated land, just a hand's breadth really and unrewarding when compared with our excellent soil? If these same people could purchase the leisure we have, would they not count themselves lucky? Further, no kind of plantation under the sun should remain unexplored, to see if it bears comparison with our soil. For as we said, the closeness or the distance of the sun is not everything. The soil itself, its inner quality, and as it seems, archaeus terrae if it is such a kind of land, plays a great part in this. Tokaj wine is the noblest in the world, and Austrian saffron the most superb under the sun, and these demonstrate, or at least give us cause to hope, that there are many other alien delicate plants yet unheard of that could be domesticated here, if only the attempt were made with a careful hand. Even if in fifty attempts just one met expectations, the costs, trouble and curiosity would be worth it. Where is he, however, who among us has ever been stirred to explore the nature of the sublime hereditary lands more thoroughly than ever before? Who has had the curiosity to experiment with new forms of plantation (I am not talking of private passion, but those that serve the good of the fatherland)? Without any doubt there is a great deal to do. Although it is not one man's work to make such a study, there are examples of how one might proceed. In Holland, an experiment is now being made with the cultivation of tea. In some parts of Germany, aloe is being tried. Who would have thought that the cochineal that used to be brought from India at great expense could be introduced to Germany? But this has actually happened in the woods of the Meissner[15] region, and there is no doubt that they can equally be found in the adjoining Bohemian mountains. It is hard to imagine that one pound of insects could be gathered for four talers. Just think how many strawberries some children might collect for four talers. The country gardens near Vienna, and other private gardens, have shown that the flower that to my knowledge has no German name, but which is called Amaranthus maximus Indicus or Blitum Americanum, can flourish here. Everyone looks at the flower, but does not know that some years ago, in France, beautiful new dyes were obtained from it. The meadows here would be suitable for it. Neither would we lack for safflower, wild saffron, woad and similar dyes, if only some thought were given to it and some work done. Just like a few years ago, potatoes were introduced into Hungary and Austria, and Spanish tomatoes – this is all well-known. There would be more of the same sort to the advantage of the general good to be found in commerce, if only the effort was made. Two major examples stand out, one of which had been briefly considered, the other not at all. The first is tobacco, unknown in Europe one hundred and eighty years ago, in Germany about sixty. Its cultivation is now commonplace not only in the Empire, but also

---

15 Saxony.

in Poland, in Turkey and roundabout, and has developed into a great trade. The hereditary lands are themselves so dilatory in the matter that they would rather spend an unbelievable amount of money annually (I would rather estimate the correct sum than be specific) than begin its cultivation here. Likewise there is little doubt that it might flourish in many places in Hungary and also in Austria and Bohemia, not as in Brazil and Virginia, but at least as good as in neighbouring Turkey. It would indeed be very fortunate for Bohemia if cultivation were undertaken there. The second example is the cultivation of silk. Austrian and Hungarian soil shows itself so wonderfully suited to the white mulberry tree. Someone told me that Austrian silk is rather like a nice soft flax. That might be true of the silk from around Niklasburg some time ago (although I am not entirely certain of this) but that is nowhere near the best Austrian soil, and even less the best Hungarian soil. Often, one soil is very unlike it neighbour in quality. All the same, while silk has not flourished here and there in the hereditary lands, this does not mean it has not succeeded anywhere. I know one example of Frankish silk that was sold with other silks, and judged to be the best in an entire shop by someone unfamiliar with its source, but otherwise experienced in the matter. Austria and Hungary have soil that is at least the equal of Franconia. Why then not find a patch of land there that could produce silk of a quality comparable to that of Franconia? I ignore for the time being that this good sometimes does better in a cold climate rather than a warm one. It must also be said that even poor silk is more suited to some everyday fabrics than fine silk, and does not lack for profits since it is used more for everyday goods than fine, which are not for everyone. In this regard, then, local silk cultivation should not be so much discounted. For who would want to deny that here and there silk might well be cultivated, and better products made than elsewhere in the world? And not only to introduce new plants, but to multiply and improve those already in the country, that would be in accord with this principal of the watchful eye, from which the country could draw unbelievable advantage. But of this sapienti & volenti satis. For anyone who wished to advance this would find sufficient things to sate his curiosity, and fill his empty hours in a both pleasurable and useful pursuit.

What can be done with plantations could also possibly be done with animal husbandry, finding in other ways something more advantageous. As regards the horse, the hereditary lands are so well-stocked that it is not necessary to do what the king of France does in Normandy: since horses are not that numerous, he directed that in some villages studs be created for horse-breeding. Which would not itself be a bad idea here, that fillies not be used for work before they reached a certain age. Otherwise, it could be of great benefit to the hereditary lands if sheep were shorn in Bohemia rather later, increasing the amount of long wool for the benefit of woollen cloth. It should also be noted here that on infertile sandy soils and heathland, as in Saxony (whose wool is at least the equal of the English, or even can be made more fine), the wool is a great deal finer in the Mark of Brandenburg and around Brunswick than that from more fertile lands in Austria and Hungary. No doubt there would be much more to be discovered in these matters by anyone who cared to investigate them. And there is a matter almost worth laughing about that I cannot here neglect: that for a long time the expensive delicacy from Italy and France, the ortolan[16], was treated as something very rare, and they

16 A small bird used as a delicacy in modern French cuisine.

were brought here by post-chaise for a doubloon a time. Some years ago, Duke Johann Friedrich of Brunswick and Hanover sent his chamber-servant to Italy, who found this delicacy on sale in the market, and thought it a disgrace that his fatherland should not harbour such a useless little bird. He therefore took the trouble of acquiring a few of them and brought them back. Then it turned out that this foreign, strange and tasty ortolan was, in skin and feathers, nothing but our familiar wren that can be caught in many places in Germany as well as it can in France and Italy. No doubt, when they are well-baked and brought to table they are good to eat. We simple Germans have hitherto done nothing other than pay good money for a foreign name. It is nonetheless true that ortolans can be kept in a particular way in a dark room, letting the light in only when they are to be fed, quickly plumping up; and then Mediterranean ortolans metamorphose into German wrens. They then perhaps do not taste so good because they have not been so dearly bought, and because they are no longer brought by post-chaise from Italy and France. That makes me also think how long the world let itself be fooled by Piedmontese Rossoli. I don't know exactly what the ingredients were, but it is actually no more that refined sugar, mixed with some good brandy (that made from syrup being the most suitable), with a little amber, jasmine or similar for taste, and while purified, a little ground almonds is added to give it a bit of body. I also recall that when a well-known curious character planted potatoes in Meissen, a peasant woman from the Vogtland[17] was amazed that anyone could devote such effort to the planting of such useless stuff, since she had more than enough in her garden at home and had no idea how to get rid of them. So this West India delicacy has long been native to Germany, but treated as a weed.

But what most of all belongs under this first economic rule concerns mines, and mainly gold and silver. As for those being presently worked, I know of nothing either good or bad, since I have no information, and am thus inclined to hold to the general rule (omnis homo videtur esse bonus, donec probetur malis). Regarding those being worked long ago, and before the Bohemian war, but which now lie idle, entire laments could be written about them. I will talk only about Jlowa or Eyl, an old royal Bohemian mining town made famous by the legend of Princess Libushe, about three miles from Prague. If the inhabitants are to be believed, the mine used to produce annually three or four hundred thousand ducats in gold after costs, which would be twelve to sixteen hundred thousand gulden in our present silver currency. If the costs were added, a lot more was extracted and put into circulation in the hereditary lands. What is happening there now? Not a grain of gold has been produced. I do not know which enemy assault led to the mines being flooded. In the meantime, the older people have died, and the younger no longer know the shafts. Little can be learned from the older books because the names of the valleys have been changed. And so they lie idle, increasingly ruined by water. In short, the kingdom has been robbed of an invaluable treasure. God willing, that it not be for ever. Doubtless the same sort of thing has happened in many parts of Bohemia, and these spurned gifts of God are a permanent rebuke to our irresponsible lack of effort.

---

17 An area near the Saxon Erz Mountains.

Nature calls through them from its pregnant womb, pleading with us to have mercy and relieve her of this burden. But nobody hears her, nobody wants to hear her. Whether this is curse or bewitchment I do not know. It cannot be for lack of timber. After such a long time, there must be more than enough there. Given the sorry loss and misfortune of the older mines, one could almost forget the failure to seek new ones. Here there would be a great deal to be done, and a king of France would lick his fingers if he were fortunate enough to have such prospects in his kingdom. But it seems we are already so rich and proud that we no longer pay attention to such petty matters. The blame cannot really be laid upon the lack of people or miners. I believe that such workers could be found in certain places in the hereditary lands. Perhaps also, means could be found to bring back those who fled during the period of war and Reformation.

XVII. Concerning the observance of the second and third oeconomic rules in the hereditary Imperial lands

I move on now to the second rule and its observance, and wish that I had something more pleasing than in the first to report. This rule concerns the working up of domestic raw goods, or their transformation in manufactures. It can be seen at a glance how we are placed with that; in the hereditary lands there is almost a flood of spun wool, flax, and linen, unworked hides, copper and tinplate, quicksilver and similar materials, that foreigners make into cloth, stockings, hats, linen, embroidery, leather, crockery, dye and countless other things that could be much better made in the hereditary lands than abroad, but which they sell back to us; while the money that they pay for the raw materials (and which is only borrowed for a short time) is drawn out of the country three, six and maybe tenfold, or with the embroidery a hundredfold. Unhappy land, this is ruinously and incomparably more than Jewish usury and to which we freely and voluntarily submit ourselves. There is no need to remark on major things, since they are in any case well-known. Small things are not attended to, but together they add up. From our quicksilver, Venice and Amsterdam supply us with sublimate, precipitate and vermilion. From our lead, we are supplied with red and white lead from other places. Our copper is made into verdigris in Montpellier. With that and our calamine, Messina crockery is made elsewhere and then imported. The Vogtland and Upper Pfalz (Palatine) send us woven woollen cloth made from our Pilsen long-staple wool. Annaberg[18] and Dutch embroidery is made from our Silesian yarn and thread and sold back to us for more than one hundred times the price. And we have a brain, eyes and hands just like everyone else, more and better raw materials than others, sufficient opportunity, enough poor people needing bread who could richly feed themselves from its manufacture if they were shown how to make it, and employed to do so. None of this happens by itself, nor by accident, for all our hard work and attention.

---

18 Annaberg: A once-flourishing mining town in the Saxon Erz mountains whose inhabitants switched, after the mines ceased to keep pace with the incoming floods of silver from America during the sixteenth century, to textile working.

There are two manufactures I cannot just pass over, since they have wounded us so deeply: tinplate and smalta, or blue dye. For many years, both were located in Bohemia, but because of Reformation or war, they moved many miles away to Meissen. What an unbelievable treasure Bohemia has lost in this way! The latter alone, consisting of little more than a mineral which is made into glaze by hand and which is otherwise little-regarded, is now monopolized by Meissen throughout the world, drawing many hundred thousand talers annually from abroad into the locality. The first, tinplate, is more complicated, giving rise to more subsistence and profit than smalta, and so much more useful for the country. It requires a great deal of tallow and wheat, from which an acidic water is made to etch the metal, to make the tin much more acceptable. Bohemia had these two fat roasts right in front of its nose, but let them be torn from its teeth, and has barely thought about how it could get the work back, at least in part. It is even so generous as to supply the people of Meissen with timber, without which those living in the Meissen hills could barely warm their houses with what they could obtain locally. I have nothing against the people of Meissen. Rather, I praise them for being so industrious in pursuing their own advantage. But I cannot praise the Bohemians for letting them do so. Apart from that, iron is about the only thing that we can boast of: the works in Upper Austria and Upper Styria, also the hammer mills in Carinthia, Carniola, Silesiaand elsewhere deserve honourable mention.

What should I say about the third rule? That the hereditary Imperial lands have as many inhabitants as it could support and feed is quite clear; and it is likewise certain that, when cloth and linen weaving flourished, the towns and cities must have had populations two or three times as great. War and Reformation are to blame for the current grievous situation. As for the war, in twenty-four years, the German hereditary lands, besides what has recently happened in Austria, have had no sworn enemies. All the same, the distress shown by many places seems so new that it is as though the enemy moved out only yesterday or the day before. Even where there has been no warfare for a hundred years, two or three hundred citizens, a good part of them poor day labourers, seems like a town. I will say nothing of the Reformation, but note only that rulers, no doubt from the best of intentions, brought ruin to so many people and their own lands, leading to the expulsion of people, manufactures and subsistence, for which, given their praiseworthy motives, I do not chide them. There should, on the other hand, be people with no less justice who, out of intentions just as good, set about finding means of bringing people back in. But there is nobody. Even though the populating of land is one of the most important issues in affairs of state deserving the close attention of offices and collegia[19]; but circumstances are so unfortunate that little thought is given to this in many privy council chambers, as if it were some American island of no concern to us that was to be populated. Rather, it has to be admitted that even now, without any war and no Reformation, the malady spreads covertly and unnoticed while, in neighbouring states, cities, markets and villages are set up for those who have fled.

---

19 Contemporary state departments or boards concerned with economic development. See introduction.

XVIII. What is considered in the remaining six oeconomic rules

There is an obvious problem regarding the fourth rule for retaining gold and silver that has been brought into the country,. Several millions are drawn into the country in return for our wine, oxen, wool, flax, yarn, hides, copper, quicksilver, iron, tin, lead, malachite and other minerals, as well as all kinds of other things that leave the hereditary lands. But, after a short while, the goods made with these materials draw two or three times as much out of the country again.

Besides these goods, cash has to be paid for Indian spices, Mediterranean dried fruits, Northern fish, all silk wares, all the shoddy stuff called French goods, plus all the other things that come from abroad. Anyone with a spark of intelligence has to see that it would be impossible to pay for all this if the gold and silver mined here every year was not used in addition to our materials, and so wasted on foreigners. It follows from this that the fourth rule applies especially to us.

The fifth rule is equally unfortunate. If one followed it and contented oneself with whatever one's own country produced, the fourth rule would also be supported. I freely admit that an abuse that has developed and become an immutable custom does not warrant the exclusion of everything foreign, and I include here spices, salted and dried fish, oil and some dried fruits. While the use of these might be moderated or even substituted, other goods should certainly be kept out. At the least, keep out foreign woollen and linen manufactures, and also bombazine, the import of which has brought down not only Austrian and German, but all European trade in fabrics, for which Europe can thank that treasure the Dutch East India Company. We should instead content ourselves with domestic goods. Besides that, French goods should be exorcised as impure spirits. That means silk ribbons, embroidery, ornamentation, buttons, beaver (which in France is made out of nothing other than Brunswick wool), other woollens and hat fabrics, feathers, baldrics, fronds, caps, masks, mirrors, clocks, combs, night-wear, head coverings, dainty shoes, pins, needles, ironmongery and thousands upon thousands of worthless stuff. They are a proper plague and death to our well-being. I cannot stop myself noting here what the well-known tract on commerce says about French goods, for I neither want to steal the work of others, nor trust myself to improve upon it. He [Johann Joachim Becher in *Politische Discurs*] says that "French goods do consist of all sorts of things. For us Germans, no clothing seems right any more if it does not come from France. I will here tell only what needs to be known of these French manufactures that are of slight utility: French razors shave our German beards better than any other; French scissors and clippers cut fingernails and hair better than ours. Their clocks work better when made in Paris for Germans, for the air is better there than in Augsburg. Their mirrors are supposed to be better than those of Venice. Their female accessories – ribbons, necklaces, shoes, stockings, even their dresses are better for being perfumed with French air. However, I would moderate this smell with brimstone before putting them on. One can travel no better than in a French carriage. Their headwear suits all German heads. And the French have better ways of measuring clothes. French wigs look better on a German head than German hair itself. Such French hair can only be combed with a French comb, only be powdered with French powder, beards only brushed with a French beard-brush or set with a French iron, German teeth can only be cleaned with a French toothbrush – while German money can only be gambled away with French cards, and only kept in a French purse. It is certain that German bread and other foodstuffs can be cut by us with French knives better than by the French themselves, for even those at Court use their fingers. I have heard from wenches that French needles and yarn are much better to sew with than German; that French plasters stick on the face better than German. Who among us Germans would have had the heart to pin a piece of wood on a woman's body and tell her that otherwise she would become hump-backed? The French have done so. They really know how to set up a woman: dresses, hair, eyes, teeth, face powders, breastplates, blouses, stockings, and shoes. They can shower them with mirrors, clocks, corals, ribbons, books. One can pray more piously with French books. They make holes in their ears and hang what they like from them; just like one coiffs little dogs. The ears should be made as long as those of an ass. In a word:

> Germany has to its great loss,
> Oh what frenzy, what a fuss!
> Foreign merchants invited here,
> Now they must pay for it so dear.
> Foreign goods but which sad to say,
> Are just strange clothes, none so gay.
> And so we Germans unabashed,
> Are rich in fashion, poor in cash.

So much for the treatise on commerce? But I must add to the above that all silken goods must be included in the prohibition. It would be different with raw silk, until its cultivation has been developed here.

It is plain from what has already been said how badly we do with the sixth rule concerning exchanging those domestic goods that we have in abundance for the goods that we need from abroad; and the seventh, that such goods should be purchased in their unworked state and then manufactured by us, so that the wages of manufacturing be kept at home. To this I must add something concerning the wages of labour. At Leiden, the centre of Dutch woollen manufacture, one hundred and twenty five cloths (each of them sixty Brabantine ells) are daily brought to market. Even in 1672, in the midst of the French war, it was one hundred a day. Since the Dutch have few holidays, one can reckon with three hundred working days a year, making on average thirty seven thousand cloths a year. In Leiden, each cloth costs in wages forty Rix dollars (Reichsthaler), not counting the cost of the wool, from the first shearing through all stages until it reaches the market hall. But cloth-making is only one third of woollen manufactures in Leiden; for another third is so-called small goods, and then also knitted goods. Taken altogether, this comes to five and a half million taler (Rix dollars) clear. The profit that the merchant manufacturers make from this could be almost double this sum. But I will assume it is half, and so about two million, or more or less ten million gulden, which is what one single Dutch city makes for itself and the state, using their labour and capital in their own manufacture. If all the best manufactories in the hereditary lands together (excluding shoemakers and tailors) could bring into this country, or help keep here, as much as one city with its labour and merchant capital made, they really would deserve great praise.

Whoever might contribute to the eighth rule, concerning the promotion of the consumption elsewhere of our superfluous goods, would make himself very useful. But there is no one. For this reason, Hungarians, and those Germans in Hungarian lands, are almost drowning in Hungarian wine in the effort of getting rid of it. There are many other examples. We often rely for the sale of our goods on foreign whim, making no attempt to persuade customers, but simply waiting for them to come and pick up the goods at our door.

As proof of the way in which the ninth rule is ignored, it should have been sufficient to have shown that because of the uncommon rage for everything foreign, such goods are favoured over anything domestic and given free passage into this country. This could be proved one hundredfold. I will only give two examples here, both of which appear to be of little significance, but from which it is far easier to come to conclusions about greater things. It is known that woad is far more practicable as a dye for fabrics than indigo, and can be grown everywhere in the hereditary lands. By contrast, indigo is listed as a non-useful good in the Imperial laws and has been prohibited several times under the name of "Devil's dye". Nonetheless, we take up this banned Indian Devil's concoction and pay no attention at all to good woad. I cite this example because the Holy Roman Empire does itself unbelievable damage in a matter that is perhaps little noticed. For as one experienced in this has told me, up to a million taler leaves Germany every year just to pay for indigo; while what had previously flowed in to pay for woad also remains outside. Many thousand cottagers who had before relied for a great deal of their subsistence on woad are now forced to suffer and starve for the sake of indigo, not to mention how much cloth and fabric smeared with it declines in quality. A similar example is provided by the case of gauze. According to the patriotic author of *Bedencken von Manufacturen in Deutschland* (1683), printed in Jena last year[20], just the lands of Saxony give fifteen thousand taler to foreigners for this; reckoned up for all the hereditary lands and the remaining empire this must amount to one half million taler. It is not as though we did not already have enough low-grade wool with which this could be made. And it is not as though no one knew about this, given how much is paid in Saxony.

So much for the observance of the nine economic principles in the hereditary Imperial lands. It is also said: if one is good, then all are good. But I say of the material gathered here: if one of these principles was ever sufficiently observed by us, then all of them were. But in fact, we do not find this true of a single one. From head to foot, this is no healthy state to be in. And does anyone still wonder, or seriously investigate the cause, why the lands are so short of money? It looks more like an Austrian miracle that everything did not go to rack and ruin long ago.

20 By Johann Daniel Crafft. See introduction.

XIX. Whether it is advisable to expose the oeconomy of the hereditary lands so openly

So both Austria's advantages and disadvantages, the former being granted by nature, the latter a matter of will, have, I believe, now been sufficiently exposed. *More than enough some will perhaps say, deriding our efforts for all time in the eyes of those, both in the present and the future, who witness here the appalling revelation of the disgrace of our broken oeconomy.* But I deny this. For you do not need to disclose something that the world already knows better than I do in describing the conditions prevailing in the hereditary lands. We would be truly witless if we imagined that any Italian, Dutchman, Englishman, Frenchman or German well-acquainted with trading and who settled here for six months would not see right through us. Indeed, he would hardly need to come here. It is enough that he knew that our raw materials went to his country and that finished goods, together with other foreign manufactures, were then sent back to us. He would soon enough come to a conclusion about our good economic order. And if one of them were to flatter us on account of our supposedly good husbandry, that would be those who privately think us fops and dandies, and seek only to hold us to the opinion of what is good about our husbandry so that they might lead us by the nose until they have quietly stripped us of everything. More, if it is a disgrace to discover a mistake, it is an even bigger disgrace to make it, and quite irresponsible not to want to remedy it. Someone might add, *what made it necessary to write down on paper something already known to the whole wide world?* It would be necessary for those who, most of all, should know it, but do not, or at least behave as if they did not – hence for us ourselves. Shortage of money is the curse of our fatherland. Everyone feels it, and everyone complains of it. However, no one can see its root and origin; or those who do see it do not take it to heart, and either cannot be of any help, or will not.

But I hear you cry, 'what do you know about all this?' In all your life you have never once visited our Treasury or attended to our merchants. Are you completely unfamiliar with both? Did not Hannibal laugh about the philosopher who ventured to discuss warfare in his presence? One should suppose that you confuse theory with practice, applying *principia generalia ad casum;* the same thing will happen to you as it did to the well-known Italian who wrote *"de arte militari".*[21] When asked by an Italian prince to lead his army in battle according to the rules he had laid down, the poor man showed himself less a general and more like someone who had never even been a corporal. I do think that I am wrong in assuming that we have no Hannibal in matters of our country's oeconomy. Otherwise, my writing would of course be unnecessary, and I could do without the derision. That prominent Italian did perhaps still open the eyes of many, and in so doing, he did better than the teacher. I am quite sure that these few poor sheets will finally fall into the hands of someone who will know how to apply them to the common good better than their writer. It sometimes happens in the council chamber that one person opens the eyes of the others with an idea that he has yet to try out, but without which the others would have been at a loss. An ordinary person can sometimes identify an illness;

---

21 Machiavelli, *Dell' arte della guerra* (1521).

but, for a cure, a physician is needed. And someone who observes a game of chance is often better positioned to judge whether he understands the game better than the one playing it. The defects in our economy and policy are now plain; but these basic rules to follow in economy and policy have been set beside these defects, showing how recovery is possible in the same way that a ship steers by the North Star. It is, however, something else to set to work to bring this about in the hereditary lands. Do we not have, among those many enlightened ministers with knowledge of the hereditary lands – ministers who are experienced, bold and in good standing with Emperor and Fatherland – a sufficient number ready to take on this challenge? I do believe that we have yet to be so far rejected by God that there should be no hope. Rather I console myself that some will be found prepared to be the chosen instruments of God in the salvation of our otherwise unhappy fatherland. O fortunate hereditary Imperial lands, and blessed day on which we will experience such salvation! Dearest, eternally praised Emperor, the figure entrusted by God with this troubled and embattled land and people; come to their aid with firm resolution and irrevocable order, helping them to escape from the mire of incapacity and want. Yes indeed, the fortunate Turkish emergency, the blessed devastation of Austria, the hoped for flight from Vienna – if all of this finally brings about an opening of eyes, the rolling up of shirt-sleeves; and if, aided by the sacrifice of part of the cargo, the wallowing ship of the hereditary commonweal survives the great storm, it can be rescued from the mighty storm and saved from sinking.

XX. From whom we might expect the reform of improper oeconomy

Yes indeed, I say, our salvation has to come from the rulers of our people. Without them, the community cannot succeed. If some of the people were to decide do without fashionable foreign goods, they could not do so without being treated as fools by their peers. If, however, the authorities were to set an example, then both – the willing and the unwilling – would have to concede. We wait in vain for any help from our merchants. Generally speaking, they know no more than how to buy up goods abroad and sell them to us. If they were asked for advice about the improvement of manufactures, which is the real basis and soul of commerce, then they would say almost regretfully, quite confidentially, admonishing us: Nothing can be done about it, otherwise you and others like you would have done it long ago. But they are quite right in saying this. For them and their kind there is no more to be done, since other manufacturers or merchant capitalists are either factors or sub-contractors; and generally understand less about the work of manufactories than Till Eulenspiegel's[22] student, the ass, knew of his ABC, who did however know how to make two sounds from it. So long as things are left up to the merchants, domestic manufactures will remain eternally undeveloped. Instead of doing something themselves, they obstruct what others seek to do. Only a higher authority will quell their common opposition to what is proposed here. I protest at this point yet

---

22 Proverbial fool or joker that flourished, according to lore, in northern Germany around the town of Mölln during the mid-fourteenth century.

again that I have nothing at all in general against commerce and trading, nor do I complain of it. However, I hold in high regard those merchants who do their duty and act for the best of the common state, from which the welfare of a country greatly depends. Indeed, I hold them in even higher regard than perhaps anyone else in the world and think them the apple of the state's eye. But the others, whose commerce causes damage to the fatherland – I cannot spare them in the least without betraying the welfare of the common weal, insofar as my work relates to it. They are to be reined in and made to work in the interest of the country, which is their own real interest too. By turning away from the improper oeconomy currently practised here, we can prevail against them. I am not joking when I say that, to begin with, as much resolution, alertness and determination will be needed as it is when a foreign foe is breathing down our necks, although without so much danger, dust and blood. The fury of merchants against those whom they think are damaging their profit, however falsely, is unbelievable. Their cunning is indescribable. The audacity with which they throw themselves into opposition is infinite. They will invoke heaven and earth, calling upon and buying up assistants and accessories from all social ranks, genders and professions, once they truly realize the seriousness of the matter. Woe to them, whoever they may be, who seek to take on those who corrupt the common weal: whether this be from an imagined good intention, which is actually nothing but gross ignorance (for they should not involve themselves in matters outside their province that they do not understand); or for money and other interests.

These merchants will find it hard to account for their responsibility to God and the world. Curses are rained down on both them and their clients by those poor people chased from house and home in the hereditary lands and driven to the edge of ruin. And if all others are supposed to hold their peace, those unhappy people dragged off into Turkish slavery, in bodily pain, with loss of liberty and with imperiled souls – they will not keep quiet. They can hear the wailing and lamentations of so many Christians hacked down with bloody sabres. For all this misfortune and evil could be accommodated if economy policy had not been corrupted by these merchants, and if the most central and best region of the hereditary lands had not been surrendered to foreigners, and the means for resistance, *nervus rerum gerendarum*, had been given away. Although the least of these unfortunates, paupers, knows the real basis and cause of their misery, their angels still call out for them, and God himself knows well whom their sighs and groans should curse. But woe to them who realize this, but think, or at least pretend, that this affects them as little as a painting has meaning for a blind man.

XXI. How the reformation of the nation's oeconomy might be effected in a manner not anticipated

Good preaching, someone will object. *A sick man might scream with pain but it doesn't help him. Show what has to be done with trade.* Now I have already stated that I did not propose to apply these rules myself, but that this was to be done by those familiar with all the qualities of the hereditary Imperial lands and responsible for their care. If I did however need to stand by my unofficial report, then I would start with the fifth rule, and ensure that the hereditary lands favour their own goods for a while, favour their own manufactures, however difficult this might be to begin with, moderating their use of foreign goods, keeping their own good gold and silver in purse. Then all the other rules would follow from this one rule. For the ninth rule is already included in the fifth. And if one wished to use nothing but domestic manufactures, the peoples and inhabitants of these lands would be compelled (most of them indeed with complete charity) to set their hands to their own manufactures, working up domestic raw materials. Thus would the second rule be set in motion. In time, artisans would need bread, and many foreigners would be thrown out of work by the prohibition of their products. In addition, they would lack our raw materials. They would be compelled to come into our hereditary lands themselves to seek work and raw materials here. They would look for their subsistence and settle down, which would meet the best part of the third rule, consisting of the role of population in promoting manufacture. If these foreigners had anything left over to share, then this avenue would cease being the magnet through which they attracted our gold and silver. Thereby, our fourth rule would be observed, and our money would remain in the hereditary lands. Since there would be some things which we could not do without – Indian spices, sea fish, for a time raw silk and so on, we would have cause, opportunity and means to exchange our surplus domestic goods mostly needed by our neighbours for the same, fulfilling our sixth rule. Thereby, our eighth rule would receive a major boost – for the improvement of domestic manufactories, the attraction of foreign artisans and the increase of the country's population would increase our own domestic consumption. With what the lands will in this way receive in coin (which will unfailingly happen in a very few years, and equal only to the annual produce of our mines), we will also gain the conviction, enthusiasm and application, in the spirit of the first rule, to advance those plantations hitherto lacking, as well as abandoned and otherwise unnoticed mines; to advance the seventh rule concerning the working up of foreign raw materials. We would benefit uncultivated stretches of land noted in the first rule; populate the lands with farming people, as in the third rule; fulfill the shipment and resale of foreign and domestic goods as noted in the sixth rule; and conclude in many ways those things remaining from the eighth rule. Indeed, I dare say quite boldly, and without joking, that within all this there is something special about Austria. With the first, third and eighth rules all together, it can overtake the improvement of all other European countries to an impossible degree. Through such human wisdom, we can gain for the hereditary lands infallible wealth and lustre the like of which has never before been seen, and has never before been hoped for.

XXII. That the practice of the fifth rule is to be undertaken by the prohibition of the four chief foreign manufactures: silk, wool and linen, together with French goods

But now we come to the big question: how do we bring it about that those residents in the hereditary lands might be content with their domestic manufactures; given that, as admitted, there is very little of it to hand, and it is not possible as at the beginning of time to put the people in untanned sheepskin. *Hic opus, hic labor est!* Quite honestly, I have to say that my fellow Austrians, who nicely and delicately care for themselves and their outer commodity, will have to swallow hard. To be less harsh, I must admit that I did not at first understand the abstinence from foreign goods in such a general way, but wanted for the time being to place in our black book only those goods whose neglect can cause our lands the greatest damage; whose proper care could bring us the greatest, most rapid and most obvious use, without the import of which we could most easily accommodate ourselves, or which could be most easily substituted. I count in first place woollen manufacture, whether as cloth, felt or worsted. And also excluding for a few years, the cheesecloth that is used too much in bread-making, until it is made in the hereditary lands. Second, all linen cloth, wherever it might come from. Third, silk manufacture of any grade. Fourth, everything that goes by the name of French manufactures and which is not included in the above three categories, whether it comes from France itself, or from Italy, England, Holland, Switzerland or elsewhere. These are admittedly very broad and general groups; but I do believe that they are, as described above, the right ones. For it is certain that these four types of foreign goods are the leeches that sap the inner strength of our body, suck the best blood from our veins. And it is certain that these four manufactures are the wasteful predators that steal sixteen million and more gulden from our purses, as though it had never been there. I was not far away when prominent persons familiar with the hereditary lands calculated that the annual loss of money that can be attributed to French goods runs to three million gulden and higher. If in addition, as mentioned in section XVIII about the consideration of Germany, fifteen thousand talers' worth of worsted yarn leave Saxony every year, it must follow that from the entire hereditary lands at least one hundred thousand talers must be paid annually for it, and it makes up barely one fifth of the woollen manufactures that we import. Hence, for this one manufactured good, at least seven million talers a year flows out of the hereditary lands. What I wrote before about the seven and a half million talers in wages and profit that remains every year in Leiden from the manufacture of wool cloth, small goods and knitted goods will make credible what I say about the seven million gulden that flows from the hereditary lands for the same goods. Silk manufactures will not be very far behind.

And indeed, after what has been said regarding manufactures in Germany on p. 60[23], that from Saxony alone over nine hundred thousand taler is paid for silk, and the author, being concerned about appearing unreasonable, made this number as low as possible. Should he not be regarded as equally unreasonable in estimating that consumption in the hereditary lands is about four times as high? Six million gulden would flow out. If everything made with linen, which also produces no less amount, were added to this, we can calculate that certainly no less than eighteen or twenty million is annually sacrificed abroad for unnecessary fine clothing, inflating the books of foreigners, many of whom are our enemies. I could say that in Vienna before the siege there were two hundred thousand people over twelve years old who, per head, spent annually ten gulden (most of them however certainly thirty and more, many even one hundred, and not a few several hundred and thousands) for foreign clothes with which to drape their bodies. It can be easily demonstrated that, in other major cities and fine towns of the hereditary lands, the higher and lower rural gentry, together with their servants and officials, then the entire

23 Section X.

Kingdom of Hungary, then the higher and lower clergy; all of these, not taking twelve years fully into account and considering the amounts spent on foreign goods aside from clothes – if these were all added together, it would make up at least eight Viennas, and amount to a loss of eighteen million. No one seems to get upset about this, nor find the large sum strange, even though millions are being played with. A neighbouring state that makes up hardly one sixth of the size of the hereditary lands sends, according to information on manufactures, three million talers clear annually abroad. It is known how much money comes in, and the country nonetheless remains in a state of some poverty, because so much flows out again. All the more plausible, then, that the hereditary lands send eleven or twelve thousand talers abroad.

Taking into account all kinds of reasonable and unreasonable scruples, I will deduct almost half and set the sum at ten million, money that we have no hope of seeing again, and in return for which, different kinds of manufactures are dumped at our door. This ten million – if it was kept in the hereditary lands for a few years, how much would it begin to animate and quicken this dull body? How it would recover and gather its strength! And if, as would happen, this ten million came into circulation and was added to that which is now in common circulation and flowed annually, like human blood through the treasure chest of the heart, into the counting-house of the ruler in a smooth and regular way suiting the Treasury – how could that not be to the pleasure and welfare of all parts of the German-Austrian state? If this went on for another ten, twenty and more years, if along with these four manufactures other industry were added. If, so far as practicable, in every branch a watchful eye was kept, then foreign consumption of domestic raw and fabricated goods would in time be brought to the maximum possible. Who would then in Europe be equal to our Austria? And what kind of foreign manufactures are these that, by doing without them, can give rise to such happiness? Their creation would need some supervision and effort, but this can be done in the hereditary lands more easily than elsewhere, as I will show below. Could we not do without French shoddy goods without any great trouble? In a few years, we could make the same more easily, and before others could do so. I will deal with this in due course.

XXIII. Why other and milder means should not be undertaken instead of the complete prohibition of foreign manufactures

The question is now how the hereditary lands might be able to exchange the oft-mentioned four sorts of manufacturers for their own domestic products rather than foreign. This is the real problem to be addressed. At once we come to the hitherto usual line of thought: manufactures must first of all be imported into the hereditary lands, privileges given out, companies created. Then, when goods are imported, impose heavy duties and onerous rights of entry, so that they are not as cheap as the domestic goods, keeping them out. Or build magazines and stock them with both foreign and domestic goods, directing that merchants may not touch the imported goods until all the domestic ones have been used up. Finally also, in order to foster the expansion of domestic manufacture, prohibit foreign goods altogether. But to my mind, these means are uncertain, tiresome, and unfailingly petty in their effects, according to our German humour. For to begin with, capitals will be lacking, since the hearts of rich people will not open up for this, given their lack of trust in the process. Second, there will not be sufficient audacity or resolution, given the same lack of faith in the outcome, and this would not be unreasonable. Third, the lengthiness of such an introduction will not render merchants well-disposed to the matter, while other factors will in time ruin through thousandfold tricks what has been begun. Fourth, eagerness to become rich quickly and impatience in expectation of profit, combined with the uncertainty about consumption, will itself undermine much from within; fifth, the length of time involved would sap us of commitment and cool our desire. Sixth, such a mild and slothful approach would lead to endless chicanery. Seventh, domestic goods would be accused first of this supposed fault, then of another, thereby falling into disfavour and discredit. Eighth, luxury, that raging beast, would not turn aside from increasing the prices of foreign goods, but raise them even more. Ninth, domestic manufactures will never fully develop so long as there is hope for those from abroad. In sum: the ultimate prohibition of foreign goods, keeping them out of our country, will never happen in this way. For our sickness is far greater and more dangerous than will respond to such weak and dilatory means.

Consequently, I approach the problem in a quite different way. The others want to introduce domestic manufactures, so that subsequently foreign manufactures can be prohibited. By contrast, I propose the prohibition of foreign manufactures, so that domestic can be introduced. A big claim! How many voices are already raised against this, even though I have hardly begun to explain it? But I will not be misled or diverted, but insist resolutely that foreign manufactures are to be prohibited, and domestic manufactures made to flourish. I plead only that a rush to premature judgement be delayed until such time as I have given the reason for my proposition, and disposed of the objections raised against it. Throughout my life, I have favoured the most simple, most conducive and most certain means, although appearing rather too strong compared with those that are too complex, neither cold nor warm, hence lacking all robustness and in the end presenting more inconvenience that rigour. Now there is nothing more simple in execution than the complete prohibition of all foreign wares in our four kinds of manufacture. For such prohibition cannot be undermined through evasion if those charged with its supervision are kept on the straight and narrow with fear and hope, reward and punishment, and domestic goods with their scorned stamps of origin are maintained against *temeratores fidei publicae*. There is nothing easier than to use some paper and ink to pass some regulation about taxes and passes, instructing a number of officials, arranging inspection and duties, the unavoidable and relentless punishment of the first or second who are caught with rotten fish, together with criminals, accomplices and fences, large or small. Nothing could be more convenient, it can all be done in twenty-four hours, so to speak. Within a year, the effect will be felt throughout the hereditary lands, both in the counting house of the ruler and the chests of his subjects. Nothing is more certain and forceful than hardship itself; and the certain gain that will result from the security of consumption will teach the country's inhabitants to reach for their own manufactures. When money no longer flows abroad, then at least ten million annually will remain in the country and turn into merchant's capital. And the aforementioned security of consumption and the associated certainty of gain will encourage the capitalists to make use of their cash. Foreign workers will, for lack of work and bread, be forced to migrate into the hereditary lands to seek both here. There are a hundred other advantages that cannot now be thought of, but which will be revealed as things unfold.

But it is not for nothing that I require vigilance, and rigorous and unyielding vigour in the execution, although this may well not be to the liking of those unused to the serious regulation of their business, and whose wilfulness and unruliness makes defiance of the law and of decrees second nature. For rigour and gravity are the soul of all major undertakings in state matters, without which nothing good can be expected. It would be far better not to have begun them at all than to create an object of general ridicule through dilatory execution. *Ubi non est rigor, non est vigor*[24]; never a truer proverb than that. This would at once secure for certain the various lands in all possible ways and means, and set a clear example, making clear to one and all that there was to be no more abuse of Viennese decrees. This would not only create clearer insight into the nature of any such crime, but also create much more confidence and mettle in setting to work, lending a liveliness to one and all. When the present King of France introduced nightly illumination into the streets of Paris he discouraged any interference with it by imposing a death sentence upon anyone who dared to do so. An unfortunate page, who perhaps imagined that this was only a Parisian bye-law and thinking to have some fun, fired his catapult at a lantern, putting the light out and damaging the lantern. He was discovered by prompt investigation, and in a few days, lay at that spot where the deed had been done, his head by his feet. Afterwards, the lanterns remained untouched. Many will think: the King of France is a tyrant. But if he were in everything so resolute as in this we would canonise him as a living saint. For this single, quick and vigorous execution protected not only the Parisian street lights, but also upheld the nocturnal security that they created, hindering most certainly many hundred fatal assaults, many thousand thefts by purse-cutters and pickpockets. Not to speak of the way in which the king established respect for himself, his laws and his government (for this was a few years after the Cardinal's death), and made no small contribution to the reinforcement of harmony in government. How could the king have served his people better than to be such a tyrant as to abolish duelling, which was at the time treated as very fortunate? And so we should, from the very first, treat like traitors those who here breach the prohibition of foreign manufactures; otherwise we should encourage such criminals, or contrary to office and duty look the other way, or permit quite irresponsible neglect in the supervision that had been ordered. For all these things and many others assist the flow of domestic gold and silver abroad, just as before, keeping us trapped in our present straits and disability, and leaving us exposed, as before, to all the dangers of Orient and Occident, enemy invasions, sieges, slavery, endless blood-letting and being cut-down with sabres. The idea that vigorous punishment of this or that malicious lad or cheeky hussy is the mark of tyranny and evil is one that the angels in heaven laugh at, for they would drink a toast to any such punishment. It would be cruel beyond all clemency, and such clemency would be truly barbaric. A ruler in such a difficult situation as the one

24 Latin for 'Where rigorousness is lacking there can be no force'.

in which we now are would doubtless earn eternal praise if each year he acted as the King of France did against duellists, making an oath in person before the sacrament to pardon no one, whoever they might be, who had earned punishment by infringing the prohibition. It is not always inadvisable to follow the example of an enemy in such matters, especially when not only is it a matter of upholding the state against the arch-enemy, but also millions of souls and of liberty. And God willing, we will in all respects make the oeconomy of our land a good example for the French to follow.

XXIV. The objection to the prohibition of foreign goods is dealt with

Now I must turn to the objections and answer them. I will be brief, to prevent this work becoming overlong. Enough will be said for those who understand the matter, while for the rest long-windedness is ill-advised. The first objection is: *given such a hasty ban on for-eign goods, where will sufficient quantities of domestic goods be found to replace them?* Answer: to be quite honest, we do not need any of the so-called French goods at all. Instead, we will do without them until they are eventually made here, a start having been made on this in many cases. We will not lack for other sorts, since they are much more beneficial than the other three, more easily imported, manufactures. It is much the same with silk goods. Besides that, it is a matter of two or three years, which will create some need in the country, but in five or six years there will be a sufficiency of everything. The heredi-tary lands would already have an abundance of linen goods as far as quantity goes if the good people whose profession this is could find enough employment. And as regards sort and quality, this could be replaced in a short time. Silesia would suffice on its own, for weaving there has practically no guild, looms being found in all places in the rooms and chambers of rural houses in which all kinds of work is done, although it seems as though only spinning is taught. Cloth making is much the same, and I know that, in some very out-of-the-way places, they are busy beyond belief. If only domestic consumption were assured for them and, for example, wool distributed every half year, how quickly cloth-making as well as wool spinning, which we do not have a great deal of given its constant sale to Holland, might be raised to a level five or six times as high as it is now? If neces-sary, it would be the same with knitted manufactures as with silk goods: to replace them with others until they could be made in the country. In short: we have already enough of the most necessary linen and cloth. Small goods would follow on from that. We could if necessary, like our forefathers, do entirely without wool products, also silk and French goods. More likely, however, we would do without them for a time. This matter will be treated in more detail later.

What is to be done with the foreign goods of these four manufactures that are already in the country? They will be sold quickly, everyone being concerned about the forthcoming shortage. Merchants would have to be kept in check so that the value not be increased. Such goods could also be put into store as the prohibition approached, and then sold by factors appointed for the purpose. If we had had the courage to do as Queen Elizabeth of England did (although in a different matter), a praiseworthy, useful, although rather unusual and costly result would ensue. When this Queen (or so I think, others attribute this to her grandfather Henry VII) decided to promote wool manufacture in her kingdom, she banned the export of domestic wool. In the first year, against all hopes, few wool workers came from abroad. The wool remained in the hands of lords and peasants. There was grumbling, since bread should have been there, and not wool. To assist in this, the Queen bought up all the wool with her own money, and put it in storage. Then, new complaints were heard: the Queen intended to create a monopoly, which would explain everything. To put a stop to this, she had all the wool that she had bought piled together and burned. Such a serious step put everyone to work. Foreigners who thought they would sit out the English prohibition lost all hope, shipped in boatloads with bread to England (which in particular hit the Netherlands very hard) and the English crown gained a new gem. This was its finest hour, and the wool burned from the first year is now made up ten times every year. So I would wish that, in general, and at the cost of the hereditary lands, all forbidden goods that at the time the ban was imposed were in the country and so really affected – as in England now, with all goods coming from France and all those detected (only because it was discovered that France drew more money yearly from England that the latter from the former) – should without further ado be burned. What pleasing smoke and a pleasant smell it would all make, the welfare of the hereditary lands, for which everyone hopes most of all, welling out of it! In marking such executive determination, those both here and abroad would see that this was in earnest, conform themselves to it and so assist in furthering the common good, as well as their own. But since it is hard to hope this of us, I counsel that at least one proceed with the related measure everywhere, by placing the goods in special magazines with the order that what has not been sold within five or six months should be quickly burned, or at least transformed into *pios usus*[25], so that it can no longer be offered for sale. And so it is with mercy I seek to have foreign French goods excluded, for it would certainly be a sin to act out of charity and spare them from fire.

What then is to be done with those goods ordered from abroad and already on the way here? Those so close to the borders that they would enter the hereditary lands within eight or ten days after the promulgation of the ban, these could probably be halted, as with those that have just entered the country. The remainder can stay where they are or where they like, and a different destination sought. If any merchant here incurred losses, he could set that off against his previous gain, consider the utility that will flow from it all, and console himself with that, if he likes. And if he does not like it, he should nonetheless be satisfied with it.

How should those merchants be treated who only work on foreign commission? They will go to ruin. I'll drink to that! For these are the very fellows that made the country poor. So it is better that they go to rack and ruin, and not the common weal. They will have to wait until domestic merchant putters-out (Verleger) take them on, or they are taken on as bookkeepers by manufacturers, or for some other kind of office or service (of which there will be many hundred times more than there are ruined merchants); or what capital they do have can be invested in domestic manufacture. If however they do not wish to seek employment in domestic manufactories and if they have no capital to invest, one should have no more sympathy with such barefaced toilers – who act only to the advantage of

---

25 Latin for 'pious uses'.

foreigners and to the disadvantage of those in the hereditary lands, but who gain no more than a daily bite of bread – than with fools twice over.

All the same, those with residence privileges and freedom of the Court should retain these, ne fides publica violetur.[26] Of course, they should retain these only if they observe the ban and regulations regarding foreign goods in their trading; otherwise not. For privileges that are not of use to the country, but to these individuals, and which to a great extent lead to the decline of Christianity (whose preservation coincides with that of the hereditary lands) and the benefit of Turkish slavery – these are not privileges, but sacrilege. And moreover, let us consider those holding such privileges, and hear how they sound: do they argue against the prohibition of foreign goods? Do they, having been granted a privilege by a country, or having freely assumed one through the benefit of residency, have to be upheld come what may? Do they exist *per modum parti perpetui, nec nisi reciproca voluntate dissolubilis*[27], or only *precario et ad libitum alterutrius partium?*[28] Are there ambiguities arising from contra-dictory interpretation, and in what sense have those with rights of residency held to them? However it turns out, their loss will not be very great if they place their capitals in manufacture, thereby pleasing the public, and seek to become domestic merchant capitalists or putters-out (Verleger). Thereupon will they become upright merchants, of great use besides the honour and boon of wishing to join such a highly estimable endeavour. And so I will be the first to call out: *Honi soit*[29], who does not honour such merchants and who does anything other than speak or think well of them! Otherwise it should be said once and for all that merchants are there for benefit of the common good, and not the common good for benefit of the merchants. If these come into conflict, then the merchants have to step back. If anyone should, by contrast, in any such case continue to support the merchants, he would show himself to be no lesser a foe and corrupter of the fatherland than they.

Foreign merchants will gather their things up and leave us alone. Good luck to them! Like a fleeing foe, one should build them gilded bridges. For in this way profit will remain solely with those living in the country. But many may well reconsider, and foreigners will per-haps prefer to become residents.

Our own manufactures will not be as good as the foreign ones. This sort of thing is on many occasions a delusion of the devil, who is foe to the rise of the hereditary lands. But presuming that this might be an unavoidable evil, it is not an unbearable one. For this reason, I raise the question of why Hungarian wine should be prohibited in Austria and Styria, and elsewhere. If one asks, why a wine is banned that is better than domestic wine, and even cheaper, then one gets the answer: so that God-given, prudently consumed, not disregarded, unspilled and unspoiled wine is of benefit to the hill regions, and the few vineyards are treated as one of the country's assets, and not neglected; that way money stays all the more in our purses. The same thing happens with Hungarian salt,

26 Latin for 'so that public confidence not be violated'. A crypto-institutionalist argumentation.
27 Latin: 'in infinity unless dissolved by mutual consent'.
28 Latin for 'as the other party's discretion and responsibility'.
29 'Shame on anyone, who…'

the Austrian variety bearing no comparison as to quality. All the same, the former is kept out, and the latter is master in its own country. This is what actually happens, and it can be applied *ad literam*[30] to domestic manufactures as well. So if we have our principles in some things, why do we not extend them to the larger and more numerous things? If we apply them to two such necessary things as wine and salt, why do we not apply them even more so with regard to the unnecessary abuses in matters of clothing? If my point was that physical sustenance was a problem in the hereditary lands, and that a prohibition on goods would limit eating or drinking, then it might quite justifiably be complained that this was too harsh, that the body could not give up its customary nourishment all at once, and that one's health would suffer. But this is not about eating and drinking, nor about health, nor about long life, nor about fasting or starvation. It is about whether the body should be draped with Silesian or Dutch cloth, with Upper Austrian fabric or with Indian bombazine, with domestic or with local silk products or stockings, with Austrian or French ribbons; and none of this has anything to do with health, nor affects either mouth or stomach; these are simply things of the imagination and the arrogant spirit of luxury. How we might bring it about that domestic goods are in no respects inferior in quality, durability and beauty to foreign goods, I will leave to explain further later.

It will prove that air and all the elements are against the work to be done here. This is something that I freely believe of merchant and pseudo-political elements. Then there is the hellish elements (since the devil takes pleasure in obstructing everything that the honour of God and human consolation can build), making a Triple Alliance, *nec tamen erit concilium contra Dominum*. Besides that, the natural elements here are not altogether against things. They are not so subtle as in Italy, nor so thick as in Holland. If at both extremes, manufacturers and merchants can do so well, why not in our moderate and temperate climate? There are all sorts of pure fables and visions about in the world. If silk manufacture in Dresden and in Vienna itself, so far as one can judge what has been tried, had already done well, perhaps there is a simpleton who can persuade himself of it.

It is impossible for our goods to match foreign goods, for we have neither silk cloth nor the Spanish wool which is indispensable for fine cloth. Here we could ask the English and the Dutch for advice, who not only have no silk in their countries, but have no hope of ever having any, nor possess very much long wool; nor any of the Spanish wool that we lack. We will need to find out where they get their raw materials from. Also, Milanese and Sicilian silk and Spanish wool will be easier to find for us, since the Spanish would prefer to supply their truest allies before others. So far as long wool is concerned, it is not only a simple matter, but as noted before, can be produced in greater quantities in Bohemia. Its neighbours will give us this wool in exchange for our money or other goods as willingly as anyone else.

What about women's fashions, the sole queen and mistress of the manufacture of clothing? Does one have to dress like other nations? It would be a good thing if we sent women's fashions to the devil. There are incomparably more nations in the world that keep a national dress than there are those who change it. Why should we imitate the few, and not the many? If we could not do without foolish variation, we would still have the liberty to be

---

30 Meaning 'literally', i.e., 'by the book'.

just as foolish as the French, and from time to time use our own imagination to invent something, so that we might remain master of our manufactures. If this does not suit, the patterns for fashionable clothes, both with regard to cut and to material, could be brought from France and made up here; this would help us in our misfortune. This would also be helpful to traders. For at the moment, when a new fashion appears, the goods have to be described from a distance. Before they arrive, the fashion has often altered. The merchant is left with losses. If the fabrics had come from this country, they would not be used fashionably, but serve only daily needs.

But where would our Germans find the inspiration to invent fresh cloth or fashionable accessories, or even just make imitations? They do not have the brains for that? Such sayings should be stuffed back in the mouths that spoke them. For the contrary is shown in abundance, and the failure of our people has no other cause than that the most skilled people are not highly regarded by us. So, they run to France and Holland. The artisans who stay are not encouraged, and know that if they do something well, something foreign will nevertheless always be preferred. All the same, there is no lack of people. There was one I know of who could have made a foreign ribbon factory after a foreign model for old Hoenig in Augsburg, who did not know how to do it. And in Dresden, I know a young man whose real skill is as a ribbonmaker, but this earned him no money. Now, a lackey, then a silk goods maker in the ducal silk manufactory, who could imitate any foreign goods if he would only apply himself, and who had made so many samples that one could not accuse him of presumption, when he spoke in his own fashion. He trusted that he could imitate anything taught him; but he could instruct those who could not so imitate.

The Imperial Court does like its lustre and gloss. It would be a laughing-stock if it were not the equal of foreign nations in this. If our affairs were so ordered that we were the equal of foreign nations in the lustre of our purses and our country's economy, the fame of the Court would to be sure not to suffer. This lustre does not consist of the foolish changing of fashion and in foreign goods, but in other things, to wit: domestic valuables. If we have to do without foreign adornments for a few years, these could be replaced in greater quantities and more profitably by domestic fabrication. If the wait were longer, there would also be more honour and lustre in being sure of moderate clothing, in the wealth and calm of home and Court, than weakening our purses with splendidly modish dresses and finery, only then to fly from every Turk, Tartar or other enemy for the lack of means. We place our honour at the worst possible time in superficial magnificence, and for it are pushed into the mire. What is supposed to make us great in the world makes us small, and a disgrace to the whole world. *Cuminum serimus, camelos deglutimus; in nugis magni, in magnis nugatores et pygamaei.*[31] I am certain that even a ducal body would be lent more sheen that the most costly foreign brocade, if through the former, the well-being of the hereditary lands could be rebuilt, instead of being led by the latter to the threshold of its complete spoliation.

---

31 Latin for 'we plant cuminseed, but swallow camels, we are great in small things (nuts) but small (literally pygmies) in great things.

It would ultimately be for the best to grow up naked as in paradise; then we would need no foreign manufactures, nor fashions, nor delights. I was once close by when I heard this remark in a conversation about domestic manufactories. I thought to myself: maybe you deserve to live naked. The comment came from a woman whose spruce demeanour would bring down upon the land the plague and the Turk as retribution. We would be very foolish if we allowed the wit of a woman to send us to the devil for the sake of some fun, or if one of his regents were to drive the Turks and Tartars to retribution.

Who will stop young wenches from having fashions sent to them, or have their own tailor or servant bring them from Paris? There are few, if any, wenches of this kind in our country, so at least I suppose. And if this were so, I have sufficient respect not to name the man of two syllables[32] who should prevent this occurring. We will finally see who rules the country, its prince or a few cheeky hussies. As for the post-chaise, the proper oversight suffices; and those gentlemen sent to Paris can be welcomed back with the gallows. The goods themselves would betray themselves through their being worn, whether for a short while or for longer. Likewise, it would be best to hang the first to be so discovered somewhere in the countryside, as a (not innocent) martyr to the common good and to justice, patience and good intention, as penitence and amendment.

Where then can the capital for domestic merchant manufacture be found? If I said that that was up to the rulers I would perhaps be right, although it is not the right answer for our times. If I then expected the money from the territorial assemblies, that would also not be unjust, but it would offend no small number. So we have to remain with what has been said before, that if there were another ten million that remained in the country, and consumption were secured to domestic goods, then there would be capital in abundance. Besides that, I have heard of a new and surprising proposal about the finding of credit to do something important, but without capital. This can be judged when stated.

How are our workers to get used to working again, for they are only used to idleness? Not all of them are like this, as I've said before. As for the remainder, I say: if the sale of wine were redirected abroad, with proper arrangements for its export, and its domestic consumption were raised through the increase of the population, then the prime instrument of idleness would be made much more expensive. If brandy were made more difficult to produce and cost more than four or five times what it does now; if masters would keep their apprentices firmly in hand; if the guilds in certain manufactures would do more to stop their apprentices carousing, and called a halt to St. Monday; if houses of correction and workhouses would do something about beggars and other idlers; if voluntary poverty and idleness was hated and scorned, as in Holland; if, finally, a competitive spirit would emerge among the artisans, this objection would soon be dealt with.

However, we will have to be careful in dealing with domestic artisans and merchant capitalists, for they will raise their prices excessively once foreign goods are no longer available. If the authorities do their work and guide their spirits, this can be avoided. Once manufactures begin to pile up in the country, the people will of themselves seek money and bread, and through their number make goods cheap. When edible goods, rents and wages for journeymen,

---

32 Leopold I, Empereror from 1658 till 1705.

plus raw materials or semi-finished goods are all paid locally, and not brought from a long way off so not subject to large freightage charges, tolls, nor any risk, then it is not possible (especially when there is certainty as to sales, and the goods are turned over quickly) that they will be of a higher value than those from abroad. It could also be said that foreigners make no gift of these to us. It would be far better if a sacrifice has to be made that it be made in respect of a fellow citizen rather than a foreigner. Console oneself with the idea already given that it is better (although every peasant cannot understand this) to pay two talers for a domestic good when the talers remain in the country, than to pay one taler for a foreign good when the money leaves the country. The public is not the poorer for what remains in domestic circulation, but is in many respects advantaged. The money can again be of benefit to the purchaser who has laid out the money in the first place. The state can be imagined as a rich man who has his money is several purses. If he takes money from one and puts it into another, he becomes no poorer thereby. For although one purse becomes lighter, the other becomes heavier to the same degree. He is master of the former and of the latter. This proposition has to be a leading principle in managing the country's oeconomy. Otherwise, it will not function properly.

Those nations whose goods we ban will become enraged, and block the passage of goods that we had previously needed to buy from them. They will spurn those domestic goods that they had previously bought from us, and abandon our alliances and even ourselves in times of danger. Let them be angry, if they wish. If they are enemies, we need have nothing to do with them. But, if they are friends, they will give us credit for placing ourselves, through the good stewardship that had been forced upon us, in a position not only to help ourselves, but also to do them real service in time of need. It can be seen how furious France became when its beloved England consigned French goods to the flames wherever they were found. Whatever the case, a friendship that is struck up only to empty our purse can go to the Devil. We find out who is a friend in need. And so other nations are not so foolish as to refuse to supply us with those goods we have not prohibited because of those that we have, compounding their enforced loss with a voluntary one. The free commerce of many places, such as Hamburg and Amsterdam, etc., does not suffer because some buyers are excluded. Even if all others should stand against us, the Spanish would, for reasons already given and out of regard for us, make up for all the others and supply us with the best Spanish wool and Mediterranean silk, the two things that we still need from abroad. After all, we could gain our silk through Turkey. But the nations from which long-staple wool has to come are not among those whom our ban will disadvantage. They will have no cause to prohibit its sale to us. And as has already been noted, if absolutely necessary, Bohemia could direct itself to the production of this kind of long-staple wool. Hence, there is no risk that our goods destined for export would go unsold. These are: wine, grain, oxen, copper, iron, quicksilver, skins, linen, all kinds of minerals. The foreign purchasers of these goods are either not among those who are disadvantaged by our ban, or cannot in any case do without our goods. If, through our good management, we can strengthen our finances, not only do we have no need of foreign alliances and assistance, these foreign nations would instead proffer it themselves. For if you have a great deal of money, then you have many allies, France being sufficient proof of this. And, on the contrary: *Point d'argent, point de Suisses.* Those whom our good order will offend, because they have previously had good fishing in troubled waters, will try all kinds of tricks to drive us mad. *Mais fin contre fin, ne fait point de fourrure.*

But it is a very harsh and unfriendly act, to ban all at once the four leading manufactures to which we are used in the hereditary lands. On first hearing, it runs against all reason, and is very alien. There will be wondrous confusion, in which no-one will be able to find his place. That is, to put it briefly, nonsense. If we managed to find to find our way out of the plague and the curse of the Turks[33], then certainly we can bear a little disorder in manufactures, from which the greatest order will follow. Domestic manufactures will, in short order, make good everything, since this concerns not the kind of goods in themselves, but only those that are to be prohibited. This involves no more than seeking to raise a renewed domestic phoenix from the ashes of foreign goods. To achieve this goal, it is better to wear poor clothes for a few years while still being master of everything, than to strut around in golden embroidery and brocade, only to end up in slavery. What cavalier would not gladly parade himself for two or three years in Silesian cloth, as it now is, if he knew that by so doing his fatherland would be assisted? What lady would not be happy to wear the silk dresses she now has to hand, and more than she needs of them, for one or three years, without yearning for foreign fashion, if she knew that it was the same for everyone else, and that, by so doing, she would make herself and her children free from the Turkish yoke? Now it is certain that this security can be created in such a way. It is nearly as certain that a cavalier who offers assistance in this way to his country's economy will do more for the state than he could in the same time do on the field of battle. Besides, it has been shown what simple means are to be observed and hoped for. So, once and for all: *Extremis morbis extrema veniant remedia.*[34] Nor is it advisable to ban one manufacture after another. For all the difficulties that would suddenly arise here would afterwards, as further problems arose, simply compound themselves.

The King of France, who is certainly very familiar with his country's oeconomy, tends not to be so harsh; instead, he merely increases the tax burden on those goods coming into the land that he does not favour. If our commerce and manufactures were in this country as those are in France, then we could certainly do as that king does, and admit some of these goods. What enters France from abroad is either raw materials for working up in France, or otherwise goods that are of minor significance compared with what France sends to other lands. I want to say: if we drew as many million [talers] annually from France as France does from us, and likewise France drew as little from the hereditary lands as these do today from France, then we would be quite happy to put higher duties on the goods coming to us from France, instead of banning them completely. But if one is arguing by example, it would be more relevant to consider that England understands better than we do how

33 This somewhat drastic language does not convey a racist sentiment here; it needs to be set against the political scenario and conflicts of the time. The Austrian lands were repeatedly endangered by a potential Ottoman invasion, and Hörnigk is here simply referring to one of the common political problems faced by Austria. See introduction for more detail.

34 Latin for 'extreme cures for extreme diseases'.

to deal with French goods, as already mentioned – and for cause that is nothing like that which we have.

Such an uncommonly harsh ban would hinder the free course of commerce, which should be inviolable. How spiteful or stupid! Who has ever heard tell that the free course of commerce means that sheer caprice should dictate whether good or harm should befall the fatherland? Which state, even that which is more than any other founded upon trade, has allowed this without any regulation? In what kind of natural law or law of nations is it written that I should, under the pretext of free commerce, allow myself to be forced to buy from my neighbours, more often from my enemy, that which I have at home, or could have, or to buy something from abroad that does not seem of any use to me. Why should I not be able to freely choose not to buy it? Here are the words of Hugo Grotius, *De jure belli ac pacis*, Book 2, Ch. 2 Para 20:

> But there is not an equally valid right obliging a man to sell what belongs to him; for every one is free to decide what he will or will not acquire.

> Thus the Belgians[35] formerly did not permit the importation of wine and other foreign wares. Of the Nabataean Arabs, Strabo says: "Some goods it is permissible to import, but not others."

No less important are the words of my highly-regarded author of *Bedencken von Manufacturen in Deutschland* p. 64:

> Commerce that is conducted with losses in a land, whereby the land and its inhabitants become poorer from year to year, is not commerce. Where however its subjects are instructed how to earn their bread, and how by keeping money in their land the people might become rich, that is the true foundation of solid commerce. For otherwise, where there is nothing but poverty, they lose by it. To have such useful commerce in his land should be the object of every prince together with his loyal counsellors and regional assemblies, to be favoured before all other policy. Money is the nerve, and to gain this should be the aim of all statutes and laws, abolishing all that stands against it.

So runs the *Bedencken*.[36] As the proverb says: a merchant who makes a loss in trade is just as much a merchant as he who gains. But it cannot be said that a trade in which a country ends up the poorer has anything to do with oeconomy or householding; it is instead more a matter of the spoliation of house and home country.

But it is not a good idea to draw the attention of foreigners with a complete prohibition. A warning of this kind seems to show great understanding, but there is nothing to it. Our prohibition will not teach foreigners anything, other than that they will see that we have resolved to deal with our economy better in future. If we depended upon them for the creation of our needs, or might persuade them to cease taking from us the goods that they now do, that would be cause for consideration. I also believe that foreign nations have for a long

---

35 *Belgae* in the original quote.
36 By Johann Daniel Crafft (1624–1697) – see introduction.

time observed rather too much of us. And that means losses for our purse. There is no danger that their eyes will be drawn to us; it is instead time that we opened our own eyes.

It is not clear that the supposition about the ten million that will remain in the land is exact, since money will have to flow out for the raw silk and long-staple wool from Spain or elsewhere. This objection is not badly conceived. But assuming that one or a few millions do flow out for this, should we really be so fastidious and discard the other eight or nine million, too? Should one give to a beggar who does not want to accept a Groschen[37] because it is worth only three, and not four Kreuzer?[38] It is for just this, and like reasons, that I reduced the proven sum of sixteen and more million to ten, although contrary to all reason.

Woe to all fairs and annual markets and all who depend upon them. They will be ruined by this prohibition. Of course they will not be ruined; far more, so to say, those who have been badly trained will turn into pious and useful children. Originally, fairs and annual markets were established to supply a country with the necessaries that it lacked. But they have in time degenerated, ruining our splendid manufactures by importing unnecessary foreign things. The result of which has been that, instead of providing us with our necessaries, they have made us into the neediest of all people, taking the precious gold and silver from our purses and robbing us of it. Fairs and the large annual markets are one of the greatest despoilers of the Holy Roman Empire as a whole. They bring foreign work in and suck German money out. Our prohibition should not seek to proscribe the bringing of all goods to the annual markets, but only the harmful ones. Even a child must grasp that, where we can make goods ourselves, but foreigners bring them to our annual markets, that does not mean the ruination of the annual markets, but calls for their useful reform. That infringes no privileges, nor, as already stated, freedom of trade. The privileges of annual markets are not contracts, but merely permissions whose granting lays in the hands of the higher authorities. The bringing in of goods must simply conform to the policy of the country. If for example a Hungarian brought his wine, his rock salt and his wool to sell in Vienna under the pretext of free trade and annual market privileges, he would soon find this out. What is right to forbid in one case is meet in another. Three kinds of people tend to oppose the prohibition of foreign goods at annual markets: the town chambers because of the loss of duties following from the restrictions on their disallowed trade and usury, discussed here and there in this treatise; the merchants because of the restriction of their unfair trade and usury, discussed at various points in this tract; and the citizenry of towns that have a right to an annual market, concerned that the lack of foreign buyers and sellers will undermine their subsistence. If that were to be so, then I would answer: it would be better if here or there one town went into decline, rather than the entire country. It can even be easily admitted that one town or another would suffer, while the state as a whole benefited. But we do not have to go so far. For the towns should not decline. They should not suffer. What foreign sellers used to bring should in future be brought by those that are local. The foreign seller who wanted also to buy from us will in any case not stay away, since the prohibition does not affect him. Indeed, he

37 See note on currency relations above.
38 See n. 6 above.

will come all the more often, the more domestic goods come to market. Some however will think it over, and say: *the penny that the local seller uses at the annual markets is already in our country, and so adds nothing for the state. But the penny that the foreigner brings, that makes the country richer.* Yes indeed, but makes us richer because that penny is gained here in our land. And indeed, while in this way a penny does come into the country, a hundred, a thousand are drawn out. One penny like this is like the eagle that eats up the others. Off with profit of this sort, that makes us into beggars. That is a really bloody coin, that sucks the marrow from our legs. It is remarkable that Martin Luther, who never claimed his whole life long to have a head for such things, more than one hundred and fifty years ago simply used his natural reason to come to a conclusion about German trade, and in particular the Frankfurt Fair. In *Von Kauffshandlung und Wucher* (1524) he writes:

> God has cast us Germans off. We have to throw our gold and silver into foreign lands and make the whole world rich while we ourselves remain beggars. England would have less gold if Germany let it keep its cloth; and the king of Portugal, too, would have less if we let him keep his spices. You calculate yourself how much gold is taken out of Germany, without need or reason; from a single Frankfurt fair, and you will wonder how it happens that there is a single *heller*[39] left in German lands. Frankfurt is the gold and silver sink, through which everything that springs and grows, is minted or coined here, flows out of the German lands. If that hole were stopped up we should not now have to listen to the complaints that there are debts everywhere and no money; that all lands and cities are burdened with rent charges and ruined with interest payments. But let that pass. So it will go anyhow. We Germans must be Germans; we never stop unless we must.[40]

If Dr. Luther were to rise from the dead and see what was happening in Germany with French goods, he would see ten holes, not one. Leipzig must have been such a hole in his time, although he does not say so; Hamburg alone could stand for six such holes; Brunswick is vigorously pursuing that end, and Magdeburg has plans. Dr. Luther would declare us Germans completely mad. One single and ordinary manufacture in such a city would be ten times more use. But no one thinks of that.

The treasury will not sing this song. Since our manufactures will be inferior to foreign manufactures, imperial duties will decline. This and similar cameralistic views are certainly the stumbling block upon which, more's the pity, many proposals must fail. It is not really the fault of the treasury, but it is rather because their revenues are so closely related that once one is affected, so all are. It is also to be deplored that to preserve one taler that is owed to the

---

39 The *heller* or half-penny was the smallest denomination coin in the central German lands in Luther's time. Until the later 1530s one *heller* would have exchanged at 1/504th of a Rhenish florin or gulden, as the official ratio was 1 florin (gulden) = 21 groschen = 252 pennies (d) = 504 heller. After the 1530s the ratio increased to 1 florin/gulden = 24 groschen = 288 pennies = 576 heller. For more detail see works mentioned above, as well as Philipp Robinson Rössner, *Deflation – Devaluation – Rebellion. Geld im Zeitalter der Reformation* (Stuttgart: Franz Steiner, 2012).

40 Full translation of Luther's pamphlet in *Martin Luther on Commerce and Usury* ed. Philipp Robinson Rössner (London/New York: Anthem, 2015).

treasury, a hundred and more others that could have served the entire country well, and the third or fourth part of what the treasury would wish to receive, is lost. Because for each taler paid as duty on foreign goods, there comes unfailingly one hundred and more talers in foreign goods into the country, and so an equal amount of money out. How easily would one hundred thousand taler (it would be about this amount; for domestic manufactories would themselves replace this in part) be used by the treasury for something else in the hereditary lands? In the second year, this would no longer be necessary, because with the retention of ten million within domestic circulation, the investment would be a great deal more, and would have a less sensible effect upon the subjects.

I conclude the objections and responses here, believing that some would wish to raise an objection not included here, that someone from the hereditary lands should say: *we do not want any domestic manufactures*. I freely admit that I do not know how to respond to this objection. But in matters concerning the general good and prevention of general decline, the saying holds *Salus Rei publicae suprema Lex esto*.[41] And in plain German: push aside anything that is in the way.

XXV. The establishment of cloth and woollen manufactures in the hereditary lands is not as difficult as one might think; first, there are ample materials and workers for the task

Now, I must fulfil both my promises, and show that the effort and trouble involved in establishing in the hereditary lands the four foreign manufactures that we have proposed for prohibition is a practicable course of action. We lack only the resolution to use the resources that all other European nations have, and hope that all can be set to work in good time, producing sufficient goods, both durable and attractive. As regards the first, sufficient raw material is needed,as is a goodly number of workers with knowledge or training, and for all things, enough linen and woollen yarn, also spun and twined silk. Regarding the weaving of linen and cloth, the principle introduced can be easily proved: everywhere in the hereditary lands where there is sufficient wool and flax, where there is enough yarn, where there are sufficient cloth-makers and weavers, there sufficient quantities of cloth and linen cannot be far off, if only one wishes it. With knitted goods and silk manufacture there is more involved. As far as raw material is concerned, there can be no shortage, since there is, if necessary, enough long-staple wool in Bohemia, and more if the numbers of single-sheared sheep were increased. There would then be no danger that those neighbouring lands who also have this wool, and who do not suffer any loss from our manufactures because they do not themselves work up very much, would emulate us, together with the Dutch, Flemish and French. But silk comes from either Asia or Italy. We have none. As regards Asia, we can travel to Smyrna as easily as anyone else can, although it is simpler and cheaper to ship it via Constantinople and the Danube to us, than to Holland through a longer sea voyage subject to piracy and shipwreck. Italy is however divided into so many different states that it is impossible for them

41 'The common weal shall be supreme zeal'.

to make common cause in such a matter, and they will all prove unreliable in this. Only one thing remains here, which is the channel through which these and all other kinds of Mediterranean goods will flow to us. And if all other states should turn from us, the royal Spanish possessions will certainly remain on our side – Sicily, Naples and Milan. So that they might not all draw the advantage from us, the others will take good care to keep an opening for us, not obstructing our manufactures, but reducing their profit. No one has to seek such simple-mindedness among the Italians. And if, finally, all foreigners refuse us their silk (which would never happen), it would only give cause to redouble our efforts to cultivate silk domestically, for which we would be all the more indebted to them; as the author of the *Bedencken von Manufacturen in Deutschland* writes, pp. 104ff., giving details of silk cultivation, among other things seeking to demonstrate that the German Empire could, through the cultivation of silk, receive annually several million Rix dollars, a large proportion of which would fall to the hereditary lands.

Where can we find sufficient knitters and silk weavers? Without more ado, I can reveal something that a good friend outside the hereditary lands told me, the author of the *Bedencken von Manufacturen in Deutschland*, the practice of which I have observed and grasped. All work done on a loom, whether in linen, silk, cloth, woollen knitting and ribbon-making, is closely related. Anyone who has experience with one or the other can, within a month, depending on the work, or eight days, be usefully employed on another. I would not state this with such certainty if I had not confirmed its truth with my own eyes. Given that the hereditary lands have more than enough linen workers, not all of them can make their living at it. The remainder could be set to work on woollens and silk. Within six months there would be something of a shortage, but after three or four years there would be quite a sufficient number working. But for this to happen, other institutions are required, in particular the provision of sufficient masters for instruction. They would have to be established in a timely manner. What has been said here of linen weaving in general (to which I must add that any linen worker who has any capability can be set to work on Nîmes serge in eight or fifteen days, which is among woollen cloth the best, most useful and lasting material, of which therefore it is hard to imagine there being a shortage) applies all the more to those weavers who engage in more elaborate work, of whom there are many in Silesia. Most of all, however, this applies to ribbon-makers. For whosoever properly understands the art of this noble occupation must also have the basics for other forms of weaving. Hence, patterned ribbon-making has to be the most advanced of all weaving skills. Any such worker who wished to work on knitted goods and brocades would be ready in twenty-four hours. They are to be vigorously encouraged in this, as well as in plain ribbon-making, leaving their ribbon-making machines for what is thought to be far more refined and profitable skill as compared with their patterned ribbon work. It can also be supposed that linen workers would do the same for the same reasons. I have not the slightest doubt that there are so many ribbon workers and trained linen workers who lack sufficient work for satisfactory subsistence that, from them alone, sufficient workers could be found for silk and satin weaving, if only there were enough teachers, looms and silk available. Thus, in at most two years, their manufacture could be fully introduced. So much for domestic workers.

If needed, because there were not in fact sufficient local workers, people could be brought from abroad. It has already been suggested that many foreign workers who already work with wool from our hereditary lands, and many of those whose goods are sold into the hereditary lands, would necessarily move here for work and subsistence because of lack of wool and sales.

Besides that, if we, like other nations, looked out for our own advantage, we should long ago have taken advantage of the war in the Low Countries. Many thousand masters and journeymen from all kinds of weaving professions have been forced by this war to move elsewhere, many of them to France. How many more would the Spanish have let us have? There will be no lack of such events and opportunities in the future, and the war could find its way into France. Then, we would also benefit from their manufacturing workers, making use of their current methods. Among other things, such thoughts should be no less a motivation for us Germans to gladly enter into a just war with that same nation. For it is not always the conquest of cities and country that is the advantage and fruit of victory. The King of France has, during the Flanders Wars, won for his kingdom no less through the transporting of artisans and skilled workers than through the conquest of cities. As for the Spanish, their discussion, like ours, is very much about the improvement of the country's oeconomy. If they were to have doubts about assisting us, we would not abandon it for all that. So it is not to be doubted, they would gladly, and to all their ability, supply us with masters for instruction, and the necessary silk, dye and knitting workers.

XXVI. Regarding the requisite amounts needed of yarn and silk

It is not only a matter of raw wool and silk and sufficient numbers of workers. The silk and wool must first be sorted, combed, carded, spun, twined, wound and sometimes also dyed. The sorting, combing, carding, winding, dyeing and the like can be easily arranged, since relatively few people are needed, compared with other work, and can be found in neighbouring places and Spanish areas. Silk winding and yarn-making can also be helped by windmills and other establishments. But wool-spinning needs more space, extent and people than all the others, and so is to be treated as the basis of the entire manufacture. As regards the spinning of flax and wool in the making of linen and cloth, it is clear that it would be easy to develop the enterprise in Bohemia, Silesia, Moravia and so on to a satisfactory level of quality and fineness. I leave the question open, however, whether the public would tolerate that cloth making in Silesia would retain the monopoly of wool-spinning. Spinning fine and long-staple wool for knitted goods is a different matter. That skill could certainly and easily be introduced into the hereditary lands, if only there was as much focus on the skill there as there is with the women who spin. Indeed, regarding the spinning of long-staple wool, five or six years ago I saw in a well-known little town, not far from Vienna (but which has now been ruined by the Turks), that a poor Dutch woman taught in three or four months, just for a piece of bread, around one hundred girls of ten to fifteen years, and with such success that the model for such spun wool is now thought abroad to be a German-Austrian rarity. I am witness that these Austrians had never before practised proper Dutch spinning. But it cannot be doubted that at the place and district at that time, if there had been need, within a year, several hundred spinners would have been produced. If this training were offered in all towns and markets of the hereditary lands, then within a year, Bohemia, with all its long-staple wool, would not be able to the work it up itself. Those towns would gain unbelievable sustenance. We would not lack a supply of such teachers from the Low Countries. Many thousand such unfortunate people suffering under French pressure would thank God if they were able to gain their daily bread in the hereditary lands with their own spinning. This will provide all parents living in these towns, and also those among the local peasantry, once their children reach a certain age, and especially the girls, with sufficient means to set their children to the learning of fine wool spinning (whether they are going to use what they learn or not). Steps would have to be taken to ensure that the local lords did not make such work an obligation, but at the least saw it as beneficial. The first teaching wage could be met either by the local authorities or from the putters-out [merchants financing these manufactures][42] involved in spinning, and would last for one or two years at the most. By that time, wool spinning would be well-established, and the usual flax spinning. One child would teach the other how to spin. The spinning wheels needed would not be too costly and could be hired to begin with. Those who wanted could buy their rented wheels with their spinning. I have no doubt at all that fine wool-spinning could in this way be quickly put on its feet, although I admit that at first it would require more oversight and care than weaving itself requires. For the last point, it is easy to say why spinning is a good thing. It is a means of enthusing children and youth, and if serious effort is made, then enough of them will be found.

Silk will I think be an easier matter than fine wool spinning. It cannot be doubted that at Roveredo and elsewhere on the Italian border spinning and twining are already practised to some extent. Teachers could easily be found in the ares, or even replaced with Milanese. For silk has the special property, involving less work, since not only has nature itself spun it through the mouth of the worm, but all kinds of spun silk and yarn and its dyes can be purchased, lending a great advantage to the development of a new silk manufacture in a country where it had hitherto not be produced, which is not the case with wool manufacture. For those who have such a fine-spun thread will hardly let another have it.

---

42 The generic German term is *Verleger*. It was very common in early modern European manufac-turing, especially cloth production, to have manufactures produced in a decentralized manner. This was usually done by domestic producers, female as well as male spinsters and weavers in their own houses. The merchants (putters-out or *Verleger*) would provide the necessary raw materials (flax, linen etc.) and thus 'finance' the prodiction of linen, fustians, cottons and other manufactures; or they would buy the finished manufactures from the producers at pre-agreed prices and sales quotas, paying upon delivery of the final product. There was an utmost var-iety of scenarios; the main aspect being that Verlegen here denotes the activity of supplying producers with the necessary means of prodiction, i.e., financial liquditiy as well as real capital. Although the alternative term 'Proto-industrialization' for the Verlag business has now moved out of fashion, a good introduction is still Sheilagh C. Ogilvie/Markus Cerman, eds, *European proto-industrialization: an introductory handbook* (Cambridge and New York: Cambridge University Press, 1994)

XXVII. How to improve the goods of domestic manufactures so that they yield nothing to foreign goods

Now, we need to consider briefly how the quality of domestic manufactures can be improved so that they are the equal of foreign manufactures. Here that humorous, or at least strange, chemical proverb occurs to me: *Accipe quod debes, et operare sicuti debet, tunc eveniet tibi, quod debet.*[43] I want to say: we have the same working materials as others, the same heads and hands as others, the same instruments as others. If the result is not the same as with others, then it must be nothing but stubbornness, or at least a stubborn lack of skill, which the authorities will take in hand, if they know what they are doing. It has already been noted that the Dutch take the cloth and linen that we have made to Holland. There, they work it up and metamorphose it into Dutch cloth – a finishing that we could well do ourselves, if God willed it. Likewise the Dutch take our Silesian yarn and make their linen fabric with it. They take our flax, process it again and specially prepare it, then spin the resulting material in their own way. From this, it might be noted that with linen the Dutch gain in two ways: the best for themselves domestically, the least for the foreigners, because they believe that the foreigners do not pay the full value of what they buy. The first is made from Silesian weft, the warp is Dutch, but made of Silesian or North German flax yarn. For the other, both warp and weft are German and Silesian. I can also report that they take our finished Silesian linen and full it in butter-milk. Fulling linen is not unknown to anyone. They understand it in Leipzig. In this way, North German products are made into proper Dutch goods. There is nothing here that we in the hereditary lands could not emulate. If our intellect were so dull as not to discover it for ourselves, then let the skilled workers come from elsewhere, and spare no cost. They will pay for themselves, even if they have to be paid their weight in gold. As soon as Germans are in France or Holland, they can do as well as those living there, or better, so long as they stay there. So they can bring their skills back and do good to their fatherland, which they owe in any case. It is not a matter of the instruments that we are not permitted to bring from France or from Holland, for that can be done neither in pieces nor complete. but it would not be a bad thing if a clever mathematical head could set to work and build the same thing here. I also note that the Swiss have learned how to prepare their hemp like the best Dutch linen. I do not simply praise their industry, but that they prefer to cultivate high hemp rather than small flax, but still know how to treat the latter as well as the former. If the Swiss can do this, then why not those in the hereditary lands? The same Swiss give us a remarkable example of their industriousness in the woollen industry too. All the world has for quite a long time had their purses made in France, and even believed that they could be brought from nowhere else. But now they are made just as well in Switzerland, and most that are used in Germany come from there, although the trading societies of Calw in Württemberg also supply some. The rise of the Swiss silk industry is widely known. And we cannot be so foolish as to criticise such people as being

---

43 'Take what should take, for things to operate as they should – then everything will turn out for you as it should'.

rather too materialistic for us, since we also doubt that we ourselves possess sufficient wit and skill to do that which they find so easy.

It would also be no little assurance of the quality of domestic goods if halls, magazines and inspection were arranged so that all finished cloth or woollen or other things were brought there to pass examination. Those that passed inspection would be the only goods allowed into the magazines and proper salerooms. Those that did not would be distinguished from genuine goods and remain as second-best and bodgers goods. Forgery or misuse of the labels given to good products after inspection would, because of the major consequences, be treated as a violation of common trustworthiness, weakening the credit of the hereditary lands, not really any less than the forgery of coins or ducal seal, a crime against the country to be punished rigorously on life and limb. In this way, not only will the products of the hereditary lands be maintained in quality, but quickly become accepted here and abroad as of credit and reputation, which will make a remarkable improvement in the sale, each buyer being assured that he was not being duped.

Further, every year, a competition could easily be held in the hereditary lands from which no master nor journeymen, whether born in the country or only a resident, was excluded; so that those who had good fortune could be granted certain privileges, advantages in money or in another fashion, this all being easily arranged so that the public might have no objection. This would not only stimulate skill at home, but also attract the best workers from abroad.

XXVIII. Concerning the regulation of guilds; the good treatment of foreign skilled hands and putting-out merchants (*Verleger*) entering the hereditary lands; security of capital for merchant capitalists (*Verleger*) regarding certainty of sales; establishment of merchant companies; prohibition of foreign horsehair canvas and bombazine, also export of domestic raw wool and flax, also of thread; protection and recognition of domestic skilled craftsmen and merchant manufacturers

There are other varied means of furthering manufactures in an acceptable manner, also necessary and unavoidable ways. An unanticipated number of these will occur of themselves in the course of time. I wish only to introduce a few here, and count the regulation of craft guilds among the most important. For many of them will be a major obstacle to those things favourable to manufacture – for example, that no master can take on more than one apprentice at a time; that no-one can become a master before completing a certain number of years, and also before that worked as a journeyman, even if in his first year he outshone all masters of that skill; that none might sell his goods cheaper than another; and so forth. These rabbles of such inane people, usually interested only in monopoly, dishonest extortion of merchant capital, must ensure that a good master has as good a chance as a bad one. They cannot force us to tread general well-being, the improvement and the maintenance of the hereditary lands into the shit. They might at one time have had their uses, or might also in the future, when manufactures are once again in a fit state, although I leave this open. But in these early beginnings, they would be the plague. Hence, I counsel that in those manufactures that are in the hereditary lands not yet established, but in course of introduction – as in silk and woollen-making – not to think of guilds until they are fully flourishing, and then to do what seems advisable. The Italians, the Flemish and the Dutch, who are here as teachers, are not used to guilds, nor are their families that are with them. They would not know how to deal with them. If then in neighbouring areas, the woollen manufacture was divided into guilds, their journeymen, if they saw their commodity here better than at home, would certainly act upon it, something of which I have particular experience. We would then be spared many wilful uprisings, disorders and thumpings by journeymen, the carousing and the inevitable St. Mondays. If our travelling lads then were not able to find work in those places where the guilds were in operation, then they would stay in the hereditary lands, which is large enough to satisfy the wanderlust of the common man. But I should not leave unmentioned that, while I mistrust the guilds, I do not wish to see good order, without which nothing can be done, overthrown. In particular, the merchant capitalists and masters have to be supported so that journeymen and workers do not demand excessive wages, or when work is taken on, they are not left in the lurch, as tends to happen now, by the carousing and wanderings of journeymen. A sharp eye is to be kept on everything else, so that the associations for clothworkers, weavers and ribbonmakers create no obstacle that might affect those working in woollen and silk. Anything of this kind would need to be nipped in the bud straight away. Wilful rebuke and complaint that some fools make about another's handiwork so will not treat it as good enough, the arbitrary setting of fines against those in their ranks who do not wish to conform to their monopoly, these are all things that cannot be tolerated at all, but are in every case to be promptly punished. In addition, those who, in conformity with the intention of the authorities, wish to move into another and finer manufacture are to be well-protected. It is to be hoped that many talented persons, of whom there is no lack among the common people, would from childhood learn in turn all kinds of spinning, yarn-making, then the five kinds of weaving – linen, the better woollen fabrics in particular, cloth, silk, and ribbonmaking. Thus, would much be done.

I consider it no less necessary that, for those artisans and workers who come here from afar, levies and other burdens should be waived for one year, also that they should be granted some practical and acceptable privileges – these to be observed and upheld honestly. To ignore the advantage that can grow from this practice would be foolishness. For then these people would not come, and we would never enjoy their presence. If we attract them with privileges, then we can be sure that we shall enjoy their presence for at least some years; not to mention what their necessary consumption of food and other goods will, in the meantime, contribute to the country. The introduction of manufactures that we might hope from them is hence a *latus per se*.[44] Those who would treat them differently, and immediately burden such pleasant guests and incomers with crude levies,

---

44 Literally 'a side of its own', a term used in business accounting meaning a (left or right) side of an account that does not need to be carried over. In the present context presumably meaning simply a separate thing.

would find themselves in the position of the woman in Aesop's fable about the goose that laid gold eggs. Above all, the authorities in towns and markets would need to be persuaded of how much good for the hereditary lands might be expected from the new manufactures, to win their approval, estimation and love for manufacturers and merchant capitalists. Especially encourage treating with leniency and politeness the foreign guests, who are rather more moral than our own people, thus winning them over and lending them encouragement.

It would be possible to loan those incoming manufacturers who seek to settle here the necessary instruments and looms for one or two years. While this would be poor capital, it would not be a poor advantage for attracting foreigners and improving manufactures. Along with which, if not free housing, at least provide a reduced rent for the same.

It would benefit manufactures incomparably more if credit for three, six, nine or twelve months were advanced to the putting-out merchants involved in the spinning of wool and silk, and those involved in weaving cloth. For many seek to do something worthwhile, but lack the capital. As for credit in the case of raw, spun or twined silk, I am convinced that enough could be found in Italy. Insurance is needed, and to arrange this is not so difficult, especially with the Milanese. For the estate assemblies on both sides, theirs and ours, are subject to the same imperial house, and each could provide and receive a national guarantee. Insofar as is necessary, a means of insurance for domestic wool could be found, for which one's word could be given. For trade, and everything that relates to it, stands and falls on credit. Also, finally, premiums would not need to be so high if domestic capitalists[45] saw how secure their capitals would be, and so were encouraged to invest them.

This security is mostly to be gained from the consumption of domestic goods, where capitals are placed. Increased consumption of this kind can only be assured by the prohibition of foreign goods, since the domestic goods will certainly be lost, especially in workers do not come in the numbers anticipated, so that it will not be so easy to proceed; starting with external consumption, thus gaining momentum in the matter. Besides that, there are other ways of easing consumption that should not be neglected, among which not least is the creation of magazines, in which not only the large putting-out merchant, but also each master who sub-contracts on his own account, can entrust their work and effects to the hands of a few factors appointed by the authorities, to whom responsibility for the sale can be given against appropriate provision, whether locally or abroad, who can also ultimately oversee shipping, this taking little time since the magazines will be constantly dealing with such cargoes. From this there follow three great advantages: that masters do not have to concern themselves a great deal with their sales, allowing them to better do their work. That buyers know where they can find the goods they need, and that they can be found there at any time. Finally, through the anticipation and securing of full cargoes, the opportunity for sale is not so easily missed.

---

45 Here Hörnigk actually uses the German term 'Capitalisten' for the putters-out/Verleger, which is exactly what it suggests to the modern ear: capitalists, meaning those financing and overseeing the several stages of manufacturing of a certain product.

Putting-out merchants (Verleger) may form companies. Whether privileges are to be bestowed on these is a matter to be decided in the individual case. I advise that one not be too hasty in this, especially in the matter of the prohibition of foreign goods, which tends to be self-defeating.

I cannot pass over a suitable means for the furthering of the sale of our wool and linen: the prohibition of so-called goods made from camel hair, and those of bombazine or cotton. For the impact of the first type of silk and other goods is great. Hence, do not tolerate those from abroad, but, as with silk goods, manufacture them at home. The disadvantage that linen suffers from cotton is however unbearable. Hence, we should not accept anything made outside or without the country unless a way was found of drawing cotton into the country, but I think it impossible that Austria and Hungary be extended to the East into warmer lands, God willing. From this it can be deduced that I include only those cotton goods among those that are to be rejected that do harm to our domestic linen industry, with which fustian and the like have nothing to do.[46]

Reason will itself dictate that hair and bombazine should be kept out, to further domestic manufacture; and conversely, to prohibit the export of raw wool and flax and their spun thread for the same purpose, so that there might be no shortage, foreign workers who had previously made a living from this and were attracted here, to be used in the future for our own land.

Finally, much would be done for the improvement of manufactures in the hereditary lands if skilled workers and putting-out merchants enjoyed more regard than they have so far. Then, not only would our best people have no cause to move away to where they are better appreciated, but foreigners would be more interested in coming to us. One single merchant capitalist or Verleger is one hundred times more useful to the state than many dozen of those who have to live as bloodsuckers, pursuing unnecessary court proceedings and engaging in all kinds of chicanery. The only prompting I need to clearly prove this thesis, or paradox, is for someone to be named. For this argument will not suit everyone. One consequence of the low regard in which trading is held is that rich merchants are almost ashamed of calling themselves traders, get their children to study instead, marrying their daughters to academic doctors, imagining that by so doing they will advance estimation of their social standing. In this way, large capitals are diverted from trade, and the most eminent family lines destroyed. If the authorities sought to prevent this, it would be of assistance to render some honour to the leading merchant capitalists (Verleger) so that there were longer any cause to despise them; ways and means would then be quickly found. In this way, the most skilled among the artisans may be encouraged to enter well-found manufactures. This is as practical as it is inexpensive; but by contrast it is unbearable if honest and trustful traders that come over here to live and produce should be faced with bad credit manners and lack of payment. Upright and honest traders will certainly not return to a place, and rather leave the country in the mire that it is. Hence, it is to be

---

46 Meaning these are to be allowed in the country.

advisable to meet any such cases with punishment, regardless of person, since such complaints are usually made by mischievous people. Those merchants and artisans, and all others troubled by those from whom they have borrowed, are to be dealt with swiftly and justly, administering justice and providing protection. I keep silent here for particular causes, until the time is right, about another infallible means of making Austria master of fine cloth-making, making a cloth that will quickly be of quantity and quality that it can be manufactured.

XXIX. On encouraging the import of French goods

Given my straightforward hostility to so-called French goods, I could almost have forgotten to report on their being imported into the hereditary lands. In the same way that, among the best wheat, weeds proliferate all by themselves, French manufactures will not be backward among others. The number of Frenchmen who, despite the prevailing maladministration of prohibitions on foreign goods, are presently in Vienna show that if everything that goes under the name of French goods were banned, there would be a far greater number of them looking to make a living. If so many of them go to Madrid, why not rather to Germany? But they should not be allowed as in Madrid to return home after six or seven years, taking the money they have made with them; rather, anyone who seeks to feed from us should settle here. Their children would soon no longer be French, but good Germans. There will be no shortage of other nationals working in French goods who seek a place. Even those wenches who wanted their French goods brought by post-chaise could use their money to bring their makers from Paris and help them settle in Vienna. And in this way, a good that was in itself unnecessary, even if legitimated through abuse, could be won to the advantage of the common good. But enough of this. Luxury would soon find counsel there, or in any case know how to replace our own inventions and the indulgence of our praiseworthy womenfolk.

XXX. Where in the hereditary Imperial lands should each manufacture be located

Before I move on from this matter to another, I must briefly note that, among other things, provision has to be made for the siting of manufactures in the hereditary lands. For here too a contribution can be made to trade, depending on whether decisions are made well or badly. Linen manufacture has already been decided, being located in Crain, Upper Austria, Moravia, German Bohemia and primarily in Silesia. The same thing goes for cloth-making in Silesia, German Bohemia and Moravia. The making of woolstuffs should, I think, be located in Bohemia and Silesia, for not only are the people acquainted with woollens, but in Bohemia the long-staple wool is available locally. It is also easier to attract young foreign lads from the neighbouring lands. Whether Prague is suitable, on account of its many authorities, courts and instances – because of these and other things one can feel a real sympathy for the good city. But nothing is impossible, if the right means are taken up resolutely. As far as silk-making is concerned, I consider that the Austrian ducal states should be brought together as a state monopoly, which because of Italy's proximity to Mediterranean silk and because of the suitability of its soil to domestic silk plantations, together with that of Hungary, would render matters simpler. To say nothing on other, more important, considerations. Vienna would in this probably be the principal magazine for French goods, there being, I think at present, goods worth more than one hundred thousand taler in storage that could be sold as French goods, and for the sake of usury, can be called and sold as such. Upon which, it occurs to me (although it does not concern manufactures) what two Frenchmen did for two or three years in a residence city. They bought up locally two hundred barrels of German wine, took it to Vienna, sold it expensively as red and white Gascony wine, and other kinds, and in this way made fools of both the Court and the city. Nobody but Frenchmen could have got away with it. I apply the same to German manufactures, that we must pay as if they were French, and say that while people were duped of their money, they did finally realize that German wine tasted as good as French. So, the Viennese will learn to their cost that Germans can make costume ornaments as well as the French. Which is some consolation for those who fear that our prohibition would result in a lack of French goods. It should also be said that here annually many thousand talers of Annaberg lace[47] is sold by the Savoyards and Flemish to the French in the lands of Meissen and Saxony, and to other settled French people. I am reliably informed that this lace is then sold on as French and Flemish lace.

If one wished, the other three principal kinds of manufacture – the making of fine cloth, silk and woollens – could be introduced to some cities. One could be placed in Vienna, the second in Leopoldstadt, the third in a city on the other bank of the Danube near the great bridge serving the new Vienna city. Rulers should have the rulerly thoughts ; this will be a proper imperial work, with the lustre, the populousness, the wealth, the commodity, price and reputation of an imperial court city, significantly increasing its strength and security with unhoped-for grandeur, raising Vienna once more from the ashes, following the chivalric rebuff of the Turkish approach and siege. Whoever might think the foundation of new cities to be a curiosity should consider what the Duchy of Brandenburg[48] has done in a few years with Friedrichswerder and Dorotheenstadt, both according to the newest standards, with more to follow. And conclude from that what a Roman emperor could not do on a grand scale.

Besides, some are of the opinion that new manufactures are better placed in villages than in privileged towns, with which rulers do not always get on. But to my knowledge, there are in the imperial hereditary lands no such highly-privileged provincial cities that are their equal in contributing to the general good and its own use and advancement. I will not stop to discuss this here. Finally, it should be noted that these provincial cities that would benefit from the introduction of new manufactures are on busy shipping routes, or are so placed that they can further the carriage and sale of goods, of which there is no shortage in the hereditary lands.

---

47 See section **XXX**. Laces made in and around Annaberg in the Saxon Erz Mountains.
48 Both nowadays located within the city state of Berlin.

XXXI. An account of what will follow from the prohibition of foreign goods and the improvement of the four principal domestic manufactures; and a brief treatment of practical oeconomic rules

And so, when Austria has arrived at the hoped-for day in this way, something of which it is capable, the day when these four principal sources of domestic wealth, the silk, wool, linen and so-called French manufacture, are brought to their requisite lustre and perfection, it will be at least the richer by what at present will be about ten million [taler] annually. These will provide also a check to domestic poverty. A new field, a new heaven of all kinds of other instances of good fortune will be promoted by this. The surplus of capitals that in a few years will inevitably arise will compensate for all remaining deficiencies in three ways. First, a praiseworthy curiosity to attempt and introduce something new or acceptable into the land. Second, courage and means to initiate great undertakings. Third, the need to seek and find advantageous investment for accumulated and idle capitals, so that they be not without use. From this, for everything else, the first rule that will repay is attempting to found new plantations. The lover of curious and useful things will find these a praiseworthy goal where much of great use can be done. For this reason, I would wish that all our respectable people venture throughout the hereditary lands to support something that costs little but which is of great use. Without trouble and cost a hundred, yes a thousand gardens would blossom instead of one. Not only a thousand things in one place, but one thing in a thousand places would be tried out, with the great advantage that one would not solely know whether a new plant would do well in the hereditary lands, but also in which place they would do best. Instruction in what and how to research this could be had from a man experienced in European and Indian plantations, of whom there are enough here and there, using seeds and other necessaries. This would involve unanticipated great successes, so that hitherto disregarded things would glorify a country or a place. It would also be especially desirable for someone to create a dictionary in which all those things that were the object of human industry were arranged in alphabetical order. This would first of all teach how every thing was planted, obtained or otherwise brought here.[49] Followed by listing its genus and difference, advantage and faults, then its preparation and use in physic and mechanics. Again, include where such a thing came from in the world, where it was circulated, what its original value was, how it was circulated in other places, how it rises and falls, what has to be taken account of in trade if it is to be preserved from fraud and harm, and so increase its profit. That would be a wonderful work, a work more wonderful than anything ever printed in economics, mechanics and commerce. It would not be the work of one man, more the result of several, and different, professions. It would be difficult, but of all praiseworthy things, of common benefit. It would cost something, but the effort would be richly rewarded. Those who sought only private profit would be unsuited to it, since they withhold what they know from fear that their penny would be reduced. People are needed *quos zelus*

---

49 Such dictionaries or economic encyclopaedias were indeed begun in the eighteenth century. See introduction.

boni publici coquat.[50] The book would not be perfect at the first attempt. There will always be something to be added to it. But it should not be neglected on account of this, for it would from the first be of considerable benefit.

I also would hope that, of all things, plantations of white mulberry trees be established for the cultivation of silk. It is regrettable that this extremely useful matter has been so much neglected by us. I can say without exaggeration that observance of this one matter in the hereditary lands would provide as much for its inhabitants as they now contribute with great complaint in extraordinary payments to the treasury. It is all the same a simple and easily-done task. The soil is suited to those trees practically throughout the hereditary lands. The trees can be planted in their thousands without affecting fields and vineyards, if sufficient care is taken. They are not that susceptible to the weather, and survive cold winters that put an end to many other trees. Mulberry trees, even the youngest and most tender, suffer the least. While the trees take eight or ten years to grow, they yield one taler a year. As they grow, this becomes ten or twenty talers. Even if silk cultivation did not succeed, there would still be the timber, the leaves as fodder, the fruit as mast. All of this would make the trouble and cost worthwhile. In short: books would be written about this project, have been written. God lend us the will to set to work. I wish the hereditary lands this boon from the depths of my heart. But a curse rather than a boon would result if the authorities used this idea to impose new burdens upon poor subjects.

Further to our matter, it would also be of benefit to improve disused mines, and to encourage the imperial administration to cultivate more, if they were inclined to do so, while also encouraging private owners through providing the means for the measure we have proposed. I cannot omit here an apparent paradox. I argued that not only should ore be mined where the benefit was greater than the cost, but also where they were equal; since what is spent stays within the country. And what is brought to the surface also stays in the country. The state becomes the richer through this, and it is as if the merchant has made a gain of one hundred per cent. Then many active people could be well-supported as workers, who would also make their contribution, their consumption also making its public contribution. Indeed, I think that mines should be exploited where the costs are higher than the gain. For in this case, it would be as if the trader had a fifty per cent return on his money. To some it would not seem prudent to use up one hundred in order to gain fifty. I agree with this, if the capital is lost. But in our case, capital and interest remain here within the land, although the capital moves from one purse to another. All the same, it cannot be denied that this is not a trade suited to the private person, for this would finish him in short order; it is rather something for the entire state, it being fitting that it should undertake this kind of thing, in this way multiplying inner nerves. For the state, subjects would soon sense this gain in their purses, and return the capital through levies to the treasury. Private persons need not always be excluded from those ventures where gains and costs were equal, or where the loss was small, if they were in the business of supplying wine, beer, bread, meat and the like to miners and others. For much is to be made there, finding with such things certain and at all times profitable consumption.

---

50 People that 'ought to be driven by the desire to promote the common good'.

For manufacturers who observed the second rule there would no smaller a field opened up, finding a new cause to sow money which was otherwise barren, and rendering it fertile. Not everything can be detailed, and there is often great benefit in small things that have been overlooked through ignorance or neglect. I do not know whether pitch should be counted as a raw material, or as something manufactured. But I do know that it is brought to Venice from as far away as the Baltic Sea, since the imperial hereditary lands has on the Adriatic Sea the most wonderful opportunity to make the same, and draw its use from the Venetians. The trials were done years ago and were judged to be good by the Venetian arsenal. There would be an endless amount of such things. So-called Annaberg lace (or rather, Meissen Upland lace)[51] is apparently a small matter, but it draws, nonetheless, many hundred thousand talers into the country. Meissen quarrymen are poorly paid, and cannot live on what they earn. Hence, their women and children find themselves compelled to find their subsistence in lacemaking. There are around ten thousand of them in a strip of land of about eight or ten miles. It is reported that each of them makes twelve to sixteen Meissner Groschen[52] a week from the work. I will however take the least, and assume only ten Groschen; which means that in fifty-two weeks about four and a half hundred thousand Rhenish Gulden[53] result, and that is only in wages. The merchant capitalist adds on at least half as much again. The French who, as described above, buy in part from these merchant capitalists, sell it on as French and Flemish goods for two or three times as much. It is a blind world that asks to be duped. It is remarkable that the yarn for this lace comes from Holland, the thread by contrast from Silesia. One pound of this lace may yield a few less talers in Silesia, but the Meissen lace is priced at around sixteen to twenty-four talers in Holland, and it can be that, in the meantime, the yarn from Grimm is taken for Dutch and mixed with it.

Those in the Meissen area make two to three hundred talers from the twenty-four talers sent abroad. So one pound of fine Silesian flax, which in its home country costs only a few Groschen, after payment for wages and rent, ends up with a value of two to three hundred talers. But Silesia has the least of this. *Nimirum vivitur ingenio*. Might it not be worth the effort to invest a few hundred or a thousand talers and learn from the Dutch how to prepare yarn? If it is true, quod *necessitas ingenium acuat*[54], this is crystal clear for those living in the Meissen hills. One could almost argue against this and conclude that we cannot really here in the hereditary lands suffer the want of which we complain, since it has taken us so long to do anything about it. Around Commodau[55] in Bohemia, a start has been made with lace, and while it has not so far advanced very far, it is nonetheless

---

51 See above, n. 1 above and section **XXX**.

52 The Meissner groschen had been the ancient currency of the Saxon and Central German lands since the fourteenth century. After mid-sixteenth century one silver florin exchanged at 24 groschen. See previous notes for references on monetary issues.

53 The Rhenish gulden was a gold coin that exchanged initially at 21 groschen but during the sixteenth century progressively replaced by large silver coins of equivalent purchasing power (Thalers). See previous notes.

54 'Necessity is the mother of invention'.

55 Komotau (Ger.) or Chomotov in today's Czeq Republic.

a worthy venture. The great advantage that the Meissen district draws from smelting and tinsmithery, even though these appear to be small things, has been noted sufficiently. I can report that one single place in the Meissen hills produces several hundred thousand threescore sets of tinned spoons, eight Meissen Groschen for one set, or half a Rhenish Gulden, and these are traded throughout the north, as far as Moscow and into Tartary. Such a small thing brings the country a few hundred thousand Rhenish Gulden from abroad.

There are perhaps many such cases where great advantages can be gained from petty things.

If the first two rules have been of assistance, the third will take care of itself, the common population as well as burghers in towns and markets increasing noticeably, citizens are also gaining in subsistence and profit. It cannot be sufficiently believed how disadvantageous for the hereditary lands is the neglect of this very necessary, but never adequately valued point – from 1650 onwards, when the Peace of Westphalia was completed[56], in the thirty three complete years since then, no provincial town has been made to flourish the way it had previously. If annually, the boys of eight or nine begging in the street were removed and, through the benevolence of godly people, first put into school, and then trained in suitable crafts, it is not to be doubted that trade would have been promoted. I am not talking here about shoemakers, tailors, smiths, potters and other craftsmen of this kind, of whom we have in the hereditary lands no shortage, but instead of those who help keep money here that otherwise runs out of the land, involving all kinds of fine weaving. There is no shortage of benevolent people. That is shown by the many annual gifts, bequests and dispositions to charities. If only it was possible to show that the state, as well as one's fellows, could benefit from such investment. Even if no one migrated here from abroad, the population of the hereditary lands would soon multiply of itself, if only the foundation of new manufactures would provide means of subsistence to young people who wanted to marry. Nothing can be done with the common artisans who have closed guilds. Young people would not be admitted beyond a fixed number, and would have to leave the country, go off to war, or remain unmarried for years; or if they wished to become a master, then find a master's widow to marry, all of which would be an obstacle for population. The shortage of teachers would also not be a problem if one considered only a medium-sized institution. I cannot let one inept, almost universal abuse pass without mention: that whoever wants to settle here in town and market has to buy himself in. On the contrary, people like this who wish to gain their subsistence in one place, but actually bring it with them, together with a great deal more, deserve to be paid to come here. No better is the practice that a new citizen has to provide himself with his own house. This rule holds back many who could otherwise be comfortably off, who lack sufficient seed capital and have to withdraw it from their occupation to put in a house; or, before being fully established, have reservations about so doing. This is without doubt an

56 The Peace of Westphalia was actually sealed by treaty in 1648 when the so-called Thirty Years War had ended; negotiations however continued and a final settlement was reached at Nuremberg in 1650.

abuse; for it does not, as intended, lead to the renovation of abandoned and dilapidated houses, but rather is the cause of such houses remaining unoccupied for longer, the towns remaining unpopulated. In those places where beer-brewing is located in the houses, that is also an obstacle: first, of industry, since citizens depend upon the brewing and pay no regard to work that could help themselves and others; and also for population, which could have been furthered by a more promising occupation. To say nothing of the fact that such beer, as in Meissen, is of little use since all those in possession of brewing privileges think that it must be drunk up, none other being available.

Since the improvement of the oft-mentioned four leading manufactures will restrict the export of domestic gold and silver, conforming to the fourth of our rules, what has been said so far speaks for itself. Further, providing the means to eliminate harmful coins[57] will provide for the schools, forest academies and colleges for all of those who have been washing around abroad for too long. The destruction of gold and silver in certain manufactures could also be done away with.

To deal briefly with the remainder of the matter, foreign goods will cease to be a matter of fascination, and glory will be made of the fact that we can produce the same thing to the same quality here as it is either produced abroad, or contracted out here; especially if the leading imperial personages showed their high regard for domestic goods and their dislike of foreign ones, giving an example to Court and country; despising no less in this way the persons who were still attached to foreign goods than the goods after which they hankered. Hence, the great hopes invested in the marriage of the present Imperial Majesty in 1673, where the point was made that not one thread of what he wore had not been manufactured in the hereditary lands. The life history of Carolo M.[58] records that he was not only moderate in his clothing, being content with the products of his kingdom, but that he could not abide seeing his Court dressed in foreign finery. He often went hunting regardless of bad weather dressed in wolfskin. The following day, all those who had been with him had thoroughly ruined clothes, while he was still wearing his dry wolfskin. Further, in the urgent search for all possible ways and means to ease otherwise unprofitable capitals, to entertain the idea to conduct ourselves all freight and shipping on sea and land, at home and abroad; making better use of the sea, improving waterways, to which end, I believe, proposals are in hand. We could be taking our goods to the door of foreigners, collecting their raw materials for ourselves, taking control of seaborne trade and shipping, opening a door for many distant and useful ventures; especially since here in the hereditary lands, not far from our coastal harbours, everything is to hand to build, supply and arm a ship. In this way, the trade long provided by the Dutch

---

57　The meaning is not entirely clear here; however, it was common in early modern German life and economy to complain about bad (debased) foreign coins that came into the country in exchange for the export of good coin (mainly silver florins), something called in common usage Gresham's law, and which sometimes caused social and economic disequilibrium and unrest. See Philipp Robinson Rössner, *Deflation – Devaluation – Rebellion. Geld im Zeitalter der Reformation* (Stuttgart: Franz Steiner, 2012).

58　Charlemagne, king of the Franks and German Emperor.

could have some prospect of being moved to Trieste and Fiume[59], and not disdained. This would in turn provide for the sale and application of our abundant domestic goods with unimagined ease, as well as products of the soil and raw materials from the hereditary lands and its neighbours. This would all provide assistance to the three magnets for foreign purchasers and money: the quality of the goods (on account of the good order proposed above); cheapness, given the good price of raw material, of subsistence, accommodation, and wages; and finally credit (arising from the surplus of capitals). Fourthly, added to this, the opportunity of rivers, which if connected would lend many places great comfort and would contribute to foreign consumption. This is especially true if the Morava were made navigable and joined to the Oder. No less beneficial would be the placing of magazines and warehouses on these rivers. If added to that, that those goods travelling outwards for sale be not burdened, the Treasury would find that for every taler foregone ten would be gained, and the lands would gain one hundred or more. For the incomparably greater amount of coin flowing in would replace everything and make it easier for the domestic population to invest. I here pass for the sake of brevity quickly over other matters, and trust myself to demonstrate only that the management of the ten million retained each year in the country is only a small beginning for our economy, because in a short time, four times as much gold and silver will be brought into circulation annually. This time is not yet come, but it will raise Austrian glory to the peak of perfection, sufficient to bring about in some matters unforeseen changes, as well as creating a situation in which we will have no cause to envy any foreign nation for their Indian kingdom, or for their industry.

XXXII. Establishment of Imperial offices of commerce

Since these are great ventures they will be no less in need of great resolution, offices, and guidance. All states, kingdoms and republics in the world were originally formed for two purposes: to be able to live in security and in comfort. Security is achieved domestically through the administration of justice, and externally by the right to wage war. Both are usually provided for by office or counsellors, which like the *nervum rerum gerendarum* are dependent on the Treasury for the funds from the subjects' purse. In many places, the task of creating security and ease in the public purse is treated as a small matter, as an appendix to the work of the Treasury, which is a great error. This is in fact the real basis of the Treasury, for the particular oeconomy of the land has to be in conformity with the general oeconomy of the land. It is clear from this tract that the extension of the latter is incomparably greater than that of the former. From which it follows that the soul of the political body is the closest concern of the council of state, and the majesty of justice the closest concern of the council of justice, that there are other affairs of state that call for particular collegia and councils that are in our land cared for the least: the general oeconomy of the country upon which we have often touched. There

---

59 Trieste, now in Italy, and Fiume, now in Croatia. These two Adriatic ports were Austria's only door to the high seas.

are countless things here which have nothing in common with the cameral administration, which require a particular treatment, and for their conduct require special knowledge and persons. Whether this should take the form, as would normally be the case, of creating such collegia quite separate from the Treasury and its offices, but connected through the Court and throughout the hereditary lands and subject to the direction of a President favouring no one collegium over another; or perhaps by creating independent directors, councils, secretaries, registrars and other officials, with rights of imperial audience and decision-making is to be determined. It would also demonstrate the importance of the matter if those of some standing might be appointed, the most experienced, best-regarded and most industrious men of state, and endowed with all necessary authority. For such a beginning this is a clear and unavoidable necessity that is as clear as day and requires no further discussion. I also leave unconsidered whether such a collegium should be named for its principal object, commerce; or whether it should be given a different name to add to its authority. It would also be advisable that this collegium – in cases involving the execution of prohibitions and other statutes connected with the economy of the land, and also those involving merchants – should acquire jurisdiction *cum derogatione* from other instances (for which some persons could be seconded) who would be pronounced there *remotis legum solennitatibus.*[60] In all, it is important that the highest administrator himself has enthusiasm for the work, devoting care and sense, heart and eye to it. Otherwise, little can be hoped for it, or everything would be done with ten times more trouble and effort.

XXXIII. The hereditary Imperial lands will exceed in independence all other state in Europe, if they so will. Conclusion

I have now arrived at the proof that Austria can prevail. I consider this to consist in the degree to which it is independent of others. However, I do not treat independence in terms of the political, as a detachment from all other forms of superior rule, in which all truly sovereign states must be equal to each other; but understand by it independence in all those things necessary for human subsistence. I have above touched on the fact that one will search Europe in vain for a country that is thoroughly independent in all things; and there is probably no more than one of this kind in the whole world. It is thus a matter of the degree to which one European land is superior to another, the standard by which the one is less dependent, the other more. I judge this dependence according to four sorts of differences. For some countries are dependent on others, firstly, because of gold and silver, which they themselves lack, but others not. Second, some are dependent on those things necessary for human subsistence, those irreplaceable necessities from its own soil; other being dependent for those things they can easily do without, or replace. Third, some are dependent on others for many kinds of things necessary for human subsistence; while other have few such needs. Fourth, some do have the kinds of goods they need, but

---

60 Meaning these economic and financial boards should be absolute from jurisdiction and put under special legislative structures.

not in sufficient quantity, or at least not sufficient to convey to others; while others have both all they need and that in sufficient quantity, even a surplus.

The reasons listed above will explain why I make a special difference for the possession of one's own source of gold and silver. Indeed, I consider the greatest dependency upon others arises from having to live in need of gold and silver, the two indispensable general tools of human action and subsistence. How many are there in Europe who can boast of such gifts of nature in their lands? Moscow, Poland, Sweden, Denmark, both the Low Countries and France – they have no gold and silver of their own. Italy, England, Norway, also the German mountains beyond the hereditary lands, these do not have very much in comparison with us. And those who would seek to qualify by virtue of their part in the Spanish silver fleet, they depend upon Spanish intentions and good will. For lack of people, these last cannot even mine their own mountains. American silver is only to be had after two thousand miles at the mercy of wave, wind and piracy, and once the foreigners have taken their share, there is little left for the Spanish. The hereditary Imperial lands alone command domestic troves granted by God with considerable quantities, running to several millions, more than in the rest of Christian Europe.

Hence the hereditary Imperial lands alone, or their supreme head, are not dependent upon others and so have the capacity, without weakening or endangering the money already in circulation, of creating hoards in such quantity as the earth conveys in gold and silver each year. Those who only receive their goods from abroad depend upon the goodwill of others. Once the latter supply these goods, and keep the gold and silver given for them, these hoards will quickly dwindle, at least if no interest is charged to the subjects. Thus, capital will decline, all coin gradually being withdrawn from circulation, and trade and industry in the land going into decline. From which it can be concluded, how might we deal with proud and unjust France, and find the means to break its pre-sumption. Austria is also supreme in this respect.

If I now come to the other difference, consisting in the necessity or lack of necessity of those goods which either occur in the country, or which do not; I find among the neces-sary grain, wine, cattle, fresh fish, wool, linen, furs and leather, all petty metals, partly minerals, common cooking salt, rock salt, timber, and everything used for building, and especially for shipbuilding; not to talk of gold and silver, which I have already mentioned. Among the unnecessary things that can be easily done without, or which can easily can be replaced by an equivalent, there are: silks, Indian spices, household goods, and Northern dried and salted fish. The latter can, by great good fortune, all be found in the hereditary lands. The other unnecessary goods noted here we do indeed lack; but only with regard to silks, only for so long as we wish. We can easily console ourselves for the shortage of dried and salted fish with out fresh fish, especially since the Dutch send only their worst and keep the best. The Italians send us their delicacies because without our grain and oxen they could not keep hunger at bay, and because for lack of sufficient food they could barely still their hunger and would not be able to eat as much at all without that we Germans sent them. Likewise, for lack of foreign wool and linen they would have to go half-naked, and would only have their warm climate to thank for the fact that they did not freeze. All European countries lack Indian spices, as we do. Here, therefore, none can claim more than any other. And so Austria is no less triumphant over all in this second difference.

As regards the third difference, having run through the second, the outcome is self-evident. Austria possesses all necessary and essential materials for human subsistence, together with a greater part of the unnecessary and superfluous, either in fact, or (as with silks) if it so wished. Others however, each and every one, lack some, if not many of the most important necessities, as well as many of the other things. From this, it follows that Austria, in the variety of its goods, enjoys an especial supremacy over all other European countries. It is superfluous to go through this in detail. It is plain that few European countries have domestic sources of gold and silver, and half of them cannot boast domestic vineyards. Not one of them possess all the lesser metals, even those who rate highly their own seapower, but find little of the materials proper to this at home. Austria however possesses them all, and so once again counts itself supreme.

In the fourth difference, the hereditary Imperial lands are without compare, and at the same time a model of bounteous nature. They not only possess all kinds of grain and treefruits, cattle and horses, copper, iron, tin, lead and quicksilver, minerals, salt, alum and rock salt, timber, wool, linen, furs and leather and more things among the necessary instruments of human life and subsistence; they also possess those things that count as delicacies and ornament. Moreover, they possess these in such number, quantity and superfluity that they are unable to consume them all themselves, but must send in some cases half or more to their neighbours and other European countries, and in some cases travelling halfway through the world. I hope that this will all be conceded without argument. Since Europe is not one land, no country is in a position to make one or other of its domestic endowments common with others; none of them has the range of endowments that we have, and few in such quantities as we possess. And so it yet again turns out that Austria is supreme over all. Austria is to such a degree supreme over all others, and so much more fortunate in its blessings, that it can only be robbed of the same either by God or from its own negligence. And it is so much more fortunate than its surrounding neighbours that there is not one or the other of them that is in need of several parts of the Austrian superfluity, so that sale of our goods to them is secured by the providence of nature itself. Austria, I state again, is supreme; but with the qualification – if it so wishes. For to mine sufficient gold and silver, and then to casually speed it on its way abroad, as if it were a foe; to possess grain, wine and other edible goods in abundance and superfluity, but not take the trouble to see to its satisfactory sale ourselves; to tread a select part of the earth suited to the cultivation of silk, but to do nothing from sheer idleness; produce sufficient wool and linen, but wear Dutch cloth, French styles and Indian bombazine – these and their like are so many signs that lead me to say that Austria is in all things a fortunate and wonderfully blessed land; but not for so long as the nation's oeconomy is run in a perverse manner. I conclude this work and hope that I have here shown what an honest man can do with heart, mouth and hand for Austria's favour. I doubt however, *odio, an amore dignus videbor*[61]; whether I will receive any thanks at all for what I have done. Besides, many

---

61 'I will be either loved or hated'.

will not yet be willing or able to digest that I have disclosed the damage, as it appears, so finely here, and more or less put my finger exactly on the sore point. And there will be people who will not think it good that I have so openly described the means of removing the evil as I have witnessed it in my travels and would wish to obstruct them. But to conceal what I have demonstrated would not, as described, be of any assistance, for our sickness is all too well-known by other nations. Such revelations cannot harm us, not can anyone prevent us from seizing suitable means. Moreover, it should also be considered that any such hindrance would bring about the greatest misfortune. If one does keep one's council, nothing will happen of itself; if one speaks openly, then it happens *ex supposito*[62], but with the hindrance of other people likewise not. In this way, keeping one's counsel and speaking one's mind would amount to the same thing, so that my writing was as little damaging as if through my silence something was made good. Quite honestly, my least concern is that other German or neighbouring rulers and monarchs would make use of these proposals and encouragement before we did; for it would be our own fault, and in any case, as the introduction makes plain, my secondary object is that others might be encouraged through Austria's example. If the latter did not wish to provide such an example, the former would do well to set to work without the example of Austria, all the better since no country in Europe can take in hand the oeconomy of their land without enforcing a greater or lesser shift in the fortunes of a hated France, an end to which we should all assist. If it should also turn out, which I do not at all doubt, that others wish to write on this matter, there would be such an outpouring of self-importance and expansiveness with which the paucity of these pages could not in any way compare. I am quite certain that there are many others in the hereditary Imperial lands intimately acquainted with their qualities. If one of them for the love of his Fatherland wished to step forward with his own insights, I would be delighted to have been the first in time, but the last and least example, although of value and goodwill; and I would freely admit that my metal would be as pure lead as compared to his. The reasons for my putting together these arguments have been shown to be unassailable. And if the way I have done so, and its application and execution are seen to be the most useful, leaving aside perhaps some disagreements, the prohibition of foreign goods and it rigorous implementation is the beginning and the end of my proposal; without which the improvement of domestic commerce and manufacture, the revival and recovery of the hereditary lands would be a vain venture, even in the imagination. To bring about a prohibition of this kind all that is needed is a solid and emphatic "Fiat"[63], with which everything can be hoped for, and without which there is no hope. The present desperate situation of the hereditary lands, through which their exhaustion is so evilly realised, should certainly impel us. We invite and seek out God-given victories against our arch-enemies, the retreat of the Turkish hordes from the Imperial residence and restored and increased security thereby. Above all, the approaching malady from the West should move us, as also the age-old gratitude that the Danube owes to its brother the Rhine. For while the latter with his Carolingian

---

62 Literally 'by attribute' or 'by implication'.
63 'So it shall be!'

and Saxon emperors and kings has gladly extended its best forces to protect the Danube, as far as it is called Bavarian and Austrian, from barbarian yoke and the invasion of the Huns and their like, it has also, disregarding its own danger, contributed greatly to keeping Turkish slavery at bay. And so the Rhine longingly awaits the time when the Danube saves and delivers it from the prevailing unbearable French dominion.[64] The small step from the Rhine to the Danube, and our own preservation depending on this, compel us to do so. Let us give them a hearing, and let us decide, to develop a righteous oeconomy that can maintain our best forces together, and rather than spoiling this oeconomy, let the French have a taste of it; in this way, the common cause will be fulfilled. Although it may not appear to be the time now to think about this, things are almost lost and I must sorrowfully end with the familiar song of Balde[65]:

> This will be sung, this will be shouted
> Said, heard,
> written about, read about,
> And what is read will be disdained.

(in Latin) In the meantime, Austria goes down. Let the Highest One decree that I am betrayed and my fears for all the world are mistaken.

---

64 Commencing in 1633 France gradually annexed the German region of Alsace (*Elsaß*), culminating with the annexation of Strasbourg (*Straßburg*) in 1681.
65 This refers to Jacob Balde (1604–1648), a poet writing in Latin.

INDEX